Genevieve Williamson

THE GOLDEN BOOK

leben vñ mūsze ss dien es got vrteil soll
gebē Die gene mit schreckē dohien Die
got nye erkāntē noch forchtē zu nichma
mag sich vbergā nicht Vor dē gotlichē
angesiecht Cristus wil do vrteil sprechen·
Vñ wil alle boszheit rechen Die die ge-
dacht dē willē sin Den wil er gebē ewige
pin Vñ wil dē gudē gebē Sy ym freude
vñ ewig lebē Sist die werlt vñ alle ding
Die in ē werlt geschaffē sint Ezu gene
vñ werdē auch zu nicht Als man wol

er werde vo pine erlost · wer in ē hymel
rich ist Der hat freude mit ihesu crist Der
von ē hymel her nidd ist kōmen Vnd
mentschlich natuer hat an sich gnōmē
· Vñ an ē mentscheit ist erstorbē Vñ mi
dem dode hat erworbē Dz wer do glaubi
hat an en Mynne vñ zuusiecht ē sal zu
ym· wir sollē gantzē glaubē habē Das
wir vō ihesu crist horē sagē Vnd sollen
alle vnß werck vñ sinne Ezu xpo kerē vn
liebe vñ vn mynne Vñ zu ym babē zu v=

The Golden Book

*The Story of Fine Books and
Bookmaking—Past & Present*

By

Douglas C. McMurtrie

Chicago

Pascal Covici, *Publisher*

1927

FIRST EDITION, NOVEMBER, 1927

SECOND EDITION, DECEMBER, 1927

TO
GEORGE O. CROMWELL
LOVER OF FINE BOOKS
AND MAKER OF TYPES
WHICH ENTER INTO
THEIR COMPOSITION I
INSCRIBE THIS BOOK
AS AN EVIDENCE OF MY
ESTEEM AND REGARD

Introduction

THE scope of the present volume was conceived by the publisher, Pascal Covici, and it was at his instance that I undertook to write it. The endeavor has been made to trace the development of bookmaking from the beginnings of written records down to the present time. In attempting to cover so wide a field I have often been led beyond the bounds of my own special interests and studies and have had to content myself with presenting a digest of the facts and of the opinions of the leading authorities. On the other hand, many of the chapters deal with subjects on which I have done considerable original work and of which I can, therefore, speak with first-hand knowledge. I have endeavored, in all instances, to make acknowledgment of my obligations to others, these acknowledgments appearing in the notes at the end of this volume.

But I wish here to acknowledge with sincere gratitude a special obligation to the Newberry Library and members of its staff who have had a large part in the making of this book. In the Wing Foundation this institution has a fine collection of incunabula and books on printing and its history which is a great asset to students of typography in the Middle West. Through the courtesy of the New-berry Librarian, Mr. George B. Utley and the erudite Curator of the Wing Collection, Dr. Pierce Butler, the books in this collection were placed freely at my disposal for study and for reproduction of a large proportion of the illustrations which appear in the following pages. Dr. Butler, who is one of the leading authorities in the coun-try on fifteenth century printing has, furthermore, been kind enough to read the proofs of all of my chapters which deal with early printing and has made numerous suggestions of which I have taken full advantage. I am also indebted to him for preparation of the material on Jenson and Aldus and on book illustration.

To Edwin Eliott Willoughby, a bibliographer of much ability on the staff of the Wing Foundation, I am indebted for the preparation of the material on wood-cuts and block-books, the study and the subjects of the incunabula, the Golden Age of typography, and private presses. His efforts have contributed largely to whatever value this volume may possess.

The New York Public Library and the John Carter Brown Library of Providence have courteously provided me with photostats of material in their collections. Dr. Charles L. Nichols of Worcester, the biographer of Isaiah Thomas, has been kind enough to read the proof of my chapter on the work of that printer. Mr. Alfred Fowler of Kansas City and Mr. Wilbur Macey Stone of New York have been helpful to me in the preparation of

INTRODUCTION

material which it has, I regret, been impossible to include in the present edition.

In reviewing the writing of this book and the study precedent thereto, it seems as though two chapters on the invention of printing required as much time in their preparation as all the other chapters put together. The reason for this is that, so far as I know, there exists no impartial statement in English setting forth the facts regarding the invention and attempting to evaluate the relative merits of the claims of Gutenberg and Coster. In view of this situation, it is hoped, therefore, that the survey of the subject here presented may be found both helpful and interesting. The discussion of the industrial antecedents of the invention may also throw some new light on the the problem of the invention.

The chapter on the beginnings of printing in Mexico will also, I venture to believe, be found the most complete statement in English of the present state of knowledge on this interesting subject.

In any one volume, it is a cardinal principle of good bookmaking that all decoration should be uniform in style and that its tone should key with the tone of the type pages. In view of the subject of the present volume, however, it has seemed wise to show a variety of initial letters and headbands, which will be found to vary considerably in design and color from chapter to chapter, in a manner which, in the average volume, would be inexcusable. I have regarded these elements, therefore, not in the light of a consistent series, but as illustrations representative of varied styles in book decoration. These have been borrowed from many sources, most of which are acknowledged in the notes at the end of this volume.

For the typographic design of this book, which has been manufactured within the usual commercial limitation of expense, I must myself accept responsibility. I am grateful for the cordial cooperation of the publisher, Pascal Covici, in its planning and production and for the highly competent assistance of Louis J. Rerra and Lee W. Robinson in its composition.

In the revision of the second edition, I am indebted to Mr. J. U. Nicolson for many helpful suggestions.

DOUGLAS C. McMURTRIE

Chicago, December 12, 1927

Contents

PAGE

Introduction   vii

Of the Making of Books   I

PART I

I Ancient Forms of Writing   9
> Pictographic writing on papyrus and clay tablets.
> The materials of the early scribes.

II The Origin of the Alphabet   18
> The Phoenician Alphabet and its antecedents. The
> evolution of the alphabet we use today.

III Paper and Its Forbears   26
> The invention of paper in China and the spread of
> the art of papermaking to the West.

IV Books in Manuscript   36
> The work of the scribes in the Middle Ages, and
> the art of the manuscript book.

V Printing in the Far East   43
> The invention of book printing in China, and the
> art of early Chinese books. The invention of mov-
> able type printing and its sterile outcome.

VI Woodcuts and Block Books   57
> The fugitive block prints, and the development of
> books with text and woodcut illustrations combined.

PART II

VII The Stage Setting for Typography   66
> The state of the related arts at the birth of print-
> ing: textile printing, binder's stamps, etc.

PAGE

VIII The Invention of Printing   73
    Gutenberg's invention, and the conflicting claims
    for Coster and other contenders. The evidence for
    Gutenberg. The early printing at Mainz.

IX The Development of Typography   107
    The sack of Mainz, and spread of the typographic
    art to other cities in Germany, to Italy, to Switzer-
    land, to France, and to Spain.

X The Venetian Masters   117
    The great period of printing at Venice. The devel-
    opment of the Roman type. The birth of popular
    priced books of convenient size.

XI Early Illustrated Books   129
    The first woodcuts used to illustrate printed books
    and the development of the art of book illustration
    in the fifteenth century.

XII The First Book in English   140
    The work of William Caxton, merchant-venturer,
    litterateur, and printer. The birth of the book trade
    in England. Wynkyn de Worde and other early
    English printers.

XIII The Study of the Incunabula   155
    The bibliographers of fifteenth century books;
    their methods and manuals.

XIV Subjects of the Incunabula   160
    What the first printed books were about. Texts that
    sold well and interested readers of the period.

XV The Golden Age of Typography   170
    Printing at Paris in the first half of the sixteenth
    century. Books of Hours and their decoration.

XVI Plantin of Antwerp   188
    The picturesque Printer to the Court of Spain. His
    economic viscissitudes. The Polyglot Bible and
    other monuments of Plantin's typography.

CONTENTS

PAGE

XVII   Master of Roman Type Design   197
     The father of English type design, and his revolu-
     tionary influence on English typography.

XVIII The French Eighteenth Century   201
     The period of graceful typography par excellence.
     The influence of Fournier, the typefounder. Work
     of the illustrators, Cochin, Eisen, and others.

XIX   The Writing Master's Disciples   205
     The work of John Baskerville, typographic ama-
     teur and pioneer, and his influence on the typo-
     graphy of the Didots in France and Bodoni in
     Italy. The development of the classic style in typo-
     graphy, and the birth of type of "modern" design.

PART III

XX   In the Track of Columbus   225
     The advent of printing to the New World and the
     beginnings of printing in Mexico.

XXI   The Press Comes to Massachusetts   235
     The dream of Jose Glover and its fulfillment in
     the establishment of a printing press in Cambridge,
     Massachusetts, in 1639. First issues of the press.

XXII The Precocious Apprentice   250
     The induction of Benjamin Franklin into the
     printing industry. His work in London; the es-
     tablishment of his office in Philadelphia; and the
     publication of the Poor Richard Almanac.

XXIII Printer—Historian—Educator   266
     Isaiah Thomas, the patriot publisher of the *Massa-*
     chusetts Spy, and his later work at Worcester.
     First historian of American printing.

XXIV A Typographical Messiah   276
     William Morris, and his service in the reestablish-
     ment of high standards in the printing craft. His
     contributions to book decoration and type design.

THE GOLDEN BOOK

PAGE

PART IV

XXV   The Processes of Bookmaking   291
An elementary description of type-setting, printing, and binding. The making of the modern book.

XXVI   On Type Design   304
What makes one type different from another. Elements of legibility and beauty.

XXVII   The Title Page   313
The historical development of the title page—the door to the book—as we know it now. Principles of sound title page composition.

XXVIII   Book Illustration   324
The various media of illustration and the work of great illustrators in ages past and present.

XXIX   The Decoration of Books   334
Borders, vignettes, and decorative initials. Their historical development and present use.

XXX   The Art of Bookbinding   340
Styles in bookbinding and their creators. The influence of Jean Grolier and Thomas Maioli.

PART V

XXXI   Private Presses   353
The work of the Doves Press, the Ashendene Press and other artistic heritors of William Morris.

XXXII   Modern Fine Printing   365
The work of Bruce Rogers, D. B. Updike, and other present-day exponents of high standards in typography.

XXXIII   Towards the Golden Book   373
The need of books for everyday use, well designed, well proportioned, executed in a workmanlike manner, at a reasonable cost.

THE GOLDEN BOOK

Of the Making of Books

THE BOOK. How our very life is woven around the conception represented by that word. From a book we learned how to read as we faltered through the staccato sentences of "The Little Red Hen." In a book we read in our youth stirring stories of the boys and girls of 1776 which gave us a far more vivid conception of history than we gained in the classroom. Between the covers of books we have re-lived the romances of many a hero and heroine of greater or less renown. On printed pages we have found the essence of beauty distilled for us by the poets, and been moved by the great verse more deeply than most of us care to confess. By the reading of history we glean from the experience of the past principles which go far toward influencing our decision on problems of the present. From biography we gain wisdom and inspiration to make our own lives richer and more fruitful. And through printed books we have obtained much of the practical knowledge, the principle and practice of the occupation, by which we earn our daily bread.

The general interest in the hypothetical question so often asked and answered: "If I were to be cast off on a desert island what books would I select to take with me?" is evidence of the indispensibility of books to the individual of culture. Yet we seldom realize the importance of books (and their offspring of magazines and newspapers) to the present organization of society. Without printed books there would be no popular education. Only the rich would be able to read, and have access to texts worth reading. The mass of the people would still live in deep ignorance and superstition. But now, books are available to all, and reading is not only the most pleasant of all recreations for spare time, but the most profitable as well.

In the field of religion, books take on an even deeper significance. Conceive the import of the Bible to the earnest believer, of the Book of Common Prayer to the devout Anglican, of the Talmud to the orthodox Jew. In point of circulation, the Bible has always been the "best seller" of all books and it will probably so continue.

In the field of science, books are the first consideration of research. The scientist—whether in the field of medicine, chemistry, or astronomy—without adequate library facilities cannot expect to do satisfactory work. The contents of his bookshelves are the most essential tools in his workshop.

There is no need to labor this argument further. The most cursory reflection will make it clear beyond doubt that books are a primary necessity of life in any civilized community. Yet while there is widespread sound appre-

[2]

ciation of literature, that is of the art of writing books,
there is almost no general appreciation of the art of bookmaking. Nevertheless, the design of books is as much
an art as architecture, or painting, or sculpture—and
perhaps of more import to the population at large in that
it exerts an esthetic influence upon more people more
frequently than any other art. And the setting of type
and printing of books is as truly a craft susceptible of
high standards as the craft of the weaver, or potter, or
goldsmith.

In view of the number of ardent booklovers and the
extent of appreciation of the literary content of books,
it is surprising that there is so little appreciation of
their design and quality of execution. It must be admitted
at the outset that present-day standards of bookmaking
are with few exceptions lamentably low. This is probably accounted for by the general lack of appreciation of
fine bookmaking, for when a demand exists for good
work in any field, that demand is inevitably supplied.

Perhaps, too, because of this lack of interest, there
are almost no "books about books" addressed to the general reader, and discussing features of books and their
making aside from considerations of literary content.
But while standards of bookmaking have been and are
bad, there are signs of light amidst the shadows. There
is even now under way a budding renaissance in the
book arts — an awakening that needs and deserves the
encouragement of all book lovers. With patronage, the
art of book design can be made to flourish; the craft of
the printer can be brought once again to a station of dignity, to a pride in fine work.

[3]

So while deploring the general standards of book-making, our view may be optimistic rather than the reverse. Conditions are on the mend rather than the decline. And those who are making good books find that they sell, which indicates an appreciation not only potential but actual—though perhaps yet limited in extent. But the evidence of an improvement in public taste, so far as bookmaking is concerned, is sufficient to indicate still greater potentialities of appreciation. The existence of this incipient renaissance is the reason for the present volume, and perhaps its justification.

This discussion of books and their makers is written from the viewpoint of the designer and printer. Personally, I confess to a real enthusiasm for good books—primarily for their content. But I take a further pleasure in a fine work of literature interpreted in physical form by an artist, just as I most enjoy a Tschaikowsky symphony played by a great orchestra under a conductor of real inspiration. To convey a beautiful passage to our brain, through a medium which esthetically affronts us, cannot fail to handicap its full appreciation. To clothe it typographically simply, appropriately, yet beautifully withal, is to treat it only as it merits. Such presentation cannot help giving us, subtly and perhaps unconsciously, added pleasure in the reading of the text.

The ambition of the true artist in the bookmaking field is to produce fine works of literature in a fine format. With reprints of the classics he occasionally has this opportunity but almost never with the best modern literature. Most books of this character are planned to sell in large quantities and are ground through the usual mill of manufacture in form or manner not one bit better than the most mediocre novel preceding them on the publisher's list. In my esthetic anguish over the modern books I most enjoy, it almost seems that the good books are, if possible, a little worse than the average in design and production. A glance through the shelves of any collection of modern first editions will demonstrate how shabbily present-day authors have been treated by the printers who acted as obstetricians to the children of their brains, in introducing them to a critical world.

The average publisher reading the preceding paragraph (if indeed publishers read books issued by other publishers) will immediately retort that there are economic limitations imposed by the cost of production and the sale price of current books. This leads me to a statement that cannot be too clearly emphasized. Good book design has almost no bearing on expense of manufacture. Taste and judgment are the added ingredients required. The artist in bookmaking, if he have his feet on the ground and is not merely a dilettante, can take almost a barbarity in the form of a book and make out of it a good volume at no increase in cost. The manner of doing this will later be discussed in detail. Let us therefore remember this precept: Sound bookmaking is not necessarily expensive bookmaking.

There is an element of public service in designing printed matter of wide circulation in that the improvement in taste exerts influence on so many readers. The typographer who has opportunity to plan a Sinclair

[5]

Lewis novel, the cover of a telephone book, the headlines and layout of a metropolitan newspaper, may make the same contribution to raising standards of public taste as the architect who designs inexpensive workingmen's houses of real beauty and charm. The campaign against banality is one in which we can all enlist with a will.

There is still another caution. By fine bookmaking we do not mean elaborate book design. Some of the finest books are made with simple types plus only the elements of taste and judgment in their setting, spacing, and positioning on the page. While a little appropriate decoration, used with discretion, often adds greatly to the charm of a volume, it is in no way essential to achieving the finest results in book design, as has been demonstrated by many master printers of ages past and present.

As in all other arts, the best in present practice is based on tradition evolved during centuries past with admixture in limited degree of principles of modern genesis, the whole colored by the personal interpretation of the designer. The best printing of any period has not been revolutionary, but evolutionary, the individual printer of genius adding some new note to the work of his predecessors. The sane book designer, therefore, studies carefully the history of his art and familiarizes himself with the printed masterpieces produced since the invention of movable types. These will be of great value not only in the development of his own taste, but in affording him sound models from which to work. If his work is to be more than routine, however, he must introduce some new note that will make it his own, that will make it creation rather than slavish reproduction.

There is still another reason for acquaintance with the historical aspects of typography, and this is that with given periods and certain countries are associated specific characteristics of type design and book planning. When the typographer has before him for design the manuscript of a book dealing with the American Continental Congress he will not want to set it in a type of wholly Italian inspiration, dating from the sixteenth century. He would choose rather a type face in keeping with the character of our own Colonial typography, and would in all likelihood set the title page in the same spirit. Yet when we deal with a volume made up of translations of French eighteenth century essays, it would be desirable, in absence of reasons to the contrary, to give the volume some of the highly characteristic feeling of French printing and book decoration during that century.

Any appreciation of modern book design is therefore based, to a considerable degree at least, on an understanding of and acquaintance with the historical development of the book. For that reason the first three parts of this volume are historical, tracing in brief outline the making of books from the earliest times, with some reference to the work of outstanding individual printers and attempting some appraisal of their contributions to the art of book design. The fourth part is given over to a discussion of the various features of bookmaking entering into the planning and production of various kinds of books. In the fifth and concluding part—which is brief—is

[7]

attempted some orientation of our present status and the formulation of a program for still further improvement of bookmaking, looking towards an ideal within the limits of accomplishment, in other words towards the "Golden Book."

I. *Ancient Forms of Writing*

HE NEXT logical step, after man had evolved a system of speech by which to communicate with his fellows, was to devise some method of communication which might be written, and thus serve for the preservation of records or to convey messages to some one at a distance. The earliest form of writing was entirely pictorial, where the picture represented an object through delineation of its shape in simple form. In the next stage, the pictorial symbols represented ideas suggested by the material objects so delineated. These two stages are "pictographic" and "ideographic" and the symbols are known as pictographs and ideograms. The Egyptians hieroglyphics are a well-known form of pictographic writing, which in its later development became ideographic.

The next step involved a radical departure and was most important—the change to a phonographic system, in which the symbols represent the sounds of spoken words. Phonographic writing passed through three stages. In the first the symbol represented the sound of a

[9]

word; in the second the sound of a syllable; in the third the simplest elements of sound—in other words, the letter sounds as we know them today.

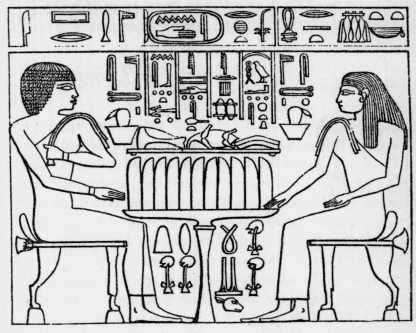

THE SEND INSCRIPTION, 4000 B. C.

The earliest writing of which we have knowledge developed in the eastern Mediterranean world, and the earliest specimen of this writing preserved to us is, as we might expect, a monumental inscription. Almost all our very early examples of writing are of this character: for two reasons. In the first place, powerful personages desired to make use of the new art to transmit to posterity a record of their fame and achievements, and,

[10]

secondly, stone and other monumental materials, being more lasting than wood or papyrus or parchment, have therefore stood a better chance of preservation.

The most ancient written record in the world is the Send inscription which is dated about 4000 B. C., preserved in the Ashmolean Museum at Oxford. The main panel of it is here reproduced (page 10). It is a limestone cornice of the false door of a tomb. At the left is seen seated S'era, a priest and royal relative of Send, king of the second dynasty. Opposite him is the seated figure of a female. There is meat on a reed-covered table between them, and at each end is a basin and water jug. Above and below are hieroglyphic symbols for incense, dates, wine, loaves, linen, flesh, and so forth, all of which are offerings to the king. This inscription constitutes, therefore, the cornerstone of the world's written literature.

As the art of writing developed, two physical processes came into common use. One consisted in applying a fluid dye to a membrane, usually papyrus; the other in incising or impressing on a plastic surface which later hardened. Broadly speaking: the former method was Egyptian, the latter grew up in the Tigris-Euphrates world. Both methods reached the classical world—the wax tablets of the Greeks and Romans, and the pen, ink and papyrus or paper which have survived through succeeding generations to our own times.

The Egyptian scribe is depicted in many ancient reliefs, writing in a standing position, holding the sheet of papyrus with his left hand and holding the reed pen in his right. A seated scribe writing an extensive document might support the roll on his lap. A scribe whose work necessitated reference to many records like census sheets or tax rolls might squat before a small desk on which were piled his rolled-up records, like a flock of college

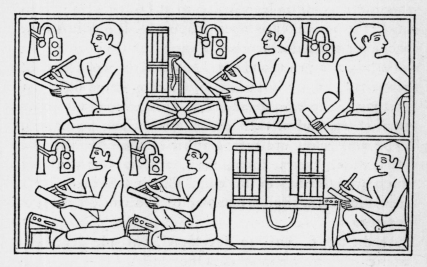

EGYPTIAN SCRIBES AT WORK

diplomas. This is graphically portrayed in a relief from the tomb of Ti at Sakkara, Egypt, dating from the twenty-seventh century B. C. In the above reproduction of this relief are seen two scribes so squatted, resting the papyrus on the desk, while their clerks or assistants are seen in a similar posture holding the sheets in their left hands.

Much of the scribe's work was done in the open, and he thus required a writing outfit in convenient form. The essential elements were: two reed pens and a protective case to hold them, a little jar of water and a palette with two round depressions in which to mix his black and red ink. This outfit was often carried over the shoulder or in the hand and the various items were, for convenience, tied together with a cord. A pictorial representation of this outfit came to be the hieroglyphic sign for "writing," "to write," and "scribe." This sign will be seen above the scribes depicted on page 12.

When writing the scribe made his ink in one of the compartments of the palette, mixing lampblack with an aqueous solution of vegetable gum which held in suspension the non-soluble black. To produce carmine ink a red iron oxide was used. The use of both red and black ink accounts for the numerous representations of a scribe with two pens behind his ear. The red was used for the introductory words of paragraphs; from this custom was derived the rubrics of European manuscripts and early printing. The word "rubric" has survived to the present day in the same meaning though it is no longer necessarily printed in red.

Of the early form of writing outfit only pictures have survived. It was later improved by combining the pen case and palette, such a case, now in the Haskell Oriental Museum, containing remains of the black and red ink, just as mixed by the scribe for the last time. An outfit of this character appears frequently in the Mastaba reliefs.

The writing implement was a cross between a brush and a pen. Perhaps by chewing the end of the reed, the scribe frayed the fibers, giving him a soft tuft to work with. His writing almost constituted brush painting on papyrus. Only with the coming of parchment, with its harder surface, did the split pen come into use.

The development of the form of hieratic writing was largely influenced by the availability to the Egyptians of a material which would readily take thin ink, would retain the color, and which was smooth enough to permit free movement of the ravelled fiber pen. This material was papyrus, made from the fibrous tissue of the marrow of the papyrus plant. Pliny in his *Natural History* describes for us the manner of its fabrication. The stems were cut into lengths of about sixteen inches. The marrow was then slit into thin strips and these were laid flat side by side. A second layer was then placed upon the first at right angles to it. The layers were then treated with gum solution and pressed, pounded, and smoothed until its surface was suited for writing. In fresh condition it was of a yellowish-white color, later turning into various tints of light or deep yellow. For extensive manuscripts a number of sheets each approximately twelve by sixteen inches in size were pasted together and made up in the form of a roll, usually comprising twenty sheets. If more than one roll was needed, the scribe himself pasted on additional material, but this was often done clumsily and the writing which came over the seams suffered accordingly.

The top and bottom edges of manuscript were the portions most exposed to wear and tear, and were, therefore, often reinforced by pasted strips. The side showing the horizontal layers was the smoothest and considered the "right side." In ancient times the reverse side was not used but later, in a pinch for space the back was utilized to finish a text. At first papyrus was evidently costly, for we find instances where an early text has been washed off and the papyrus used over again.

The height of the rolls was usually a little in excess of twelve inches. These were then divided laterally into rolls approximately six inches tall or sometimes into rolls somewhat over three inches tall. Such small rolls had the advantage of being easier to handle and less liable to breakage. For letters, the normal leaf, halved vertically, was used; where necessary the whole leaf was utilized or it was cut into four strips.

The writing on papyrus was in columns arranged something like the columns of a newspaper. Each column constituted the equivalent of a page in our modern books. A section of a roll looked therefore something like this:

```
xxxxx   xxxxx   xxxxx   xxxxx   xxxxx   xxxxx
xxxxx   xxxxx   xxxxx   xxxxx   xxxxx   xxxxx
xxxxx   xxxxx   xxxxx   xxxxx   xxxxx   xxxxx
xxxxx   xxxxx   xxxxx   xxxxx   xxxxx   xxxxx
xxxxx   xxxxx   xxxxx   xxxxx   xxxxx   xxxxx
xxxxx   xxxxx   xxxxx   xxxxx   xxxxx   xxxxx
```

There was a normal length of about thirty-eight letters to each line. Papyrus as a material for the preservation of records was far from satisfactory. There was danger of piercing it in the process of writing, and in guarding against this the up and down strokes often became almost indistinguishable. When it had dried out it became highly fragile—almost as brittle as dead leaves.

What remains of ancient papyri are best preserved between sheets of glass.

Following papyrus, the next writing material was parchment. This was prepared skin of animals, principally of the sheep or of the calf. That from the latter animal is the best and is known as vellum. Uterine vellum—the finest and whitest of the varieties of parchment, was made from a calf's intestines. In parchment is avoided the fragility of papyrus and the coarseness of primitive paper, but is was expensive and heavy.

Parchment has a rather picturesque history. It is related that Eumenes II, King of Pergamum, was deprived in the second century, B. C., through the jealousy of the Ptolemys, of an adequate supply of Egyptian papyrus. Necessity is the mother of invention, and in having recourse to the ancient use of skins as writing material, some improvements were made in their preparation, and there was obtained a product of fine quality which soon gained renown. The material became known in the natural course of events, as *Pergamena*, from which is derived the English word *parchment*.

Passing now to the western Asiatic world, the evidence regarding methods of writing is not as plentiful. An examination of clay tablet documents indicates that the end of the stylus (cut from a river reed) was either square or round. The impressions were wedge shaped, from which was derived the term cuneiform writing (Latin *cuneus*—wedge). We have no pictorial representations of clay tablet writing earlier than the eighth century B. C., during the Assyrian Empire.

ANCIENT WRITING

Breasted thus describes a relief depicting a scribe in the act of recording the plunder of a captured city: "At the left is an official reading from a tablet, while before him stands a scribe with a thick clay tablet supported on the left hand. He has paused a moment in his writing, and raises his right hand with the stylus poised between the thumb and the palm of the hand, the fingers being stretched straight out . . . When the scribe actually applied the stylus to the clay he bent all of his fingers and held the stylus in the closed fist."

In practically all the reliefs of the period showing the process of writing, we find pictured one scribe writing on a clay tablet with a stylus and a second writing on papyrus with a pen, in just the manner of the Egyptian scribes. Now arises the question of when the pen began to invade the realm of the stylus. There was interpenetration of the two influences. The clay tablet was not infrequently encountered in Egypt after 1400 B. C., but thereafter the stylus yielded in progressively greater degree to the pen. By the end of the twelfth century papyrus was being imported into Phoenician cities.

The introduction of pen, ink, and papyrus writing from Egypt into Western Asia was synchronous with the development of the first alphabet—the so-called Phoenician alphabet—written without vowels. This was the next great forward step in man's mastery of the art of bookmaking.

II. *Origin of the Alphabet*

T THE foundation of bookmaking stands the alphabet—the development of which has made writing and reading an almost universal function of mankind and no subject is of more fascinating interest than its origin. Our present alphabet is derived from the alphabet of the Phoenicians, the seafaring people of the Mediterranean. The word comes from the Greek names for the first two letters: *alpha* and *beta*. It may be defined as a series of symbols representing the sounds of a spoken language, and in its perfect form would have one symbol and only one for each sound. This ideal has never, however, been attained. Furthermore, most spoken languages evolve to a pronunciation quite different, in many instances, from the sounds indicated by the symbols.

The Phoenicians were using the alphabet on which our present letter system is based in the ninth century, B. C., and perhaps earlier. Whence they derived their alphabet has been the subject of very extensive discussion and argument. According to the commonly accepted view, it was derived from Egyptian hieratic writing, one theory holding that it came to the Phoenicians along with papyrus as a writing material—which was of course of Egyptian origin. Alan H. Gardiner has but recently shown the existence of a hitherto unknown script of Egyptian origin, the "Sinai" script, which is clearly an intermediate stage between Egyptian hieroglyphic writing and the Semitic alphabets on which the Phoenician was based. The Sinai script is most probably a form of the proto-Semitic posited by Praetorius.

The inscriptions on which this new but apparently sound theory is based were discovered by Flinders Petrie in the ancient copper and malachite mines of Sinai and in the ruins of a temple of the Egyptian Goddess Hathor at Serabit el-Hadim. Petrie dates them, on archeological evidence about 1500 B. C.

On the basis of these new contributions, the genealogy of our alphabet reads thus: Egyptian Hieroglyphic—Sinai script—Old Semitic (north)—South Semitic—Phoenician—Greek—Latin.

This theory of Egyptian derivation has recently been challenged by Sir Arthur Evans who has argued, on the basis of his field studies, that the alphabet originated on the Island of Crete and was taken to the mainland by the "Cherethites and Pelethites" or Philistines, who founded colonies on the shores of Palestine. From the sixteenth century B. C., and undoubtedly earlier, there was in use in Crete a hieroglyphic writing that was probably a growth out of indigenous prehistoric elements, but which also shows some possibilities of Egyptian influence. There was also a linear script.

In 1889 Evans came into possession of a bead-seal of cornelian, with figures on all four sides, that was said to have been found at Sparta, but he found later that it came from Crete, and he succeeded in obtaining more of the same character. In November, 1893, he reported to the Hellenic Society that he had discovered a series of gems which showed hieroglyphics of sixty symbols which were distinct from both Egyptian and Hittite symbols. He went to Crete and found many such stones worn about the necks of prospective mothers who believed that they were milk producers, and called them "milk stones." Evans succeeded in buying some of these stones and in taking impressions of others. Some show merely pictorial forms, others are decidedly quasi-alphabetic. In April, 1896, he obtained in Crete from underneath a prehistoric sacrificial stratum, a slab of a table which had carved upon it a small early shrine of the Cretan Goddess in the Palace at Knossos. This proved that it belonged to the early part of the second millennium before our era. This is believed to have had connection with the incidents pertaining to the legend that the baby Zeus had been fed with mingled milk and honey. This table had an inscription which reads from left to right, and consists of eight or nine characters and two stops. Supposing it to have been symmetrically arranged, it would originally have consisted of about fifteen characters and perhaps four words.

More seal-stones, found later, huge jars with marks which some term "mason" marks, but which Evans found to be a well advanced system of writing, all tended to reinforce his belief. Excavations brought forth parts of tables inscribed with script prevalent throughout the concluding period of the Palace history—the twelfth century before our era may be regarded as their latest limit—and this would make them older by several centuries than the oldest known specimen of Phoenician writing. The hypotheses of Evans, however, while of

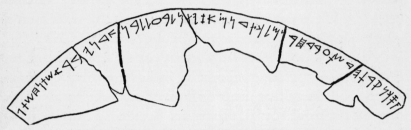

BRONZE BOWL WITH PHOENICIAN WRITING
NINTH CENTURY B. C.

very great interest, must be as yet accepted with qualifications so far as the Cretan origin of the Phoenician alphabet is concerned.

The earliest example of clearly alphabetic writing which has been preserved to us is the Moabite Stone. There was controversy over its possession, which resulted in its being broken into pieces by the Arabs but it has since been patched together again, and this priceless relic now rests in comparative safety in the Louvre. On it is an extensive inscription in the alphabet of Moab, commemorating the deeds of King Mesha, who had thrown off the sovereignty of Israel following the death of King Ahab. The events dealt with are presumed, with reasonable certainty, to have taken place in the first half of the ninth century, B. C. The oldest example of writing in the Phoenician alphabet proper is a fragment of a

EGYPTIAN HIERATIC	SEMITIC PHOENICIAN	HELLENIC EARLY GREEK	ROMAN EARLY LATIN	PRESENT DAY

25 CENTURIES B. C.	IO TO 9 CENTURIES B. C.	7 TO 4 CENTURIES B. C.	200 B. C. TO 300 A. D.	

THE EVOLUTION OF FOUR LETTERS OF OUR ALPHABET

bronze bowl found about fifty years ago in Cyprus, which bears, around its edge, a dedication inscription. This bowl is, in all probability, about as early as the Moabite Stone.

The early Phoenician alphabet consisted of twenty-two letter symbols, which represented consonants only— a characteristic which it shares with the other Semitic languages. This alphabet was taken over with some changes—among which some of the characters were inverted—by the Greeks, and we have had recent testimony of the extent of the Greek obligation to Phoenician sources in the discoveries of von Gärtringen on the

ABDEGNRS

LETTERS CUT IN STONE ON THE TRAJAN COLUMN
AT ROME, 114 A. D.

island of Thera. There were many differences in alphabet and dialect in different sections of Greece and it took a good many centuries for the Greeks to attain an approximation to uniformity in these matters.

The earliest examples of Greek writing which have come down to us cannot be dated earlier than the seventh century B. C., and by this time the vowel characters had been added.

The Latin alphabet was in turn derived from the Greek, undoubtedly through the agency of the Chalcidian Greeks in Italy. We have several examples of the early use of this alphabet which we use today, chief among which is an inscription, which occurs on a fibula found at Praeneste, near Rome, and reading, "MANIOS MED FHEFHAKED NUMASIOI," which may be translated "Manius made me for Numasius." The most interesting feature, however, is that the writing reads from right to left. This is dated by authorities either fifth or sixth century B. C.

Then there is an earthenware jug of odd shape, which was discovered in Rome between the Viminal and Quirinal hills, the probable date of which is early fourth century B. C. This bears the inscription: "DVENOS MED FECED," also reading from right to left—"Dvenos made me."

SYRIO VIATIC

ROMAN INSCRIPTION OF 1261 A. D.

Finally, and most important of all, is a portion of a pillar found under a pavement in the Roman Forum. This is of approximately the same age as the Praeneste fibula but the inscription on it is undoubtedly of Roman origin. It is written in what is known as the "Boustrophedon" manner, *i. e.*, it reads up the column; then down, the text turning and reversing its direction, rather than

[24]

going back to the starting point of the preceding line. The next development was the change to a left to right direction of writing.

There are, of course, many non-roman alphabets in use today. Russian and other Slavonic languages have derived their alphabets from the Greek. Hebrew and Arabic are the Semitic alphabets of most importance, while on the Asiatic continent we find the alphabets of the Indo-Iranian group. But into the details of the non-roman alphabets we cannot here enter in detail.

Suffice it to say that the development of alphabetic writing forged one more link in the chain of mankind's progress from barbarism to culture.

III. *Paper and Its Forbears*

N THE development of printing consequential progress would have been impossible without paper. It is perfectly clear that papermaking was a Chinese invention dating at least as early as the Christian era. It has also been demonstrated that the art of paper manufacture was transmitted from the east to west, the manner of its transmission and the chronological sequence of its first appearance at successive points constituting one of the most intriguing instances of historical ratiocination that can be called to mind.

The year 105 A. D. seems to be taken conservatively as the date of the invention of paper, for it was then that the new process was first reported to the Emperor by Ts'ai Lun, who is generally credited with the invention. Whether he was responsible personally for the idea or whether he was merely the official through whom a discovery of this kind was made public is not certain. The record runs thus: "In ancient times writing was generally on bamboo or on pieces of silk, which were then called *chih*. But silk being expensive and bamboo heavy, these two materials were not convenient. Then Ts'ai Lun thought of using tree bark, hemp, rags and fish nets. In the first year of the Yuan-hsing period [A. D. 105] he made a report to the Emperor on the process of paper-making, and received high praise for his ability. From this time paper has been in use everywhere and is called the 'paper of Marquis Ts'ai.' " So not only was paper an Oriental invention but, contrary to common belief, rag paper was first produced in China.

This record receives amazingly clear confirmation from the recent Chinese discoveries of Sir Aurel Stein. In the sealed dust bin of a watch tower near Tun-huang in western China he made rich finds of early documents in Sogdian script on paper, one group of which dates not later than 737 A. D. One of these documents, dating earlier than 137 A. D. and therefore constituting one of the oldest pieces of paper in the world, is here reproduced from the original in the British Museum.

The Ts'ai Lun story is also given credence by the discovery—also by Stein—of fabric from the first century B. C. containing fibers of the paper mulberry tree of China and Japan. This use of the bark fibers was thus a helpful preliminary to the later invention.

A mere recital of dates of the earliest known manufacture of paper in various localities tells much of the subsequent history of this universal substance for writing and printing. We have found paper first in Central China 105 A. D.; at Tun-huang, farther westward, before 137 A. D.; at Turfan in Chinese Turkestan 399 A. D.; at Samarkand 751 A. D.; at Bagdad in 793 A. D., in Egypt 900 A. D. or earlier; at Fez in Morocco about

1100, at Xativa in Spain 1150; at Herault in France
1189; Cologne, Germany, some time in the neighborhood of 1320, in England 1494; in Philadelphia 1690.

How graphic a story this schedule tells! Chart it on a
map and it is even more impressive. During the period of
the transmission westward of the secrets of papermaking,
there was a lively trade between the west and the east
along the "great silk ways" and there was consequent
interchange of culture. There was too the permeating
influence of religion as the belief of one or another sect
spread eastward. The Buddhism of India spread over
China and Japan and, though the fact is little known,
the missionaries of Nestorian Christianity penetrated as
far as Chinese Turkestan. And the envoys of Moham-
medanism were far from inactive.

Other specimens of paper of only slightly later date
than those discovered near Tun-huang have been found
by other explorers at various points in Central Asia. They
are usually found together with documents on wood or on
silk, showing that the use of the earlier substances had
not been entirely supplanted. By the fifth century, however, the use of paper had become almost universal.

Military conquest was next to serve the spread of culture. During the early part of the eighth century the
Arabs conquered the territory now known as Russian
Turkestan. During a battle, the Arabs took as prisoners
some Chinese papermakers, who taught the art to their
captors. Thus paper was introduced into the Arabic
world at Samarkand. An eleventh century writer tells us:
"Among the specialties of Samarkand that should be

SPECIMEN OF CHINESE PAPER, A. D. 137

mentioned is paper. It has replaced the rolls of Egyptian papyrus and the parchment which was formerly used for writing, because it is more beautiful, more agreeable, and more convenient." Soon the art spread to other cities, among them Bagdad and Damascus.

The next point of appearance was Egypt. Here papyrus had been the standard writing material. Toward 850 paper was displacing it. By 950 papyrus was entirely supplanted. An Egyptian letter written toward the end of the ninth century closes with these words: "Pardon the papyrus." Paper was already the vogue for stylish correspondence.

Papermaking then traversed northern Africa to Morocco and was introduced into continental Europe via Spain. Its spread in Europe was not as rapid as might be expected, due in the first instance to the satisfactory qualities as writing material of the parchment then in general use, and also the paucity of demand occasioned by the fact that few people could read or write. It was not until the invention of printing that the paper industry became active.

What were the methods of manufacture of the paper entering into the first European books? One point of exceptional interest is that the methods of the early papermakers differed in but slight details from the methods followed now in the mills turning out hand made papers used for the finest books printed today. Like the arts of the weaver and potter the craft has changed but little since its early days.

The essence of papermaking is to mix disintegrated

fiber with water, spread the mixture evenly over a screen or mould through which the water drains off leaving a film of matted fibers which, when dried, is paper. The only changes of method have been in the treatment of the fiber and the construction of the moulds.

It is possible that the Oriental papermakers may have poured the water-mixed fibers or pulp on the moulds, but at least since the eleventh century when the art came into Spain the method has been to dip the mould into a tub of pulp, bringing to the surface of the screen the desired amount of fiber.

The rags were first macerated and the resulting pulp placed in a tub or vat. The mixture was, when possible, kept warm and it was kept in constant agitation by a workman stirring it with a pole. The mould was a screen bordered by a frame to give it strength. Another removable frame placed over it, and known as the deckle, determined the size of paper to be made. The mould was plunged into the liquid perpendicularly and then turned to a horizontal position under the surface. When withdrawn the screen carried on its surface the fibrous material which was to form the sheet of paper. The vatman then shook the pulp on the surface of the mould, first in one direction, and then in another, the two directions being at right angles to each other. This process crossed and matted the fibers, and made paper as strong in one direction as another. Incidentally, papers with most of the qualities of hand-fabricated papers are being made today by machine (being called mould-made papers) but the one feature in which true hand-made paper cannot be duplicated mechanically is in this knitting of fibers in all directions. The fibers in a machine-made paper practically all run in one direction.

The wooden deckle, limiting the size of the sheet, was then removed, leaving the paper with a feathery and slightly uneven edge which has come to be known as the "deckle." The mould was then passed to a second workman known as the "coucher" while the vatman started to dip another sheet using a second mould but the same deckle. After the proper amount of water had been drained off the sheet, the coucher turned the mould face down on a piece of wool cloth or felting. As the mould was lifted again the wet sheet of incipient paper adhered to the fabric. Another felt was laid on top of it ready to receive the next sheet from the vatman.

These operations were repeated until a hundred and forty-four sheets of paper, separated from each other by pieces of felt, were accumulated. The pile was then placed in a screw press and pressure was applied to expel as much water as possible. After the pressing the felts were removed and returned to the coucher for further use and the pile of paper, with nothing now between the sheets, was pressed again. The leaves were then parted, arranged in different order, and pressed again. The more often this was done, the smoother the finish became. This finishing was a refinement, however, and many of the earliest papers give evidence of no further treatment subject to removal from the felting.

The paper was next dried, by hanging it in "spurs" of four or five sheets together, over cow-hair or horsehair cords. If hung up individually the sheets would have wrinkled badly but in groups they dried fairly flat. A final process more necessary for writing papers than for book papers, was sizing, the sheets being dipped in a glutinous liquid and subsequently pressed and dried. The size made them impervious to ink.

After a lapse of four or five centuries hand-made paper is still manufactured by practically the same methods. The great changes have come in the manufacture of paper by machine. The process in use today was invented in 1798 by Louis Robert, who was in the employ of the Didots at the Essonne mills in France. The process was introduced into England by Henry Fourdrinier, after whom the modern papermaking machines have been named.

The screen of the single hand mould is replaced by an endless band of wire mesh over which the pulp, prepared in mechanical "beaters," is flowed. As the screen, which is constantly shaken from side to side, moves forward, more and more water seeps through it, leaving the film of fiber on top. A roll of felt soon meets it, and by superior adhesiveness, picks the web of matted fiber off the wire screen and carries it through steam heated drying rolls which serve the double function of pressing out and evaporating the moisture. Soon the web of paper is well enough formed to hold together and the felt leaves it to continue alone through further drying rolls. At the end of the machines, some of which are several hundred feet long, the completed paper is wound on a roll. If it is an uncoated paper such as that on which this book is printed it is finished, except for being "sheeted" or cut off the roll in sheets of convenient size. Newspaper and paper for the large edition magazines go directly in rolls to rotary presses without being cut into sheets.

The papers ordinarily used for printing fine illustrations, for color printing and the like, while still in roll form go through another process called coating, wherein a mixture of casein or glucose, clay, and some other ingredients are applied to its surface, making it extremely smooth and suitable for receiving the impression of fine screen plates. The product is known as "coated paper." At first all coated paper was glossy, but in recent years an improvement has been introduced in the shape of clay coated paper without shine or gloss. This is known as "dull coated" and is generally used by the best printers for work in which halftone illustrations must be used. Another method of achieving smoothness of finish is by a process of burnishing between rolls traveling at different velocities, which is known as supercalendering.

Among uncoated papers the two main varieties are "wove" and "laid," according to their textures. The screens of laid papers have fine wires in one direction, bound together with heavier wires at right angles to them, and placed an inch or so apart. These secondary wires show in the texture of the paper and are known as laid marks. They may be observed in the sheet on which this page is printed. All the earliest hand-made papers were laid papers and it was not until the middle of the eighteenth century that "wove" paper was developed, its introduction being credited to John Baskerville, the fas-

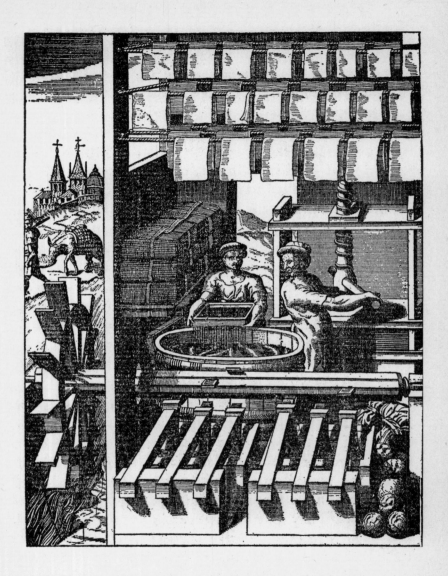

THE ANCIENT METHOD OF PAPERMAKING

tidious printer of Birmingham, England. This was made over a fine texture wire screen which showed no pattern of wires. The French called it *papier velin*, and the members of the Didot family of celebrated French printers did much to bring its manufacture to perfection.

The most vexing problem in the field of paper today is the constant deterioration in quality of material entering into its manufacture. The price of rags makes their use impossible for papers used in any quantity. So it has come about that most modern paper is composed mostly of wood pulp, often in a very crude state. The newspapers of the present day, for example, practically disintegrate in a period of ten or twenty years, while the newspapers of the Revolutionary period are in almost as good condition as the day they were printed. Wood pulp properly treated, however, makes fairly satisfactory paper and, for economic reasons, we must content ourselves with it for ordinary use. But for books and records designed for the use of posterity there has not yet been found a substitute for paper manufactured out of good old-fashioned rags.

IV. *Books in Manuscript*

L ATER than clay tablets and papyrus rolls, we find books in much the form of those with which we are familiar, but of course written by hand. It was books such as these, laboriously written by scribes, that have preserved to us all we have of the history and literature of ancient times. Some of our most precious intellectual treasures were saved by the tenuous thread of a single existing copy, which was discovered by an appreciative enthusiast and made mankind's heritage forever, first through duplication by manuscript, and later through the medium of printing.

The word manuscript is explained exactly by its Latin derivation: *codices manu scripti*, books written by hand. Manuscripts are differentiated, on the one hand, from the inscriptions on stone, metal, or wood which preceded them and, on the other hand, from the printed books which succeeded them.

The first great period of manuscript books is found— strange to say—in Ireland, in the sixth, seventh, and eighth centuries. Within a century after the coming of St. Patrick to the Emerald Isle there was a vivid renaissance, cultural as well as religious. The influence of this went beyond the insular limits and Irish missionaries and monks invaded the Continent while, reciprocally, continental students made pilgrimages to Ireland to study the classical languages. During this time there were produced in the Irish monasteries, manuscripts of splendid calligraphy and illumination which have never been surpassed for originality of design and skill in execution.

The most celebrated example of the work of Irish calligraphers and illuminators of this period is the Book of Kells which has been termed, by more than one writer, "the most beautiful book in the world."

The scriptorium of an ordinary Benedictine monastery has been well described for us by Madan. It was a large room usually over the chapterhouse and when no special room was assigned for the work of the scribes separate studies were often made in the cloisters. Every scribe thus had a window to himself but his den was always open to the cloister walk. It was only in special cases that a scribe had a private room in which to work. For fear of injury to the manuscripts, artificial light was taboo, so all work had, of necessity, to be done during the daylight hours. Access to the scriptorium was denied to any except high officials of the abbey so as to guard the scribes against interruption. The scriptorium was in charge of an officer known as the *armarius*, whose duty was to provide parchment, pens, ink, knives, awls, and rulers. Scribes were usually forbidden to make corrections in the text even when the original they were copying was obviously in error. Absolute silence was the rule.

When a scribe wished to borrow a book he made certain signs to his fellow workers for example: in requesting a pagan work he gave the general sign, followed by scratching the ear after the manner of a dog! In addition to the monks, there were some secular scribes who came to the monasteries for special duties, such as rubrication or illumination.

The scribe worked about six hours daily. He was given his parchment in sections, each sheet separate but folded and arranged in the order in which it would appear in the book as finally bound. After the decision as to the style and size of the writing, the limits of the written page were ruled in blind with marginal lines, the parchment being held in place with awls. Inasmuch as parchment has two distinct sides, a quaternion or signature is arranged so that the two facing pages have the same character. That is, both are hair-side or both are flesh-side. In addition to the line limiting the margins, guide lines for the individual lines of writing were ruled with a blunt instrument which caused a little furrow in the parchment. The scribe was now ready to write.

When he finished the quaternion which was proofread in comparison with the original by a second person, the sheets were then sent to the hands of the rubricator who inserted titles, notes, headlines, and the like. If illustration was provided for, the sheets next went to the illuminator and, after he had completed his work on the volume, it was ready to be bound.

Accuracy in the transmission of classic texts was, of course, of prime importance, for the tendency to error in successive re-copyings by different hands at different times was very great. The ingenuity of expert textual criticism in repairing the mental lapses of the scribes and unravelling the meaning of obscure passages is in some instances remarkable.

Illumination added much charm to manuscripts. The earliest texts were of course the plainest but as wealth increased and the demand for beautiful books in manuscript form became greater, the first move was to make the first letters of new sentences larger and sometimes color them. Then the extremities of these initial letters were flourished and soon the flourishes became extensive, and ran into the margins. Next the margins of opening or important pages were decorated with an independently designed border. Finally, miniatures were introduced into books and, where the miniaturist was a real artist, the results are superb indeed.

The principal colors used in the embellishment of books were red, blue, and gold. More infrequently, purple, yellow, green—black and white, were used. Sometimes whole manuscripts were lettered in gold or in silver, and in these cases the parchment was often dyed purple, giving a very rich effect. Until the twelfth century gold was applied in powder form; after that usually in leaf form, and burnished, producing a glittering effect of much splendor.

In the transmission of literature, there is no story more romantic than the tale of the discovery of the manuscript of the Bible in Greek, written not later than 400 A. D., the oldest text of the New Testament which has been preserved to us, and in several respects the most interesting. It is well told by Madan. "Constantine Tischendorf, the well-known editor of the Greek Testament, started on his first *mission littéraire* in April, 1844, and in the next month found himself at the Convent of St. Catherine, at the foot of Mount Sinai. There, in the middle of the hall, as he crossed it, he saw a basket full of old parchment leaves on their way to the burning, and was told that two baskets had already gone! Looking at the leaves more closely he perceived that they were parts of the Old Testament in Greek written in an extremely old handwriting. He was allowed to take away forty-three leaves; but the interest of the monks was aroused, and they both stopped the burning, and also refused to part with any more of the precious fragments. Tischendorf departed, deposited the forty-three leaves in the Leipzig Library, and edited them under the title of the Codex Friderico-Augustanus, in compliment to the King of Saxony, in 1846. But he wisely kept the secret of their provenance, and no one followed in his track until he himself went on a second quest to the monastery in 1853. In that year he could find no traces whatever of the remains of the MS. except a few fragments of Genesis, and returned unsuccessful and disheartened. At last, he once more took a journey to the monastery, under the patronage of the Russian Emperor, who was popular throughout the East as the protector of the Oriental Churches. Nothing could he find, however; and he had ordered his Bedouins to get ready for departure, when, happening to have taken a walk with the steward of the house, and to be invited into his room, in the course of conversation the steward said: 'I, too, have read a Septuagint,' and produced out of a wrapper of red cloth 'a bulky kind of volume,' which turned out to be the whole of the New Testament, with the Greek text of the Epistle of Barnabas, much of which was hitherto unknown, and the greater part of the Old Testament, all parts of the very MS. which had so long been sought! In a careless tone Tischendorf asked if he might have it in his room for further inspection, and that night (February 4-5, 1859) it 'seemed impiety to sleep.' By the next morning the Epistle of Barnabas was copied out, and a course of action was settled. Might he carry the volume to Cairo to transcribe? Yes, if the Prior's leave were obtained; but unluckily the Prior had already started to Cairo on his way to Constantinople. By the activity of Tischendorf he was caught up at Cairo, gave the requisite permission, and a Bedouin was sent to the convent, and returned with the book in nine days. On the 24th of February, Tischendorf began to transcribe it; and when it was done, conceived the happy idea of asking for the volume as a gift to the Emperor of Russia. Probably this was the only possible plea which would have gained the main object in view, and even as it was there was great delay; but at last, on the 28th of September, the gift was formally made, and the MS. soon after deposited at St. Petersburg, where it now lies. The age of this manuscript is supposed to be not later than A.D. 400, and has been the subject of minute inquiry in consequence of the curious statement of Simonides in 1862, that he had himself written it on Mount Athos in 1839-1840."

When the lava of Vesuvius in eruption poured over Herculaneum and Pompeii it blackened and apparently destroyed many rolls of papyrus in private libraries in the devastated area. But, strange to say, what appeared to be destruction turned out to be preservation, for in the excavations at the beginning of the nineteenth century many of these blackened rolls were recovered and it was found that, by very careful treatment, they could be put in condition which would permit unrolling them. Many were deciphered and some consequential additions were made to our store of Greek and Latin literature.

Very fortunately, copies of the manuscripts were made at the time, for the originals have since suffered by disintegration, and it is the facsimiles which are now of the greatest value.

There are countless stories of the vicissitudes of celebrated manuscripts, but we have not space to recount them here. The ravages of time, the perils of military conquest, the bigotry of religious zealots, and the carelessness of the ignorant and unthinking all conspire to cut us off from the records of ages past. Yet, on the other hand, the efforts of the scribes served to counteract these influences and to preserve for us, up to the time when the printing press began to function, those texts on which our cultural foundations are established.

V. *Printing in the Far East*

HE heights of literary glory to which China attained in years far past are hard to conceive when we ponder the chaos both intellectual and political which is rife there today. In the development of bookmaking the history of the art in the Far East must be considered entirely independently from its origins and progress in Europe, for in the East books were printed nearly six centuries earlier. These earliest books were of course block books—that is books printed from wood blocks on which text and illustrations had been engraved —but movable types also were invented in China long before Gutenberg's epochal discovery. They would un-doubtedly have been invented earlier had the Chinese written language been adapted to their use. Because of the vast variety of characters movable type composition offered no great advantage and even after it was invented it fell into disuse, because it was easier to engrave on wood the ideographic symbols.

In Europe, with its alphabetically written languages,

the invention of movable types meant—to all intents and purposes—the invention of printing. In China, however, the invention of printing as a practical book-making process meant the invention of block printing.

With this distinction in mind, let us consider the origins of printing in the Far East. The essential feature of printing is the preparation of a form in relief, which can be inked, and from which successive impressions can be drawn. Passing over the early efforts at reduplication by means of seals and stamps, we find the earliest block prints now extant were printed in Japan about 770 A. D. It is probable, however, that block printing had been done in China early in the eighth century.

During this period, Japan was strongly under Chinese influence, an influence traceable in large degree to the Chinese origin of Japanese Buddhism. Shotoku, the Empress of Japan, reigned from 748 to 769, and to her zeal for Buddhism we must credit the earliest undisputed record of printing wood blocks on paper. She ordered to be printed a million Buddhist charms which were to be placed in miniature pagodas and distributed. This took place about the year 767. The facts are clearly attested by Japanese historical records and, in addition, a number of the prints are still extant. Several can be seen today in the British Museum. These charms of the Empress constitute, therefore, the earliest printing known.

Our next certain date which is attested by existing evidence is 868, and the printing this time is Chinese. Furthermore, the example is not a slip of printed paper, but a complete printed book, *and with a woodcut frontis-*

piece. The manner in which this book and other material of like importance were discovered reads like a fairy tale.

In the northwestern part of China a little finger of civilized territory stretches out into the desert of Turkestan. Near the city of Tun-huang are the "Caves of the Thousand Buddhas," cut in rock into the face of a cliff. From an early stone inscription we learn that this cave colony dates from the year 366 A. D. In 1900 a mendicant priest raised money for restoring one of the caves to its former magnificence and was engaged in "improving" one of the original frescoes when he found that the wall on which he was working was not of stone but of brick. Investigating a little further he found that the brick closed the mouth of a chamber piled high with manuscript rolls. Seven years later, Sir Aurel Stein, the British archaeologist celebrated for his research in the field of Chinese history, came to Tun-huang. He tells us in his *Serindia* of his discovery of the secret chamber and of his nerve-racking negotiations for a part of its treasures.

The manuscripts found in the walled-up chamber ranged in date from the fifth to the tenth centuries. It is thought that the cave was sealed in 1035 to prevent its precious contents falling into hostile hands. It appears then to have been forgotten for nearly nine hundred years. When opened, all the manuscripts were found to be in well-nigh perfect condition, a situation made possible by the climate of Chinese Turkestan which, like that of Egypt, is conducive to the preservation of ancient materials. In other parts of China with a different climate the same documents might have perished through disintegration.

Among these documents was found one of the most sacred landmarks of cultural history—the first printed book known. This is the Diamond Sutra which is now one of the proudest possessions of the British Museum. Toward the end of the text occurs the explicit statement that it was "printed on May 11, 868, by Wang Chieh, for free general distribution, in order in deep reverence to perpetuate the memory of his parents."

This book is the work of no tyro and gives evidence of a considerable antecedent period of evolutionary development. In other words, in this example, we find the arts of book printing and illustration in an advanced rather than a primitive stage. This is demonstrated most graphically by the woodcut frontispiece which is here reproduced, and which represents, therefore, the earliest dated woodcut, antedating by many centuries the St. Christopher later to be discussed in Chapter VI. The plate shows Sakamuni seated on a lotus throne, attended by a host of divine beings and monks and discoursing with his aged disciple Subhuti. This copy of the Diamond Sutra is made up of six sheets of text almost a foot in height and about thirty inches long, and a shorter sheet of paper on which the woodcut is printed. All these sheets are pasted together and the whole strip made up into a book in roll form.

There were also found in the chamber numerous single sheet prints, which served as charms or votive

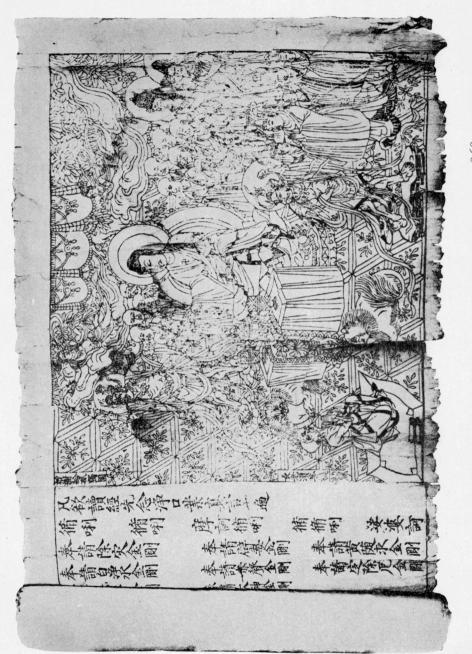

THE DIAMOND SUTRA, CHINESE BLOCK PRINTED BOOK, A. D. 868

offerings. On them are printed illustrations and text and they have, in many respects, kinship to the early European "heiligen" or sacred block prints. A small Buddhist sutra is the earliest known representative of a new form of book, differing from the roll form hitherto in vogue. This book is printed on one side of a long strip of paper, but broken up into pages, and folded accordion fashion. The unprinted backs of the pages were then pasted together giving a final result which resembles to a surprising degree, the form of the modern book.

The early origins of block-printed books in China are also attested by documentary evidence. There is a record of books seen by Liu Pin in the Province of Szechuen in the year 883. After enumerating several secular books he writes: "Most of these books were printed with blocks on paper, but they were so smeared and blotted that they were not readily legible." This Province of Szechuen [then known as Shu] was evidently the center of printing activities in China, as is confirmed by several other historical references. It became independent in 907 as the Empire of Shu, and bookmaking received great impetus from the interest of a far-sighted statesman, Wu Chao-i, about whom this story is told. "When Wu Chao-i was poor, he wished one day to borrow books from a friend. The friend showed by his look that he did not wish to lend them. Wu was grieved and said, 'Some day, when I come into a position of power, I shall have books cut in blocks, so that all scholars may have the opportunity of reading them.' When later he served the king of Shu as prime minister he fulfilled his promise. This was the beginning of printing [*i. e.*, of official printing]."

The central empire, under the premiership of Fêng Tao, who had served four dynasties and seven emperors, conquered the state of Shu in 929, and in taking it over, acquired the art of block printing. The value of this art Fêng Tao was quick to recognize and in 932 he and his associates issued the memorial initiating the printing of the Confucian classics, one of the great enterprises in Chinese cultural history. This memorial stated: "During the Han Dynasty, Confucian scholars were honored and the classics were cut in stone. . . . Our dynasty has too many other things to do and cannot undertake such a task as to have stone inscriptions erected. We have seen, however, men from Wu and Shu who sold books that were printed from blocks of wood. There were many different texts but there were among them no orthodox classics. If the classics could be revised and thus cut in wood and published, it would be a very great boon to the study of literature. We therefore make a memorial to the throne to this effect."

Fêng Tao's prime interest in this project was not in the printing but in the editing of these classics—the establishment of a correct and definitive text. The editorial task was entrusted to the Kuo-tzu-chien, or National Academy. The most expert calligraphers were then to write the text which would be transferred to the blocks and engraved. Through twenty-one years, during which the empire was torn by civil strife, the work went on, and the project finally reached a successful conclu-

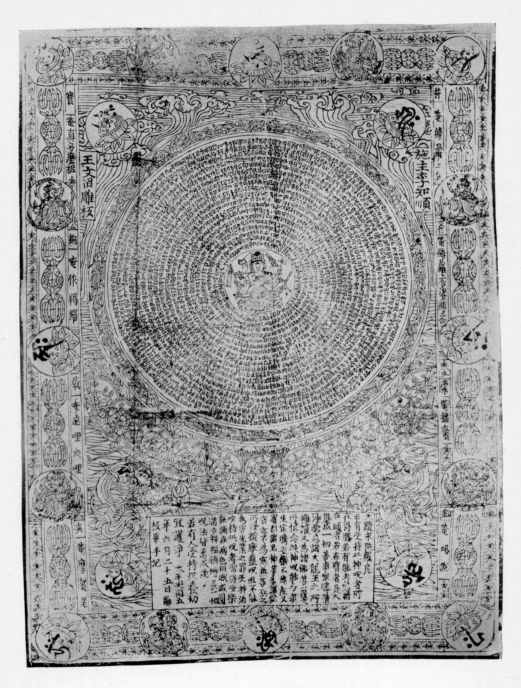

BLOCK PRINT OF CHINESE CHARM, A. D. 940

sion in the completion of the full text, commentaries included, in one hundred and thirty volumes.

And many other books followed them. One example of a block-printed book dated 1187, the *T'ang Liu sien shêng wên tsi* is now in the fine Chinese collection at the Newberry Library, Chicago. A page from it is reproduced herewith. This work, in twelve volumes, contains the collected poems and essays of Liu Tsung-yüan, who lived 773-819 A. D., one of the most celebrated writers of the T'ang dynasty.

We must here leave the further development of block printing in China. The art spread westward in Asia, but met in the Mohammedan world, which lay between it and Europe, a seemingly impenetrable barrier. Islam was uncompromisingly opposed to the duplication of its sacred writings through the medium of print. The reason for this prejudice is not clear, but in all probability it was simply conservatism. The Koran had been given to Moslems in written form and that was, therefore, the only form fitted for its transmission.

So we find the Asiatic peoples using the art of printing for many purposes—not only for books but for playing cards, paper money, and many other miscellaneous uses as well. In Europe, the monasteries were busily at work copying manuscripts by the most laborious possible method, and for centuries there was no penetration of the art as practiced in the East among the peoples of the West. The conquests of the Mongols under Jinghis Khan, however, broke through the barrier and, from the middle of the thirteenth century to the midpoint of the

[49]

臨淄王隆基起兵討韋氏并其黨皆伏誅隆基

寫平王

其不以臨尾誅五章　　韋氏著其撥基封　　世者等稍法　　中　故而獨歸惡
撥泯自淄本日氏之分　　立為漢中注載以　　戒之所知之義逆宗雖　不為獨歸惡
亂實為平意必進回　　　為封　王撥以亂　　之豈以大深崔所不　　義章要皆氏
之嘉王蓋待載為宗　　　為甲王基　　封　　不立著義意湜以能　　而推防黨氏何
績賴意欲劉久平之繼　　上王非　為　　　　深法禍必所初不　　　　原開黨要出
故之書故自幽之王隆故　　涾自字是　　　　切若本不以不　　　　頭禍惟皆於
下書故取求考王隆基絕　　自何為時　　　　著此之從誅　　　　始落氏也
書綱曰力之何基基　　此　　尹何之中　　　　明其所弒賊謀　　　　亂貽正中
隆目臨此言未　　　　　　　氏之自宗　　　　也所弒君亂之　　　　胎章宗
基上淄即前始恕　而　　　　立自罪波　　　　為自起之　　　　　禍氏寵
為書削綱始盖其為　　　　發罪謂弒　　　　哉起之書　　　　本自信
平臨平月請自為自　　　　明然宗睿　　　　後而書其　　　　己是以
臨溷王日相綱自　恕　　　烈謂上未　　　　　賊黨於　　　　而以綱
王溷難法六目其　　　　　相若上即　　　　特而孤本　　　　浸長目
所起　之即舉之　不　　　自書書位　　　　書孤弒也　　　　冊則
以兵興意庚事不　立　　　書討甲　　　　　受其或而　　　　制楚
恕討復也子不封　然　　　討　　　　　　　裝惡日以　　　　則楚
其韋意唐是然也　　　　　　　　　　　　　職之韋綱　　　　肆客
章復唐也是以也烈　　　　　　　　　　　　等故此氏目　　　見
自氏室然先甲相若　　　　　　　　　　　　所不何陰　　　　客
為既社以王隆相相　　　　　　　　　　　　以五也談　　　　妻
之以稷則原王隆　　　　　　　　　　　　　治宗張書　　　　淫
罪　之不謂首既基　　　　　　　　　　　　黨楚正于　　　　而
　　　　　　　　　　　　　　　　　　　　賊客能書福　　　　不

PAGE FROM BLOCK PRINTED BOOK OF 1187

fourteenth, Asia and Europe were in contact, and there was interchange at many points, cultural as well as commercial. The Mongols penetrated to Russia, Hungary, and Poland. At Tabriz there grew up a colony of international character, which served as the crossways between the East and the West. There is no categorical evidence attesting the direct transmission of the Chinese art of block printing to Europe, but the late Professor Carter in his very thorough study of the origins of printing in China concluded, on the basis of much circumstantial evidence, that such transmission took place.

Until comparatively recent years we knew of no early block printing between the Asiatic and European worlds. In 1880, however, in excavations in Egypt near El-Fayyûm were discovered a great quantity of ancient documents which are now preserved in the Archduke Rainer Collection at Vienna. The documents date from the fourteenth century B. C. to the fourteenth century A. D., a range testifying to the spectacular importance historically of this find. Among the fragments numbering over a hundred thousand, were about fifty examples of block printing. They are all in Arabic but vary widely in the style of writing reproduced. Based on this feature, they have been dated approximately between 900 and 1300 A. D. The subjects are religious: passages from the Koran, prayers, charms, and so forth. There is text and decoration—but no illustration, in accordance with Moslem precept.

There is no definite evidence regarding the origin of the art of block printing in Egypt but the prevailing opinion is that it came from China, via Persia. Nor is there evidence of a connection between the Egyptian printing and European block printing. All that can be said is that the late Egyptian examples synchronize quite closely with the probable beginnings of the art in Europe.

There was one important influence in the spread of the art of block printing, and that was the use and manufacture of playing cards. These are clearly of Chinese origin. Cards were first known as "sheet dice." When made on bone or ivory they evolved in simple forms to dominoes, in more complicated forms to Mah Jong; when made on paper to playing cards.

The use of playing cards in China is traced with certainty as far back as 969 A. D., and they are probably still more ancient. When first known in Europe in the closing decades of the fourteenth century, they were recognized as an Eastern invention. In China they were early produced by the method of block printing and in Europe, soon after their introduction, the same process of manufacture was used. Again, the evidence regarding transmission of the printing art is not conclusive. To quote Professor Carter: "While it is not safe to say with certainty that playing cards in coming from China to Europe brought block printing with them, the evidence is at least sufficient to suggest that among the possible ways by which block printing may have entered the European world, the use of playing cards holds an important place."

We now come to the consideration of another important Chinese invention: the invention of movable types at a period antedating the experiments of Gutenberg by over four hundred years. The inventor was Pi Shêng and his types were made of china rather than metal. As the event is one of such major importance in cultural history, I am quoting the original record in full:

Under the T'ang Dynasty, block printing, though carried on, was not fully developed. In the time of Fêng Ying-wang [Fêng Tao], first the Five Classics and then in general all the ancient canonical works were printed.

During the period *Ch'ing-li* [1041-1049] Pi Shêng, a man in cotton cloth (i. e., a man of the common people), made also movable type. His method was as follows: He took sticky clay and cut in it characters as thin as the edges of a cash. Each character formed as it were a single type. He baked them in the fire to make them hard. He had previously prepared an iron plate and he had covered this plate with a mixture of pine resin, wax and paper ashes. When he wished to print, he took an iron frame and set it on the iron plate. In this he placed the type, set close together. When the frame was full, the whole made one solid block of type. He then placed it near the fire to warm it. When the paste [at the back] was slightly melted, he took a perfectly smooth board and rubbed over the surface, so that the block of type became as even as a whetstone.

If one were to print only two or three copies, this method would be neither convenient nor quick. But for printing hundreds or thousands of copies, it was marvellously [*lit.* "divinely"] quick. As a rule he kept two forms going. While the impression was being made from the one form, the type were being put in place on the other. When the printing of the one form was finished, the other was all ready. In this way the two forms alternated and the printing was done with great rapidity.

[53]

For each character there were several type, and for certain common characters there were twenty or more type each, in order to be prepared for the repetition of characters on the same page. When the characters were not in use, he had them arranged with paper labels, one label for each rhyme, and thus kept them in wooden cases. If any rare character appeared that had not been prepared in advance, it was cut as needed and baked with [a fire of] straw. In a moment it was finished.

The reason why he did not use wood is because the tissue of wood is sometimes coarse and sometimes fine, and wood also absorbs moisture, so that the form when set up would be uneven. Also the wood would have stuck in the paste and could not readily have been pulled out. So it was better to use burnt earthenware. When the printing was finished, the form was again brought near the fire to allow the paste to melt, and then brushed with the hand, so that the type fell of themselves and were not in the least soiled with clay.

When Pi Shêng died, his font of type passed into the possession of my followers and up to this time it has been kept as a precious possession.

There is confirmation of this invention by other Chinese historians. Types are also reported to have been cast in tin, but these as well as the china types did not take well the water color ink. So wooden types were made, and their making clearly described in 1314 by Wang Cheng. The characters were engraved first on a wood block and then cut apart. They were set up, using a case in the form of a revolving table. Some wooden types of Chinese origin, dating from the early part of the thirteenth century, were found by Paul Pelliot in the caves at Tun-huang, and examples of them are to be seen in Paris and in New York.

PRINTING IN FAR EAST

Our scene now shifts to Korea, a kingdom which had acknowledged the sovereignty of the Mongol Empire, though kings of the Koryu line had nominally occupied the throne. With the Mongol overthrow Korean government became rather chaotic and things went from bad to worse until the country was redeemed by the Korean hero, General Yi, who established a new line of rulers who gave Korea a vigorous and enlightened administration, which encouraged literature and the arts. In the Korean annals for 1392—still antedating Gutenberg by half a century—we find record of the establishment of a department of books, among the responsibilities of which were "the casting of type and the printing of books." There is some evidence pointing to movable type printing in the earlier part of the century, but this is our first sure date. The "department" is known to have actually begun work in 1403, in which year, at the private expense of the new king, T'ai Tsung, "several hundred thousand type had been cast."

Here in Korea, movable type printing became more than an experiment. Between 1403 and 1544, there were eleven royal decrees concerning the casting of new fonts of type. A type of small size was produced in 1420, and a new larger face in 1434. These types were produced by casting in sand, using wooden types as models, as is recorded by Song Hyon, writing at the end of the fifteenth century. Some early Korean types preserved in the American Museum of Natural History give unmistakable evidence in the texture of their metal surface that they were sand cast. In my judgment they were imbedded in a plastic base which was ribbed with half-round or round rods which fitted into a semi-circular concavity in the feet of the type, and thus served as guides to alignment.

The fundamentals of printing thus came into being, and further steps would have been only a question of development. The early work with movable types in the Asiatic world, however, seems to have been largely sterile, and there is no evidence that the Chinese invention had any influence whatever on the invention of movable types in Europe. The reason for this, as we have already pointed out, was that, for the Asiatic peoples with their non-alphabetic languages and the vast number of characters employed in writing them, block printing was the logical method of reproduction. The result was that the experiments with movable types were abortive and—with the single exception of the printing in Korea—ended almost where they began. In Europe, however, with its alphabetic languages, the invention of movable types marked a new era in the intellectual history of mankind.

VI. *Woodcuts and Block Books*

HE probability that European block print-
ing was derived either directly or indirect-
ly from the Far East is strengthened by
the fact that early woodcuts were impressed there in the same manner as they
were printed in China. On a block of wood a desired picture or text was cut in relief. The block was then inked
with a water color ink and the paper laid upon it and
rubbed on the back with a brush or frotton. Originally,
this ink was probably black, but it has faded, in almost
all instances to a weak brown. This method differed radically from that used in printing textiles and that used
later in printing from type.

We first hear of playing cards in Spain and Germany
in 1377. So rapidly did their use spread that by 1397
the provost of Paris forbade working men to play cards
on working days. By 1441 Venice found it advisable to
prohibit the importation of printed playing cards and
pictures and the edict speaks of the local industry which
the new law is designed to protect as once flourishing in
Venice but now because of competition fallen into decay.

[57]

The fact that card playing was forbidden to Parisian workingmen argues that by 1397 an inexpensive method was employed in their manufacture and the language of the Venetian edict of 1441 gives us reason to believe that the method was block printing. The fact that no playing cards now exist which can be dated, with any certainty, before 1450 is no valid objection to their having been printed in the last decade of the fourteenth century, for cards are quickly destroyed by use.

Just as in the manufacture of playing cards, block printing supplied the poor with an inexpensive means of amusement. So employed in the making of sacred image-prints, or as they are often called *Heiligen*, it met a need which was aroused by a growing wave of austere, puritanical and deeply personal religious feeling which, especially in Germany, was pervading the lower and middle classes. The printing of *Heiligen* went, it would seem, side by side with that of playing cards. Both were manufactured by the same process, both were sold to the same classes and, as we have seen, both are coupled together in the Venetian edict of 1441.

Very few of the early woodcut *Heiligen* bear the year on which the block from which they were printed was engraved. The two earliest existing dated woodcuts are likenesses of two of the most popular saints, the Virgin of 1418 (a date open to some question) and the St. Christopher of 1423 (the first date on which we can with certainty depend). These dates, however, by no means mark the beginning of European block printing. Besides the evidence of the Venetian edict, the pictures them-

THE ST. CHRISTOPHER WOODCUT OF 1423

selves display a mastery of technique probably attained by years of experiment. There is good reason to believe image prints were being made as early as 1400.

The famous print of St. Christopher, preserved in the John Rylands Library at Manchester, is reproduced on the preceding page. Even apart from its early age, its artistic merit, in spite of its conventional design, is sufficient to command interest. The gigantic St. Christopher with an uprooted tree for a staff is depicted carrying the infant Christ across a stream. On one bank is represented the secular life; a miller bringing grain to a mill and a peasant carrying flour to his home; on the other, the spiritual life, a hermit holding a guiding beacon. Beside the date 1423 is a crude Latin couplet which may be translated:

Each day that thou the likeness of St. Christopher shall see
That day no frightful form of death shall make an end of thee.

These two prints with an image of St. Sebastian of 1437 preserved in the National Library at Vienna are the only existing woodcuts which bear a very early date. It is agreed, however, that some of the undated *Heiligen* are older than the earliest of those which bear dates. Yet the time of the making of an early woodcut is very difficult to determine. A very specious error into which those assigning dates to wood engravings often fall is the assumption that the print showing the poorest technique is the oldest, whereas it is merely the worst. The fashion of the clothing represented in an engraving is no certain guide to the date, for later woodcuts are often copies of earlier ones. The fact, too, that blocks were kept for years and prints were made from them long after the engraver had died complicates the matter of dating. Woodcut blocks of the fifteenth century, in fact, are now preserved in museums and impressions from them can still be taken, although all the ancient prints made from them have perished.

Heiligen were primarily intended for illiterate persons. The ease and rapidity with which block printing duplicated copies, however, soon appealed to those who wished to make broadside sheets, such as letters of indulgence, cheaply and in large quantities.

From a picture with a simple Latin couplet like the St. Christopher, to a series of pictures with a more or less connected text is a simple step. When it was taken the block-book had evolved. How the early block-books were made cannot be determined with certainty. Conservative authorities at present hesitate to date any existing block-book before 1450. Block-books may be divided into two classes, those printed on one side of the paper by rubbing and bound with the blank sides of the sheet facing each other, much like a Chinese book, and those printed on both sides of the sheet on a printing press. Those of the first class of block-books are undoubtedly the earlier.

One of the earliest block-books and one of the most frequently printed [it is known to have gone through eleven editions] is the *Biblia Pauperum*, the Poor Man's Bible. It is a series of forty pictures representing incidents from the life of Christ and Old Testament scenes which prefigured them. A similar and equally popular xylo-

PAGE FROM BLOCK BOOK: ARS MORIENDI

Temptacio dyaboli de vana gloria

Quarto dyabolus temptat hominem infirmum per
complacenciam que est superbia spiritualis
per quam deuotis et religiosis atqz perfectis magis est infes-
tus Cum eum homine ad deuiandum a fide aut in despacio-
nem aut ad impacienciam non potest inducere tunc aggre-
ditur eum per sui ipsius complacenciam tales eidem iaculans
cogitaciones. O qz firmus es in fide qz fortis in spe et qz con-
stanter pacies in tua infirmitate o qiam multa bona operatus
es maxime gloriari debes quia non es sicut ceteri qui infi-
nita mala perpetrarunt et tamen solo gemitu ad celestia reg-
na peruenerunt igitur regnum celorum tibi uere negari
non potest quia legittime certasti. Accipe ergo coronam
tibi paratam et sedem excellenciorem pre ceteris optinebis
Per ista et similia dyabolus instantissime laborat hominem inducere ad spiritualem superbiam siue ad sui ipsius
complacenciam.

Pro quo notandum qz ista superbia multum est vitanda
primo quia per eam homo efficitur similis dyabolo nam
per solam superbiam de angelo factus est dyabolus.
Secundo quia per ipsam homo videtur committere blas-
phemiam per hoc qz bonum qd a deo habet a se presumit
habere. Tercio quia tanta posset esse sua complacencia
qz per hanc dampnaretur. Unde gregorius Reminiscen-
do quis boni qd gessit dum se apud se erigit apud auc-
torem humilitatis cadit. Et augustinus. Homo si se
iustificauerit et de iusticia sua presumpserit cadit.

FACING PAGE FROM BLOCK BOOK: ARS MORIENDI

graphic volume was the *Speculum Humanae Salvationis*
—The Mirror of Human Salvation.

With the *Ars Moriendi*, a title Caxton later quaintly
translated as "The craft for to deye for the helthe of
mannes sowle," we reach the climax of the artistic and
literary merit of the block-book. It is a manual to instruct
the sick man to prepare for death and beat off the demons
who crowd around his bed hoping to lure him into some
sin in his dying moments. It is the most thoroughly mediaeval of all the block-books, yet its appeal is universal
for in it, despite its theological language, may be heard
the lyric cry of the human soul brought face to face with
the unknown.

Space forbids the mention of more than a few of the
more important of the remaining block-books. The
Cantica Canticorum consists of sixteen leaves each with
two pictures illustrating the Song of Songs as an allegory
of the Virgin Mary. The Book of Revelation is made
vivid in the *Apocalypsis Sancti Johannis*. Still religious in
character is the *Mirabilia Romae*, the Wonders of Rome,
a guide book for German pilgrims. Secular works are
found only in block-books known to be of a late date.
About 1475 appeared the *Kalendar* of Johann Muller
and Johann Hartlieb's *Die Kunst Chiromantia* [The Art
of Palmistry]—examples of popular literature while
the *Ars Memorandi* [The Art of Cultivating the Memory,] published a little later, may serve to remind us
forcibly that a fifteenth century block-book dealt with a
subject still popular in our magazine advertising.

Reproduced on pages 62 and 63 are two pages from

a block-book edition of the *Ars Moriendi* printed in the Rhine district about 1465. Both the pictures and the text which faces it sets forth the manner in which devils tempt the dying man to trust too greatly in his own merits and to be unmindful of his sins. They are depicted offering him crowns and exhorting him to vainglory by such utterances as "Exalt yourself!" "You deserve a crown!" God, the Father, Christ, the Virgin and the saints are represented in the background watching the dying man's struggle with his demoniac tempters who in the picture which follows in the original volume are shown routed by the Good Angel. Its right-hand pages are devoted entirely to type.

Although eventually destroyed by typography, the block-book did not leave the field to its rival without a long struggle. A small illustrated work with a large circulation could be cut upon blocks, and then, like the stereotyped editions of today, could be printed again and again without the cost of composition. As late as about 1530, for example, a xylographic adaptation of the *Biblia Pauperum* appeared in Venice. For larger works and those intended for a smaller and more discriminating audience the more legible book printed from movable types soon won the victory. Although absent from the earliest products of the printing press, woodcut illustrations soon began to appear in these type-printed books which were intended for richer buyers than the poor who bought the block-books, and in which the art of wood engraving was destined to attain still higher standards of excellence.

[65]

VII. *The Stage Setting for Typography*

BLOCK BOOKS must be considered, not the forerunners of typography, but in a way competitors—the two arts developing almost simultaneously though along independent lines as we have seen in our discussion of the development of the art of wood engraving. Each was an effort to solve the problem of how to produce books at a cost which would put them within reasonably easy reach of the public at large.

Any invention depends almost as much on the state of knowledge in the related arts as on the idea to which the mind of the inventor gave birth. This is particularly true of inventions of a mechanical character. The inventor borrows one known process from one art, a second method from another, and building on these and other established industrial practices, adds the new idea and lo! we have an invention. It is of interest, therefore, to consider what the related industrial arts had to offer the inventor of printing in his quest for the one best way to produce books quickly and economically.

One of the most important contributory factors was the spread of rag papermaking throughout Europe. The manufacture of paper had begun in Italy and southern

THE STAGE SETTING

France in the thirteenth century and in the fourteenth the art was introduced in northern France, Flanders, Lorraine, and the valley of the Rhine — in other words into the territory destined to be the cradle of printing. From the end of that century onward, scribes began to make use of paper, in addition to parchment, for books intended to sell at modest prices. A supply of paper was therefore available for the printer-to-be. It was an essential antecedent to his invention.

The next point of importance is that there was already in use a printing process making use of engraved relief blocks: namely the art of printing textiles. Our knowledge regarding the origin and development of cloth printing has been greatly augmented in recent years by the studies of R. Forrer, supplemented by those of Joseph Dépierre. These authorities have shown that the art of direct printing of designs on fabrics by the use of engraved wood blocks was known in Egypt in the sixth century A. D., and was practised in Europe as early as the twelfth century, probably in monasteries where decorative arts of varied character were held in esteem. These printing processes were so developed and perfected in the fourteenth and fifteenth centuries, that there were produced many cloth prints of real artistry, examples of which have been preserved to us in various public and private collections.

The printing of pictures on textiles was regarded in the middle ages as a form of painting, as we learn from the reference to it by Cennino Cennini, the Florentine painter, in his treatise on the arts, written in 1437.

The process was most frequently used in the portrayal of religious subjects for altar cloths and other items of ecclesiastical decoration, which could by this process be produced at much less cost than tapestries. The best known of the examples date from the twelfth century (Siegbourg), end of the fourteenth century (Sion), and the beginning of the fifteenth century (a print attributed to a master of the Cologne school picturing the infancy of the Virgin). On this latter appears a legend of thirteen gothic letters arranged in the form of a scroll.

Not only have there been preserved examples of the picture-printed textiles but, through a stroke of good fortune, one of the printing blocks was discovered in 1898, in demolishing the Cistercian convent at La Ferté-sur-Grosne (Province of Saone-et-Loire, France). This was a block of wood cut in relief, depicting part of the Crucifixion scene, and bearing an inscription of several words in uncial letters. The large size of the block, which measured approximately nine by twenty-four inches, points to its use for printing a fabric to be viewed from a distance. The costume and arms of the centurion and two soldiers who are pictured indicate a dating in the last quarter of the fourteenth century.

Another known process which could not fail to be suggestive to the prospective inventor was that used by the illuminators in stamping decorative initials in the blank spaces left for them by the scribes. The illuminator made use of stamps engraved in relief on hard wood or metal and probably mounted on handles similar to those used for binders' tools. Color was applied to these stamps and they were then impressed on the paper by hand. The clearest evidence of this practice may be seen in a thirteenth century manuscript produced in the scriptorium of the Vauclerc monastery, and now preserved in the Bibliothèque Municipale at Laon, France. On the reverse of pages on which large initial letters appear, can be felt the embossing resulting from vigorous pressure in the impression of the stamps. Ridges of ink around the edges of the design of one initial provide additional confirmation of the process used.

There were three vital elements in the development of printing with movable types: (1) the press; (2) a thick ink on a varnish base; (3) cast metal types. The combination of all three was essential in order to make fruitful the invention of movable types. The extent to which the inventor of printing was indebted to the allied arts will be apparent from a consideration of what was available to him at that time. With regard to the first factor, presses of essentially the same construction as the printing press were used in a number of different lines. Screw presses were used for expelling the moisture from damp sheets in the process of papermaking, for the printing of fabrics, for the pressing of grapes and olives. So all that was necessary was to provide the proper base on which the type might rest and an impression member in the form of a platen. As to the ink on a varnish base, this required only an adaptation of the oil paints which were in current use at the beginning of the fourteenth century in the decorative arts and even for painting.

With relation to the third element, the idea of movable types for the imprinting of letters and the *successive* use of them to make words and sentences was already known. This procedure had been developed by the book-binders who required letters for the stamping of their bindings, and these letters were made up in much the same form as the gilding tools used by hand finishers to-day. The only difference was that these letter stamps were cut in intaglio instead of relief. They were used for lettered inscriptions on dated bindings of 1436, 1442, and 1451, as has been pointed out by Falk. But these stamps were also cut in relief, as exemplified in the binding of a manuscript missal of the fifteenth century described by Zedler. On the cover of this book the word *Missale* and the name of the binder *Hene Crans* are impressed with relief stamps, and a manuscript note inside, complaining that several of the signatures were transposed by the binder, refers to him as *impressor*.

As early as the thirteenth century, metal founders had made use of single letters engraved in relief on metal or on wood to impress in the sand in which the molten metal was poured the letters of an inscription which it was desired to have appear in relief on the finished casting. There is attributed to Etienne Boileau, Provost of Paris in the thirteenth century, a regulation forbidding the Guild of Metal Founders to produce castings bearing a legend similar to those on seals or coins, but making an exception of those which bore only letters impressed one at a time. Letter punches were used also by founders of bells, pewter vessels, and other metal objects. Punches were employed by the engravers of dies for coins and medals, some being used for parts of the design and others for single letters in the inscription.

The process of casting small objects was, of course, well known to the medallists and goldsmiths, both of whom had carried the art to a high degree of perfection. It is interesting to note, in this connection, how often a goldsmith figures in the first attempts at printing with movable types. Hans Dunne figures in the Gutenberg lawsuit at Strasbourg, for example, as having furnished the inventor with "what pertains to printing." Waldfoghel at Avignon (see page 101) was a silversmith, Nicholas Jenson was skilled in the making of coins, and there are other instances of a like association. A capable goldsmith would have been able not only to engrave type models or punches, but would also have been equipped, from his experience in casting gold and silver, to cast types in sand moulds, if that process was used in the production of the most primitive types.

So far as the engraving of metal was concerned, the art was well known at the time the invention of typography was brewing. A spectacularly early testimony regarding it appears in the records of the Dukes of Burgundy under the date of 1398. A "block of lead" costing twenty-two livres is provided for the painter Jehan Malouel, "to cut in it several stamps (or prints) necessary for the making of pictures of several subjects for the said church (Eglise des Chartreux at Dijon)."

The *ciripagus* is described by Paulus Paulirinus in a manuscript on the industrial arts written between 1459 and 1463, as one who engraves skillfully in brass, iron, or wood both pictures and text with the object of printing them on paper.

We thus see that the inventor had at hand, subject to observation, all the elements of typography but two. One was the combining of letter stamps or types so that a series of them assembled to reproduce the letters of a text could be printed together at one impression. The other was a satisfactory method of producing these types in such form that they could be assembled easily, distributed, and re-assembled in another order, and when together could be held firmly so that successive impressions could be drawn from them with reasonable convenience.

Here was the problem. The end in view — the economical duplication of texts without variation due to errors — must have engaged the minds of hundreds who devoted their lives to the laborious task of duplicating these texts in manuscript. The problem was awaiting an inventive genius who could conceive the one best way of accomplishing this purpose. I have pointed out the known industrial processes at his disposal with no idea of minimizing the importance of the invention yet to be made, but only with the desire to give a clearer view of his task and make possible a more accurate conception of the manner and method of his approach.

The stage was now set for the greatest invention in the history of mankind.

VIII. *The Invention of Printing*

THERE have been many events in political history which may well be called epochal. Magna Charta, the French Revolution, the Armistice in the World War—all these were of major importance. But in cultural history, there is no event even rivalling in consequence the invention of printing with movable types. To this must be credited the present status of popular education, and the comparatively high average level of intelligence. While we are often dismayed at the tide of ignorance and superstition, there is, of course, no comparison between conditions at the present time with those before the coming of the printing press.

Since the typographic art has made so vital a contribution to cultural development, the question of who invented it becomes one of high historical importance. Though the birth of printing made a great impression on Europe in the fifteenth century, and in spite of the fact that the first printer dealt with the very tools of publicity, we have surprisingly little exact knowledge on the subject. When asked: "Who invented printing?" we must answer that we lack conclusive evidence making possible a categorical reply. We can add, however, that much direct evidence, and ninety per cent of the direct and circumstantial taken together, dictates the ascription of the honor to Johann Gutenberg of Strasbourg and Mainz.

Before going into detail regarding Gutenberg it may be well to state that the credit for the invention has been disputed with much acrimony, the argument being largely nationalistic in character. At one time or another almost every country has had some contender for the honor. The main question at issue, however, is whether printing with movable types was invented by Lourens Janszoon Coster at Haarlem, Holland, somewhere in the vicinity of 1430 or by Johann Gutenberg at Strasbourg or Mainz, Germany, in the neighborhood of 1445.

The Dutch claim was not advanced until some time after the invention is supposed to have taken place. The first report to lend it color appeared in the "Cologne Chronicle" printed at Cologne in 1499. In it we find the following passage, following Pollard's translation or paraphrase:

This right worthy art was invented first of all in Germany, at Mainz, on the Rhine. And that is a great honour to the German nation that such ingenious men are found there. This happened in the year of our Lord 1440, and from that time until 1450 the art and all that pertains to it was investigated, and in 1450, which was a Golden Year, men began to print, and the first book that was printed was the Bible in Latin, and this was printed with a letter as large as that now used in missals.

Although this art was invented at Mainz, as far as regards

the manner in which it is now commonly used, yet the first pre-figuration (Vurbyldung) was invented in Holland from the Donatuses which were printed there before that time. And from and out of these the aforesaid art took its beginning, and was invented in a manner much more masterly and subtler than this, and the longer it lasted the more full of art it became.

A certain Omnibonus wrote in the preface to a Quintilian, and also in other books, that a Walloon from France, called Nicolas Jenson, was the first inventor of this masterly art — a notorious lie, for there are men still alive who bear witness that books were printed at Venice before the aforesaid Nicolaus Jenson came there, and began to cut and make ready his letter. But the first inventor of printing was a Burgher at Mainz, and was born at Strassburg, and called Yunker Johann Gutenberg.

From Mainz the art came first of all to Cologne, after that to Strassburg, and after that to Venice. The beginning and progress of the art were told me by word of mouth by the Worshipful Master Ulrich Zell of Hanau, printer at Cologne in this present year 1499, through whom the art came to Cologne.

This passage states very clearly that printing was invented by Johann Gutenberg at Mainz, but it adds that it was "pre-figured" in a more primitive form of printing in Holland.

The next important document, and the principal one on which the Costerian protagonists base their case, is a passage in *Batavia*, a history of Holland by Hadrianus Junius, a Dutch physician and historian, which was printed at the Plantin office at Atwerp in 1588. The book had, however, been written in 1568 so we may accept this latter year as its date. Of this passage relating to printing we will give a full summary.

[75]

Junius advances a positive claim for the city of Haarlem to the credit for the invention of printing. He says he obtained the information on which his story is based from aged residents of Haarlem of good reputation. Lourens Janszoon Coster (*Coster* meaning *church warden* or *sexton*) lived in Haarlem 128 years earlier [1440], and members of his family were still living there. One day, while walking in the forest, he whittled letters from the bark of trees and found, by impressing them on paper, that they made a print of the letters. Having a keen mind, this first essay led him to attempt greater things. With the help of his son-in-law, he invented a superior kind of black ink. This son-in-law, Thomas Petrus, had four children, who have all held positions of honor. Then Laurentius began to make pictures and to illustrate or perhaps explain them with printed words. Junius had seen some of his first works along this line. The leaves were printed on one side only. The book was written in our own tongue and entitled *Speculum nostrae salutis*. With such books it was the custom to paste the blank sides together so that they might not appear unpleasing. The essence of the story continues thus:

Then he substituted lead forms for the wooden ones; still later he made them of tin that they might be more resistant and durable. The old wine pots which were manufactured from these tin forms, are still in the house of Laurentius [Lourens]. This house was occupied by his great grandchild Gerrit Thomaszoon, a prominent and excellent citizen, who died only a few years ago at a ripe old age.

The new invention spread rapidly because of the readiness

[76]

with which persons bought the pictures, and soon not only the family but strange workers were employed in the art. This however, proved a misfortne, for a certain man named Johannes proved untrue to his employer and brought bad luck to him.

This Johannes diligently learned all the secrets of the art and then on Christmas Eve when all were at the church, he stole all the forms and indeed all the equipment of his master and left for Amsterdam, from thence to Cologne, and then to Mainz, which was out of striking distance, and set up a book printing establishment and reaped the fruits of his theft.

It is known that his first work appeared within a year [1442] with the same letters [*iis ipsis typis*] which Laurentius had used in Haarlem, being a Doctrinale of Alexander Gallus, a well-known and universally used grammar, accompanied by the tracts of Petrus Hispanus.

This is the story about as I heard it from aged persons, who had had it handed down to them from their forefathers. One of my aged teachers, a man with a remarkable memory told me that as a boy he often listened to a certain bookbinder, a man eighty years old, named Cornelis, tell of things that happened while he was an assistant in this same printing establishment.

This Cornelis told him how the art had been discovered, as he had heard it from his employer, how the art had developed, and also how the theft had been accomplished, although he felt very badly about this part of the story, and wept when he told it to my informant, wished on the thief all kinds of dire things, and cursed the nights when he had slept in the same bed with him.

It is quite evident that the story is not a fabrication by Junius but that it was current tradition in Haarlem. This is proved by the fact that the claims of Haarlem are mentioned by three earlier witnesses: Johann van Zuren, Dirck Coornhert, and Lud. Guicciardini [*circa* 1560].

The strongest point in the story, as Pollard has pointed out, is the bookbinder Cornelis, there being documentary evidence of a binder of that name having been employed between 1474 and 1514 to bind the account books of the Haarlem Cathedral, and he continued his binding business, in conjunction with which he was also a bookseller, until 1522, the date of his death. The first known printer at Haarlem was Jacob Bellaert, whose first recorded work dates from 1483. Cornelis had a shop on "der Cruysstraet" and we know that in 1492 he there sold a book printed by Jacob Bellaert. We also know that in 1560 there was in that same street a house known as "Den Bellaert." Kruitwagen, in a recent attack on the Junius story, has suggested that some facts recalled from his associations with Bellaert might have been woven by Cornelis into the Coster tale. This, however, is pure speculation.

Regarding Coster, contemporary records show that he was a resident of Haarlem from 1436 to 1483 and that he was an innkeeper and also a dealer in wine, candles, oil, and soap. No mention is made in the records of any activity as a printer.

There is also a mention in a manuscript pedigree of the Coster family prepared about 1559, preserved at Haarlem, which refers to Lourens Coster as "having brought the first print into the world" in 1446. There is one other scrap of evidence. In the bindings of the Haarlem church account books of 1474, 1489, and 1514, bound by Cornelis, have been found Donatus leaves of primitive Dutch printing.

Another piece of Dutch testimony which, however, favors the claims of Mainz, appears in a manuscript chronicle, written between 1515 and 1520 by an anonymous Benedictine monk in the monastery at Egmond, a town about twenty miles from Haarlem. From internal evidence it is apparent that he was personally acquainted in Haarlem. Yet he apparently knows nothing regarding the invention of printing there, for he writes: "In the year 1440 the printing of books took place at Mainz and Joannes Fust was undoubtedly the inventor of that art."

This is the extent of the historical record pro and con on which rests the case of Haarlem. Bear in mind that the first statement of any kind, either in manuscript or print, connecting the name of Coster with the invention of printing is dated over one hundred years after the event. There are other weaknesses in the story which have not been adequately emphasized in discussions of the subject. In the first place, the earliest Mainz printing, of which we have a multitude of examples, was not in the types of the primitive Dutch printing. The Doctrinale of Alexander Gallus (otherwise known as Alexander de Villa Dei) and the Petrus Hispanus tract mentioned in the Junius account are not known to have been printed in Mainz types, but are known to have been printed in the types of the early Dutch typographer or typographers.

Attempts have been made to discredit the Junius record on printing because he recorded a legend of Loosduinen, according to which Countess Margarethe von Henneberg brought 364 children into the world at one time. Mother and children soon died and were buried in the same grave, and the events were noted on a tombstone. Junius says the story is incredible, but there was the record on the tombstone. As Junius was a physician as well as a historian, he must have had his own opinion of the probabilities in this case, but nevertheless recounted the record as it stood. The story about the invention of printing is categorical and set down with thoroughness and appears to me to represent truthfully the Haarlem tradition of the day.

But in such an important matter, a first record over one hundred years removed from the event would in itself be disqualified as not dependable. If this was all there was to the question the Haarlem claim would be thrown out of court without further ado.

There is one drawback to this disposition of the case. We have an extensive body of primitive Dutch printing which is clearly Dutch, in the first place because the text of some items are in that language, and in the second place because the type designs are based on calligraphy which is distinctively Dutch in character. Of some of the books and pamphlets there are preserved some complete examples, but most of them are known to us through fragments only. By the study of these, however, we are able to identify—not one or two—but *eight* distinct types. Not one of these types can be tied up with the work of any known printer, nor can we establish the place of printing nor the date of issue of any one of the dozens of publications represented.

Iameth gflhigt a inal̃ sins vroribus   Iob flagellabat a demone et ab vxore

Achioꝛ fuiꝶ ligatꝰ ꝑ holoferni faꝛtitꝛꝰ
Xꝓs ligatꝰ fuiꞇ ad collũpnã ꝑ pilati milites
Achioꝛ ꝓꝑ veritatẽ cꝋ dixeaꞇ fuiꞇ ligatꝰ
Ihꝓs ꝓꝑ veritatẽ cꝋ ꝓdicaueãꞇ fuiꞇ flagellatꝰ
Achioꝛ ligabaꞇ q̇ noluiꞇ hoꝝm locꝰ placꝛꝺa
Xꝓs ligaꞇ̃ ꞇ cꝑ repꝶ̃ꝺiꞇ iuꝺeos displicꝛꞇia
Achioꝛ ꞇ ligaꞇ̃ q̇a gloriãꝺei magniꞇꝺicauiꞇ
Xꝓs flagellaꞇ̃ ꞇ cꝑ noꞇm̃ sui pꝶ̃s maꞇfeſtabaꞇ
Potãꝺũ ãꞇ q̇ꝺ due gẽtꝛs xꝓm flagellauerũꞇ
et ille ꝑ duas vxoꝛes lamech pꝶ̃figuꝛaꞇꝛ fuerũꞇ
Due vxoꝛes lamech appellabaꞇ cella ꞇ aꝺa
Due gẽtꝛs ꞇuerũꞇ gẽtilitas ꞇ ſynagoga
cella ꞇ aꝺa mariꞇũ ſuũ ꝑꝛ vbeibꝛ afflixꝛrũꞇ
gẽtilitas ꞇ ſynagoga ſaluatoꝛẽ ſuũ flagellauerꞇ
Gẽtilitas ꝑbeãuiꞇ eũ flagellis ꞇ virgis
Synagoga ꝑbeãuiꞇ eũ lignis ꞇ verbis
Hꝛc flagellaꞇio ĩ xꝓo duobꝛ moꝺis ꝑpetrata
Olim fuiꞇ ĩ bꝛi iobflagellaꞇione pꝶ̃figuꝛata
Bꝶꝰ iob fuiꞇ flagellatꝰ duobꝰ moꝺis
Quia ſathã flagellaꞇiꞇ eũ ꝑbeibꝛ ꞇ vxoꝛ ꝑꝺ
Dr flagello ſathariꞇ ſuſtinuiꞇ ꝺoloꝛeꞇ ĩ carne
De flagello ligue habuiꞇ cõturbaꞇꞇem ĩ coꝛꝺe
Nꝋ ſuffeciꞇ dyabolo cꝑ flagellauiꞇ cꝛꝺꝶ exꞇꝛ
Niꞇa eꝺã inſtigarꞇ vxoꝛeꞇ ꝗ irritaꞇꞇ coꝛ inꞇꝛ
Sic nꝋ ſuffeciꞇ mꝺeiꞇ ꝗ xꝓs ꝛꝺebaꞇ flagellis
      Geneſis iij capꞇo

Nill̃ eꞇã affligerꝛꞇ eũ acutiꞇis verbis
A plãta prꝛ vſꝗ ad Þtꞇꝛ ĩ iab ſaꞇtas nꝋ eaꞇ
Sic ĩ carne xꝓi ĩ gñuſꞇ ncꞇhil remãebaꞇ
Eꞇ quãto caꝛo xꝓi eãꞇ noꝛilioꝛ ꞇ teneꝛioꝛ
Tãto fuiꞇ ꝺoloꝛ ipꞇius amaꝛioꝛ ꞇ aſpeꝛioꝛ
O hꝋ cogiꞇo qñta ſuſtinuiꞇ xꝓs ꝑ te paſſionꝛ̃
Eꞇ ne tꝛadas aĩaꝶ tuã ĩꝛꝺꞇꝛ ĩ ꝑꝺicionꝛ̃
Attꝛꝺe ſi vncꝗ talꝛ penã audiuiſti ꞇ viꝺiſti
Qualis fuiꞇ paſſio ꝺñi nꝛi ihꝓ xꝓm
Aꝺuꞇe quãta habuiꞇ xꝓs ad te dilꝛcꞇꞇonꝛ̃
Qui tãta ꝑ tue ſalute ſuſtinuiꞇ paſſionꝛ̃
Cõſiꝺꝛã ſiꞇ qñtũ tu vſꞇa vicꝛ ꝑꝗ xꝓm ſuſtinuiꞇꞇi
Nꝋſꞇi gꝶꞇuꝺis ꞇ qꞇitã ſeruiꞇꞇ ꞇibi reꝺꝺiꝺiſti
Diꞇne bonꝰ q̇ꝺ ꞇacꝛ alꞇꞇris ꝺiebꝶ Niꞇe tue
nꝋ coꝛrũꝺꝛꞇ miꞇme ſanguis ſue gutte
Noli ergo nꞇũſaꝛ ſi cõꞇigꝛꞇꞇ te moꝺicã ſuſtinꝛ̃
Sed ſanguinꝛ̃ ihꝓ xꝓi oclꝶ metaliꞇbꝛ ĩtuere
Amaritudinꝛ̃ tuã cũ ſanguinꝛ̃ xꝓi cõmiſcꝛꝛe
Eꞇ viꝺꝛtur tibi ꝗꞇꞇꝛꝗ ſuſtineꝶis eꝶ dulce
Suſtine ĩ hac vita moꝺica flagellaꞇionꝛ̃
Eꞇ ĩ futuꝛo effugias ꝑpꝛꞇuã ꝺãpnacionꝛ̃
Poſtula a ꝺiꞇo uꞇ ĩ hoc ſꝛꝗo ita coꝛꝶipiaꝶis
Nꞇ poſꞇ moꝛꞇꝛ regnũ ꝺei ſiꞇ ꝑeã ĩgregi nꞇaꝛꞇꝶ
O bꝺꝛ ihꝓ uꞇ ĩ hac vita poꝶte nꝺos ꞇ flagella
Eꞇ poſꞇ moꝛꞇꝛ nꞇrãm guſtemꝛ̃ cꝛlica mella
      Iob ij° capꞇo

PAGE FROM THE MIXED EDITION OF THE SPECULUM

Off der heiligē drier kōnige dag zwo vren vñ m...
ist der mane nuwe · Vnd sint sonne vñ māne ...
xxv gde des steinbocks · Saturn9 in dem xxv...
des lewens vnd geet hindersich · Jupiter ē ge x...
der wagen · Mars in dem ersten grade des scorpions · Ve...
dem xv gt grade des wassergiessers vnd geet hintersich Ve...
in dē ij gde desselbē zeichens ¶ Off den xxj dag desselbē m...
iij vre nach mitternacht ist ō mane fol · Vnd ist die sonne i...
grade des wassergiessers · Der mane in dem · x · grade des l...
Saturn9 in dem xxv grade des lewēs vnd geet hindersich...
in dem xxiij grade der wagē · Mars in dem xx... des sco...
Ven9 in dem xi grade des waszeegiessers vñ geet hindersich
curius in dem xxvj grade desselben zeichens

¶ Februarius

Off den virdē dag Februarij das ist oÿ passen ... ...
vren nach mittage ist ō mane nuwe · Vnd sint son...
mane in dem xxv grade des wassergiessers · Saturn9 in dem...
grade des lewens vnd geet hindersich · Jupiter in dem x...
der wagen vnd geet hindsich · Mars in dē xv gde des scor...
Venus in dem iiij grade des wasze giessers vñ geet hin...
Mercurius in dem · x · grade der fische vnd geet ... ...
den xix dag desselbē mandes · x · vren ... ... in de...
fall · Vnd ist die sonne in dem · x · grade der ... ...

des lewes vnd geet hindersich · Jupiter in dem ... grade ...
gen vnd geet hindersich · Mars in dem xxij grade des sco...
Venus in dem iiij grade der fische · Mercurius in dem ersten
fische vnd geet hindersich

FRAGMENT OF THE ASTRONOMICAL CALENDAR FOR 1448

Inasmuch as the history of printing in Holland from 1473 on—at which date printers of the German school introduced the art at Alost and Utrecht—has been exhaustively studied and is well known, the existence of this body of unidentified printing presents a puzzle which challenges the wits of a bibliographer not committed blindly to one camp or the other. When we add that the technique of this printing is primitive to a degree, considerably ruder than the earliest examples of German printing, the puzzle becomes even more complicated.

When, where, and by whom was this printing done? The answer to this is perfectly clear: we have not a shred of definite evidence on which an answer could be based. The identity of the primitive Dutch printer or printers is still a mystery. The *Gesamtkatalog der Wiegendrucke*, the latest and most complete of the incunabula bibliographies, with praiseworthy conservatism lists the printing as done by the "Printer of the Speculum."

There is just one thread of connection between the unidentified early Dutch printing and the work of known printers. In 1481, Jan Veldener, an itinerant printer then working at Utrecht, used in an edition of Epistles and Gospels in the Dutch language, two halves of one of the double compartment woodcuts which had been used in the *Speculum*. In 1483, while at Kuilenberg, he used a number of the *Speculum* blocks cut in half so that they would fit a smaller book. This shows that he must have acquired all or nearly all of these historic wood cuts, and as he is known to have used them first at Utrecht the assumption, in the absence of evidence to the contrary, is that he found them there. For this reason Bradshaw provisionally attributed the various editions of the *Speculum*, of the *Donatus*, of the *Doctrinale*, and so forth, to Utrecht. As Pollard says, "the presumption that Veldener found the blocks of the *Speculum* there constituted a grain of evidence in favour of Utrecht; and if a balance is sufficiently sensitive and both scales are empty, a grain thrown into one will suffice to weigh it down." The attribution has been often repeated without the emphasis on its provisional character with which Bradshaw accompanied it and there has been considerable resultant confusion. I share with Mr. Pollard the opinion that it would have been better to disregard the grain and not attempt, in our present lack of knowledge, to assign the books and fragments to any one city.

The most interesting product of the early Dutch press is the *Speculum humanae salvationis* [in Latin] or *Spieghel onser behoudenisse* [in Dutch]. This is a series of scenes from Bible history placed two on a block, each picture being enclosed in a border of architectural character, with a column of descriptive matter under each picture. There are four known editions of this publication. In three the text is set in movable type, while in a fourth the text of part of the pages is set in type while for other pages it is engraved on a wood block. For three and a half centuries this mixed character led to the presumption that this edition was the earliest of all and marked the boundary line between block books on the one hand and movable type printed books on the other. Ottley, however, in 1876, upset this neat hypothesis which had seemed to fit "like the paper on the wall" by demon-strating from the comparative wear and tear on the blocks in the various editions, that the "mixed" edition came third instead of first. Under these circumstances, it indicates that the printer had become weary of re-setting the book each time it was reprinted and in consequence decided to replace the type composition by engraved blocks which could be used again and again without un-due labor. This hypothesis has, however, been vigorously contested by Hessels, with much show of reason, so this must be regarded as an open question until there has been opportunity for further study of the existing copies and fragments of the various editions of the Speculum.

What are these early Dutch books? The principal item is an extensive series of different editions of the Latin grammar of Aelius Donatus. Numerous editions of the *Doctrinale* of Alexander Gallus, another popular school book, the *Distichs* of Dionysius Cato, the *Facetiae Morales* of Laurentius Valla, the *De Salute Corporis* of Guilelmus de Saliceto and the *Singularia Juris* of Ludo-vicus Pontanus, with a treatise of Pope Pius II. Some of the Donatus fragments appear to have been printed on one side of the leaf only and appear extremely primitive.

There are a good many examples of this early Dutch printing now to be seen at Haarlem but, as Kruitwagen has pointed out, not many of them were found there but have, on the contrary been acquired by purchase in com-paratively modern times.

In 1446 there was entered in the diary of Jean le Robert, Abbot of St. Aubert at Cambrai, note of the purchase of a Doctrinale "jette en molle" and two others, one correct and the other incorrect in text, are mentioned in 1451. These words would indicate some relation to the process of casting, though just how the books were produced is not quite clear. Between 1471 and 1474 a copy of the Dutch printed Saliceto book is known to have been purchased by Conrad du Moulin, Abbot of the Convent of St. James at Lille.

How were these early books produced? W. L. Schreiber, the leading authority on early woodcuts has advanced the theory that they were engraved on metal in intaglio, but his arguments are not convincing, particularly because we have no books the text of which was apparently printed by this method. Gottfried Zedler, who has recently studied the primitive Dutch printing, believes Coster was their printer and that he produced his types by casting in sand using wooden hand-engraved originals as models.

We may now leave the Dutch printing for the moment and discuss the evidence tending to show that printing was invented in Germany sometime in the neighborhood of 1445 by Johann Gutenberg. Here our knowledge is less fragmentary but still far from satisfactory for the decisive proof of any hypothesis.

I shall first briefly sketch the story as it is advanced by the Gutenberg advocates and then discuss the evidence in a rather unusual order, starting with the most trustworthy and unimpeachable evidence and proceeding then to the points in controversy.

INVENTION OF PRINTING

Johann Gänsefleisch, called Gutenberg, was born at Mainz about 1400. In young manhood his family was banished from Mainz and settled at Strasbourg. Here we find him in 1439 engaged in a lawsuit. He had entered into a partnership with two associates to develop several inventions. On the death of one partner, his brother claimed his rights in the partnership. The records of the litigation are a little hazy as to just what activities were involved but there seems every likelihood, especially in view of Gutenberg's later activities that at least one of the inventions the partnership was developing was printing. In 1441 and 1442 Gutenberg borrowed money, presumably to further this work. About the middle of this decade, Gutenberg moved to Mainz. Here, in 1450, he borrowed the considerable sum of 800 guilders from Johann Fust, a goldsmith and capitalist, "to finish the work." Toward the end of 1452, Fust advanced a second sum of like amount. In 1455 we have record of the judgment in a lawsuit brought to recover these sums together with interest and for forfeiture of the tools or equipment which he was to make with the proceeds of the first loan. In Gutenberg's reply there is mention of expense for workmen's wages, house-rent, parchment, paper, ink, etc. and also of money to be devoted to "the work of the books." Peter Schoeffer, Fust's later partner and son-in-law, appears as a witness on his side, and there appeared for Gutenberg two of his servants, Bertolf von Hanau and Heinrich Keffer who are probably the men we later find working as printers at Basel and Nürnberg. This all sounds very much like a suit over money advanced to

[85]

finance a printing project of considerable importance.

On January 17, 1465, Archbishop Adolf of Mainz appointed Gutenberg as his servant and courtier for life by reason of the "grateful and willing service which he had rendered to himself and to his order [*Stift*] and may and will render in the future." Whether this was for political service in support of Adolf's cause or a reward for his work in the typographic field we have no means of knowing.

From a document of February 26, 1468, we learn that Dr. Kunrad Humery received from the Archbishop of Mainz "some letters, an instrument, tools and other things relating to printing" which he had, at one time or another, procured for and loaned to Gutenberg. A contemporary copy of this document, unquestionably genuine, is preserved at Würzburg. We are by this enabled to fix with reasonable certainty the date of Gutenberg's death which must have occurred slightly earlier. There are a good many other earlier documents bearing on Gutenberg's activities to which we shall not refer for the reason that they have no possible relation to printing. Many of them relate to Gutenberg's borrowing money, none of which seems ever to have been returned. Others relate to annuities to Gutenberg, duties paid by him on a large store of wine, a breach of promise suit brought by a lady of noble birth, Anna zu der Iserin Thure, and the arrest in Strasbourg of the town secretary of Mainz to hold him as hostage for a debt Gutenberg considered due him by that city.

Various of these documents have been published at

different times by different authors among whom may be noted: Schelhorn, 1720; Joannis, 1727; Senckenberg, 1734; Schöpflin, 1740, 1741, 1760, 1761; Köhler, 1741; Fischer, 1800, 1801; Oberlin, 1801; Léon de Laborde, 1840; Schmidt, 1841; Dziatzko, 1889; Schorbach, 1900, 1925, 1926, and possibly others. They were first arranged in systematic form and published in 1882 by J. H. Hessels, the late Costerian advocate, and again by Schorbach in the *Gutenberg Festschrift* in 1900. Except for three later finds by Schorbach, they have been critically discussed at considerable length by Hessels in his *Gutenberg Fiction*, London, 1912.

When we come to consider the early productions of the German press, we find the earliest of them represented to us by fragments, no one of which bears any indication of the name of the printer, place of printing, or date of issue. These characteristics they share with the fragments of early Dutch printing, which we have already discussed, but with this salient difference: that we are able to associate all of the types with types which were used later by known printers, all of them located at Mainz or in the immediate vicinity.

With the known use of certain types in a given condition, at dates which have been established with at least approximate accuracy, it is possible to make a reasonably satisfactory deduction, judging by the condition of the types and how primitive is the technique of their use, regarding the probable date of printing of the various pieces with which we have to deal. The earliest examples of movable type printing in Germany, were set in a type known as that of the 36-line Bible, which was certainly printed at Mainz or Bamberg not later than 1460. The same types are also known to have been in the hands of Albrecht Pfister of Bamberg and used by him in books printed in 1461 and 1462.

These types of the 36-line Bible are classified by German bibliographers as having passed through three successive states. (1) types of the Paris Donatus; (2) types of the astronomical calendar; (3) types of the 36-line Bible.

The consensus of present-day bibliographical judgment is that the earliest of the fragments which have been preserved to us is part of a single leaf of a sybilline poem in German, which is generally referred to as the "Fragment of the World Judgment" because of the fact that the particular section of the poem which has survived deals with the Last Judgment. From the position of the watermark in the fragment, we are able to compute its probable position in the full sheet; and from the known text of the complete poem it has been estimated that the book of which the fragment was originally a part was made up of 37 leaves or 74 pages of 28 lines to the page.

The familiar little Latin grammar by Aelius Donatus, which figured so frequently in the issues of the early Dutch press, was a most natural thing for the first German printer to experiment with. For with a school-book of this character, he could depend on a ready sale. We are not disappointed, therefore, in finding the next three issues of the press, arranged in chronological order according to the condition of their types, to be three different editions of the Donatus. The fragments of two are preserved at the State Library at Berlin and that of the third in the Bibliothèque Nationale at Paris. Each of these editions was set in a format of 27 lines to the page.

The first representative of the second form of this type is a fragment of a single sheet astronomical calendar. The fragment bears no indication of the year for which it was printed but on the basis of astronomical data, it is believed by many authorities to relate to the year 1448. If this is so—and the sequence of many other pieces which have been identified, in their relation to issues of known date, do not make it impossible—the calendar was, therefore, printed at the end of 1447.

As the "Fragment of the World Judgment," to which we have already referred, is considered more primitive in typography and technique than this calendar and the still earlier editions of the Donatus, it is thought to have been printed about 1445 or 1446. There is some speculation in this deduction, of course, but there is much more evidence in favor of the presumption than against it. Competent authorities regard it, therefore, as the earliest piece of printing with movable types now extant, and as such, it becomes a very precious document indeed—now the prized possession of the Gutenberg Museum at Mainz.

The only man in Mainz or in the vicinity, who, on the basis of existing evidence, we can so much as suspect of being interested in or engaged in the practice of printing at this period was Johann Gutenberg. The majority of scholars are united in ascribing this, the issues of the Donatus, and the astronomical calendar, to his press. Bear in mind that this book of seventy-four pages or thereabouts appeared a full ten years before the probable date of the so-called Gutenberg Bible, which has been widely hailed as the first printed book in the world. And furthermore, that at least sixteen editions of the Donatus and several other pieces of printing appeared in all probability before that Bible. Then again, these issues of the press, which are known to us only through unique copies of fragments, probably represent a small proportion of the printed editions of which all trace has disappeared.

On the basis of this evidence it therefore seems likely that printing was being done in Mainz and the vicinity for a period of at least ten years before the appearance of the celebrated Bible. This situation seems, further, to be in accord with experience in the development of other inventions. The 42-line Bible has superficially been spoken of as the first book ever printed and the finest book ever printed, but it would be a miracle if the two attributions coincided. The first telephone was not a perfect instrument, nor was the first phonograph, nor the first electric light. Is it reasonable then to presume that the art of printing sprang full-grown and perfect from the brow of Jove? It is not.

The honor of being the printer of the great 42-line Bible has been contested to Johann Gutenberg—and with much reason. The sense of poetic justice has led many to ascribe it to him when their better judgment would have told them it was more likely brought to completion, if not produced in its entirety, by the partnership of Fust and Schoeffer. The plan for this book was perhaps Gutenberg's and the technique of its manufacture was unquestionably his, but we certainly cannot consider it to have been printed by Gutenberg individually. It seems to me, however, that this is no discredit to Gutenberg. The greatest honor we can do his name is to say that he was the printer of that smaller book which we have been discussing, completed ten years earlier. In its production he was blazing virgin territory, encountering problems the difficulty of which we can only surmise, and evolving from his own brain the fundamental principles of that art which of all arts has made the greatest impress on civilization. It is for this reason that the "Fragment of the World Judgment" is placed as the frontispiece to this volume.

The first *dated* example of printing preserved to us appeared in the year 1454, which is thus the earliest date we can set, beyond the sphere of speculation or controversy. This was an "indulgence." At the solicitation of the King of Cyprus, Pope Nicholas V granted indulgences to those of the faithful who should aid by gifts of money the campaign against the Turks. Armed with Papal authority, Paulinus Chappe, as representative of the King of Cyprus, went to Mainz to raise money for this cause. These indulgences would ordinarily be written out by hand but, as there were a considerable number to be distributed, he enlisted the aid of the printing press

[91]

Forma plenissime absolutionis et remissionis in vita

Forma plenarie remissionis in mortis articulo

or presses which he found then in active operation at Mainz, and had forms printed ready to fill in with the name of the donor.

All of these indulgences which have been discovered look remarkably alike, but on close examination we find that they may be divided into those which have 31 lines and those which have 30 lines. It was then recognized that the type of the 31-line indulgences was different from that used in the 30-line indulgences, but so similar that it could only indicate independent use of similar types by different printing offices.

The 31-line indulgences make use, in addition to the small type in which their text is set, of a large type which has already been identified as the type of the 36-line Bible, and therefore that used for printing the "Fragment of the World Judgment" and therefore, in all probability, belonging to Gutenberg.

The 30-line indulgences, on the other hand, have employed for the display lines a slightly smaller type very closely resembling that of the 42-line Bible but not identical with it. There is one other clew, however, to the identity of their printer—there was used a decorative capital M which we find later in the possession of Peter Schoeffer.

The first three known varieties of the 31-line indulgences were dated 1454 and the fourth variety is exactly similar to the three except that in printing the date was changed to 1455. There are three known issues of the 30-line indulgence, one of 1454 and the other two of which are dated 1455.

The other piece of printing dated 1454, appearing in December of that year, was the *Manung Widder die Durken*, a warning of Christians against the Turks. This was a leaflet of twelve pages.

The next important date in our chronology is 1456, in August of which year Heinrich Cremer, vicar of a church at Mainz, completed the rubrication and binding of a copy of the great Latin Bible already referred to as the 42-line Bible, from the fact of there being 42 lines to the column on most of its pages. Cremer made note of the date at the end of the two volumes of a copy of the book now preserved in the Bibliothèque Nationale at Paris. The printing of the Bible was, therefore, completed not later than 1456, and possibly earlier.

This is the book commonly referred to as the "Gutenberg Bible" and generally regarded as the first printed book as we have already noted. The book itself bears no note of the time or place of printing nor of the identity of its printer. The warm adherents of Gutenberg, whose name is legion, confidently regard this book as the masterpiece of his printing career. I think I am stating the truth when I say that the majority of temperate bibliographers who are not special pleaders believe the book was either produced in its entirety or in any event carried through to completion by Fust and Schoeffer under whose remarkably competent auspices the magnificent Psalter was brought out just one or two years later.

All features of this book have been studied with meticulous care by Schwenke, Dziatzko, and other German bibliographers, and a good many facts have been learned

est anima ei9 cu ea: tristemq̃ delinuit
blandicijs: et pergens ad emor patrē
suu̅ accipe inquit michi puellā hanc
cu̅iugem. Quod cu̅ audisset iacob: ab-
sentibus filijs et in pastu pecoꝝ occu-
patis siluit donec redirēt. Egresso autem emor patre sichem ut loq̃retur ad
iacob ecce filij eius veniebā̅t de agro:
auditoq̃ ꝙ acciderat irati sunt valde.
eo ꝙ fedam rem opatus esset in isrl̄: et
violata filia iacob rem illicitā perpe-
traꝪet. Locutus est itaq̃ emor ad eos.
Sichem filij mei adhesit anima filie
vestre. Date eam illi uxorem: et iunga-
mus vicissim conubia. Filias vestras
tradite nobis: et filias n̅ras accipite:
et habitate nobiscu̅. Terra in potestate
vestra est: exercete negociamini: possi-
dete eam. Sed et sichem ad patrem et ad
fratres ei9 ait. Inueniā graciā coram
vobis: et quecu̅q̃ statuitis dabo. Au-
gete dotem: et munera postulate: et liben-
ter tribuā ꝙ pecieritis: tantu̅ date michi puellā hanc uxorē. Respōderūt filij
iacob sichem et patri eius in dolo: seui-
entes: ob stuprū sororis. Non possu-
mus facere ꝙ petitis: nec dare sororem
nostrā homini incircu̅ciso: ꝙ illicitū
et nephariū est apud nos. Sed in hoc
valebim9 federari. Si volueritis esse siles
n̅ri: et circu̅cidat̅ in vobis ois mascu-
lini sexus: tunc dabim9: et accipiemus
mutuo filias u̅ras ac n̅ras: et habita-
bim9 vobiscu̅: erimusq̃ un9 ppl̄s. Si
aute̅ circu̅cidi nolueritis: tollem9 filiā
nostrā et recedem9. Placuit oblatio eoꝝ
emor et sichem filio ei9: nec distulit ado-
lescens quin statim ꝙ petebat̅ expleret.
Amabat eni puellā valde: et erat in-
clitus in omni domo patris sui. Ingressi
q̃ portam urbis locuti sunt ad ppl̄m.
Viri isti pacifici sūt: et volūt habitare

nobiscu̅. Negotientur in terra et exerceā̅t
eam: que spaciosa et lata cultoribz in-
diget. Filias eoꝝ accipiem9 uxores: et
n̅ras illis dabim9. Vnū e quo differt̅
tantū bonū. Si circu̅cidam9 masculos
nostros ritum gentis imitātes: et sub-
stancia eoꝝ et pecora et cuncta ꝙ possidēt
nostra erūt. Tantu̅ in hoc acquiescam9:
et habitātes simul unū efficiam9 ppl̄m.
Assensiq̃ sūt omnes circu̅cisis cunctis
maribz. Et ecce die tertio ꝙando grauissi-
mus vulnerū dolor est: arreptis duo
filij iacob simeon et leui fratres dine gla-
dijs: ingressi sunt urbem confidēter:
interfectisq̃ omnibz masculis: emor et
sichem pariter necauerūt: tollentes dinā
de domo sichem sororem suā. Quibus
egressis irruerūt sup occisos ceteri filij
iacob: et depopulati sunt urbem in ulci-
onem stupri: oues eoꝝ et armenta: et
asinos cunctaq̃ vastantes que in do-
mibz et in agris erant: paruulos q̃ eoꝝ
et uxores duxerūt captiuas. Quibus
perpetratis audacter: iacob dixit ad
simeon et leui. Turbastis me: et odio-
sum fecistis me chananeis et pherezeis
habitatoribz terre hui9. Nos pauci su-
mus: illi congregati prutent me: et dele-
bor ego et domus mea. Responderūt. Nu̅q̃d
ut scorto abuti debuerīt sororem nostra̅?

Interea locut9 est deus ad
iacob. Surge et ascende bethel et habita
ibi: facq̃ altare dn̅o ꝙ apparuit tibi
quā̅do fugiebas esau fratrem tuū. Iacob
vero conuocata omni domo sua ait.
Abicite deos alienos qui in medio uestri
sūt: et mu̅damini: ac mutate vestimen-
ta u̅ra. Surgite et ascendam9 in bethel
ut faciam9 ibi altare dn̅o: qui exaudi-
uit me in die tribulationis mee: et soci9
fuit itineris mei. Dederūt ergo ei omnes
deos alienos quos habebā̅t: et aures

PAGE OF THE 42-LINE BIBLE

regarding the manner of its production. The type body size at the beginning was such that forty lines made a column; the size was then reduced so that forty-one lines filled the same space, and it was then finally reduced so that forty-two lines came within the depth of a column. After printing began it was evidently decided to increase the edition for the early pages were reset and sent to press a second time. Six presses were at work on the book simultaneously. Paper was purchased in large quantities rather than in job lots, and the total consumption of paper and vellum was extremely large.

The production of such an important piece of work does not dovetail at all with what we know of Gutenberg's circumstances during the period in which it was being completed. On the other hand, had he had such a book practically completed in 1455, the capitalist Fust would have been disposed to back him more liberally rather than proceed against him. As Pollard points out, "the inventor who lacks organizing power and whose invention never thrives till it has passed into other hands is no unfamiliar figure, and such a conception of Gutenberg perhaps accords better with the known facts of his career than that of a living incarnation of heroism and business ability such as his German eulogists love to depict."

In 1457 appeared one of the greatest books ever printed—a book which is a never-failing source of amazement and an object of admiration to all amateurs of early printing. I refer to the first edition of the Psalter

Dñicis diebz post festū trinitatis · Inuitatoriuȳ ·

Regē magnū dñm venite adorem9 · Ps venite ·
Dñicis diebz post festū ephie Inuitatoriȳ ·

Adorem9 dñm q̄ fecit nos · Ps venite aȳ Seruite ·

Beatus vir qui
non abijt in
consilio impioȳ et in
via pctōȝ nō stetit : ᷑ ī
cathedra pstilētie nō se
dit · Sed ī lege dñi vo
lūtas ei9 : et in lege eius meditabit̄ die at
nocte · Et erit tanq̄ lignū qd̄ plātatū est
sec9 dcursus aq̄ȝ qd̄ fructū suū dabit in
tpȳ suo · Et foliū ei9 nō defluet : ᷑ oīa q̄cūqȝ
faciet prsperabūt · Nō sic impij nō sic : sed
tanq̄ puluis quē picit ventus a facie tre ·
Ideo nō resurgūt impij in iudicio : neqȝ
pctōres in ᵭsilio iustoȝ · Qm̄ nouit dñs
viā iustoȝ : ᷑ iter ūpioȝ peribit · Gla Ps

PAGE FROM THE FUST AND SCHOEFFER PSALTER OF 1457

Volětes sibi ꝥparare infrascriptꝯ libros magꝫ
cū diligētia correctos. ac in hmōi lra moguntie
impꝶos. bn̄ ꝫnu̅atos. venͣt ad locū habitatio-
nis infrascriptū.

Primo pulcram bibliam in pergameno.
Item scōam scōe beati thome de aquino.
Item quartū scriptū eiusdē.
Itē tractatū eiusdē de eccīe sacris ꝫ articlis fidei.
Itē Augustīnū de doctrina xͥpiana. cum tabula
notabili pͦdicantibꝰ multū pͥficua.
Itē tractatū de rōne et ꝫsciētia.
Itē mgͤrm iohāne gerson de custodia lͥngue.
Itē ꝫsolatoriū timorate ꝫscie venerabilis fratris
iohānis nider sacre theologie pͦfessoris eximij.
Itē tractatū eiusdē de ꝫtractibꝰ mercatoꝛ.
Itē bullā ꝑij iꝑꝫ scōi contra thurcos.
Itē historiā de pͤsentacōe beate marie vͥginis.
Itē canonē misse cū pͤfacōibꝰ ꝫ iꝑaratoꝛis suis.

antiphōnis in magna ac grossa littera.
Itē iohānne ianuensem in catholicon.
Itē sextumdecretaliū. Et clemeūnā cum aꝑaratu
iohānnis andree.
Itē in iure ciuili. Instituꝫōnes.
Itē arbores de ꝫsanguinitateꝫ affinitate.
Itē libros tullij de officijs. Cū eiusdē paradoxis.
Itē historiā griseldis. de maxia ꝫstantia mulieris
Item historiam Leonardi aretini ex bocatio de a-
more Tancredi filie sigismūde in Buiscardum.

hec est littera psalterij

which was the first *dated and signed printed book*. On the last page appears this colophon:

The present copy of the Psalms, adorned with beauty of capital letters, and sufficiently marked out with rubrics, has been thus fashioned by an ingenious invention of printing and stamping without any driving of the pen, and to the worship of God has been diligently brought to completion by Johann Fust, a citizen of Mainz, and Peter Schoeffer of Gernsheim, in the year of the Lord 1457, on the vigil of Feast of the Assumption.

Here at last we stand on firm ground regarding identity of printer and place of issue. The capitals referred to in the colophon are floriated initials of lacy design printed in three colors. The register of these colors in all the existing copies is so perfect that printers have been puzzled in an effort to determine the method by which it was obtained. The large type is printed throughout in red and black and the entire effect cannot be otherwise described than as magnificent.

There are two editions easy to distinguish the one from the other. The first has 143 leaves, the second contains some added rituals and comprises 175 leaves. There are also at least three variations in typography of the first page of the text. The differences have been studied by Weale and Martineau, but there is more work still to be done in order to put us in possession of all the facts regarding the ten existing copies of this book, all of which, by the way, are printed on vellum. The copy at Vienna is known as the virgin copy, having never been used in a church. Its vellum pages are practically as pure and white as the day it was printed. Under the colophon of this copy only appear the illuminated arms of Fust and Schoeffer.

By this time, I fear these descriptions of early books printed at Mainz will have become tiresome, but there are just two others which demand special mention because of problems arising in the effort to identify their printer or printers. One is the 36-line Bible; the other the *Catholicon*.

The 36-line Bible is much rarer than the 42-line Bible, but eight copies even approximately complete being known to exist, whereas thirty-two practically perfect copies of the other edition were known to De Ricci. As we have already noted, the book is set in the type used for the earliest German printing. In view of the early origin of the type it was natural to assume that this Bible antedated in issue the 42-line Bible. But according to patient studies by Dziatzko of the text of the book it contains numerous errors which can only be accounted for by assuming it was set up from the 42-line Bible as copy. This circumstance, known dates of completion of rubrication and other evidence points to its being printed about 1460 or perhaps earlier. As the type belonged earlier to Gutenberg and later to Pfister, and as Pfister shows himself to have been inexperienced when he printed his first books about 1461 there are some reasons why we should ascribe the book to Gutenberg and no very weighty reasons why we should not. Certainly this volume has a much better claim than the 42-line edition to be called the "Gutenberg Bible." There is but one perfect copy thought to exist outside of public collections. Should it ever come on the market we may confidently expect the bidding to reach dizzy heights.

The *Catholicon* is a Latin dictionary written by Joannes Balbus in the thirteenth century. It was a folio, printed in two columns of a small type which was none too good, and three varieties have been differentiated. It contained a colophon which reads as follows:

By the help of the Most High, at Whose will the tongues of infants become eloquent, and Who ofttimes reveals to the lowly that which he hides from the wise, this noble book, *Catholicon*, in the year of the Lord's Incarnation, 1460, in the bounteous city of Mainz of the renowned German nation, which the clemency of God has designed with so lofty a light of genius and free gift to prefer and render illustrious above all other nations of the earth, without help of reed, stilus, or pen, but by the wondrous agreement, proportion, and harmony of punches and types, has been printed and finished.
Hence to Thee, Holy Father, and to the Son, with the Sacred
    Spirit,
Praise and glory be rendered, the threefold Lord and One;
For the praise of the Church, O Catholic, applaud this book,
Who never ceasest to praise the devout Mary.
        Thanks be to God.

Many have considered Gutenberg the probable author of this colophon, preserving to the end his policy of anonymity—perhaps for cogent business reasons. The identity of its printer has been argued with much vigor pro and con. At present the question must be considered as still open. The printing office in which it was produced had a short life and the stock of the book was "remaindered" to Schoeffer not later than 1469 (at which date it appears in his list of books), and perhaps earlier.

All of this time the Fust and Schoeffer combination had been prospering, turning out well printed books with regularity. There was a lull of a couple of years following on the sack of the city in 1462, but in 1465 we find them publishing some editions of the classics. Fust died and Schoeffer continued alone but, though successful in a business way, his publications never rivalled the brilliance of the early fruits of the partnership. In 1469, as we have intimated, appeared a single sheet list of books which is here reproduced, constituting the first "publisher's list." It is also the first type specimen, the last line, set in large type, reading "hec est litera psalterij" (this is the type of the Psalter).

We see, therefore, that our knowledge of Johann Gutenberg the man is many times more complete than our knowledge of Lourens Coster. And our information regarding the earliest German printing is an hundred fold more specific than that regarding the primitive printing of the Dutch school.

A myriad of fifteenth century statements claim the invention for Germany and a lesser number, more specifically for the city of Mainz. From 1470 on, public statements by disinterested authorities award credit for the invention to Johann Gutenberg. None of these claims was once contradicted by a Hollander. Even Ulric Zell, in 1499, tells us the same thing, only leaving us to speculate on the character of the Dutch "prefiguration."

It may be well at this point to recall that there have

[100]

been several other pretenders to the honor of being the inventor of printing. Pamfilo Castaldi of Feltre, Italy, according to an obscure chronicle of the seventeenth century, was the inventor of movable types, and his native town gave the story such credence that in 1868 a monument was erected in his honor. The story has not been taken seriously by historians, but in denying him this honor recent researches have shown him to have been the first printer in Milan. One wild story places the invention at Kuttenberg in Bohemia of which city Johann Gutenberg is asserted to have been a native. Another ascribes it Jean Brito who printed at Bruges about 1477 to 1488. The honor has been claimed by some advocates for Johann Mentelin, the early printer of Strasbourg. None of these tales appears, however, to be well founded.

The remaining claim has some basis of fact and the circumstances are of much interest. In 1890 Abbé Requin discovered at Avignon, France, five notarial protocols in Latin dated 1444 and 1446 which show that Procopius Waldfoghel, a silversmith of Prague, was interested in a method of "writing artificially" and in painting colors on textiles. One document mentions "two alphabets of steel, two iron forms, one steel screw, forty-eight forms of tin, and various other forms pertaining to the art of writing." Another deals with a promise made by Waldfoghel to give instruction in the art of writing. We hear further of promises not to disclose to others the art so taught, of making twenty-seven Hebrew letters cut in iron "according to the science and practice of writing" and of instruments of "wood, tin, and iron."

But these and other references in the documents do not indicate the invention of printing with movable types. Perhaps their individual letters were successively impressed on paper in the "writing" of a text. Then again no fragment of early Avignon printing has ever come to light. The record is one of intense interest but it does not seem to bear directly on the invention of typography.

In 1469 printing was established at Paris by three Germans who had been brought thither by Guillaume Fichet and Jean Heynlin, as is told in more detail in Chapter IX. We can hardly conceive of two intelligent men with more information regarding the beginnings of the art, which it is evident they had followed closely, or with a more disinterested viewpoint regarding the invention and the identity of the inventor. In 1470 Fichet writes to Robert Gaguin, a scholar and author of eminence, a letter praising printing and its service to the cause of humane letters, and stating categorically some facts regarding the invention. This letter, which was printed and bound in a copy of Gasparino's Orthographia dedicated to Gaguin, is a discovery of comparatively recent years. Because of its importance, I published a year or so ago a full translation and transcript of the text with an introduction and notes. I consider it the most weighty document bearing on the invention controversy.

In the course of this letter Fichet writes: "It is said that there, not far from the city of Mainz, a certain John surnamed Gutenberg first of all men thought out the art of printing." This informed non-partisan statement can hardly be impeached.

INVENTION OF PRINTING

The colophons of the books printed at Mainz were meanwhile claiming the honor of the invention for that city. In some verses by Magister Franciscus, a press corrector, following the colophon of the Justinian of 1468 printed by Schoeffer, it is stated that two Johanns, both of the city of Mainz, were the renowned first printers of books, and that with them was associated a Peter. This has naturally been interpreted as referring to Johann Gutenberg, Johann Fust, and Peter Schoeffer.

Johannes Andreae, Bishop of Aleria, writes (Rome, 1468) that the sacred art of printing had risen in Germany. In 1471 Ludovicus Carbo speaks of the Germans having invented printing. There are so many references crediting the art to Germany and to Mainz that they need not be listed further.

In 1474, Joh. Philippus de Lignamine published at Rome his *Chronica*, the first reference to printers being under the year 1459 and giving the names of Jacobus with the surname of Gutenberg of Strasbourg and a certain other one named Fustus. In 1483, Matthias Palmer of Pisa stated under the year 1457, that Johannes Gutenberg zum Jungen, Knight of Mainz, invented the art of printing in 1440, and by his full and accurate listing of his name gave evidence of clear knowledge regarding his identity.

Adam Wernher and Johann Herbst, two professors at Heidelberg, in 1494 wrote some verses in honor of Johannes Gensfleisch (Gutenberg's family name) whom they called "the first printer of books" and "the first inventor of the art of printing." Jacob Wimpheling in

1499 praises Joannes Gensfleisch for his invention at Mainz. These verses were preceded by an epitaph on Gensfleisch, "inventor of the art of printing," by Adam Gelthus, a relative of Gutenberg, whose remains, it is added, rest in peace in the Franciscan Church at Mainz. In 1499, Polydore Vergil says that a certain Peter, a German, invented the art of printing at Mainz in 1442, but in later editions "Joh. Gutenberg" is substituted for "Peter." In the same year we encounter the *Cologne Chronicle* naming Gutenberg as inventor but making the puzzling allusion to the "prefiguration" in Holland. In 1501, Jacob Wimpheling says that the invention was made at Strasbourg by Johann Gutenberg of Strasbourg and that it was perfected later at Mainz.

In 1505, in a German translation of Livy printed at Mainz by Johann Schoeffer, the son of Peter Schoeffer and the grandson of Johann Fust, appears a reference to Johann Güttenbergk as inventor of printing in 1450, and of Johann Fust and Peter Schoeffer as improvers and perpetuators of the art. This statement, which was repeated in a number of subsequent editions, tends to weaken later references, in books printed by Johann Schoeffer, to his grandfather as the first inventor of printing.

Most of the testimony is to the effect that the art was invented at Mainz and the inventor was Gutenberg. It is also worthy of note that there were thirty or more published references to the origin of the invention before there was a whisper regarding the city of Haarlem.

One of the strongest arguments in support of Guten-

berg is that Fust and Schoeffer, though they were ag-
gressive self advertisers in their colophons, never during
Gutenberg's life claimed credit for the invention, which
they would have claimed without question had they been
entitled to it. Peter Schoeffer was still actively at work
when Guillaume Fichet made his statement regarding
the invention of printing by Gutenberg, yet neither he
nor any of the many others living who must have known
the facts entered any denial.

The cause of Gutenberg was seriously hurt by some
over-enthusiastic advocates who, in the last half of the
eighteenth century, unblushingly forged numerous
"original" documents in support of his claims. These
forgeries have now been shown up, but they have served
to cast suspicion on the authenticity of all the Gutenberg documents. The situation is further complicated by
the fact that the original record books containing the
proceedings of the Strasbourg trial of 1439 have
perished, and we have to depend therefore on the text at
second hand. The text of the Helmasperger Instrument
which gives us the information regarding the Fust-
Gutenberg lawsuit, is also a transcript, though an early
one, but the fact that such a suit took place is attested by a
mention of it in the *Encomium Chalcographiae* of
Arnold Bergel (or Bergellanus), 1541.

If we endeavor to regard the Strasbourg trial of 1439
as an entire forgery, it is certainly a clumsy one. Had an
ingenious fabricator written the minutes of this trial with
the idea of abetting the cause of Gutenberg, he would
certainly have made the references to printing clearer
and more precise. As they now stand they could not well

be more cryptic. I could occupy considerable space in discussing both sides of this question, but it is not worth while. Even if we leave the records of this trial out of consideration by our jury, the case is still strong enough to justify a verdict in Gutenberg's favor.

Weighing all the evidence, we must conclude on the basis of present knowledge, that printing with movable types of cast metal (which constitutes the invention of printing) was invented in Mainz or the vicinity some time between 1440 and 1450. We must also, *on the basis of the testimony now before us*, credit that invention to Johann Gutenberg.

IX. *Development of Typography*

OUTSIDE of Mainz, the first cities into which the typographic art was introduced were Bamberg and Strasbourg—both in the near vicinity. It is possible that Gutenberg himself may have printed the 36-line Bible at Bamberg, and Albrecht Pfister is known to have printed at least ten books, to which we shall later refer. Most of his publications were addressed to a popular audience, and few copies have survived their contemporary popularity.

At Strasbourg, Johann Mentelin was printing by 1460, and perhaps earlier, turning out for the most part large and unwieldy volumes which defied everyday use and have thus come down to us in better condition. Mentelin's associate and successor was his son-in-law Adolf Rusch whose name does not appear in a single one of the books he printed. He was the first to print with a type of strongly roman character, and his font was distinguished by a capital R of bizarre design which has led to his being usually referred to as the R-printer. Heinrich Eggestein, who began printing at Strasbourg about 1464, seldom signed his typographic productions and many of the other early books printed in that city fail to state the name of their printer.

Soon after the beginnings of printing at Strasbourg and Bamberg, the city of Mainz was sacked in the course of a conflict over the authority of rival ecclesiastics. During the succeeding period all industrial enterprises suffered serious dislocation and printers, trained in the mysteries of the new art of typography, found themselves without employment. Realizing the value of their services to other communities they scattered in several directions and set up business wherever they thought the prospects good. It is thus that we find almost all the first printers in Italy, France, and Spain to be men either with German names or specifically designated as Germans. Konrad Haebler, one of the world's leading authorities on fifteenth century printing, has recently devoted an imposing volume to the work of German printers in foreign countries.

Conrad Sweynheym and Arnold Pannartz apparently started toward Rome. We may conceive that they stopped to pass the night at the monastery at Subiaco, a little town not far from the Eternal City. Here, it is more than likely, the abbott, foreseeing the service a printing press could render to his work, and likewise sensible of the fame that book production would bring to his convent, persuaded the typographic pilgrims, by adequate inducements, to stay their journey and set up their press in his monastery. However this may have been, the two German printers did there establish their shop, and proceeded to

magis utimur. Recte si ita nixisset ut locutus est. Seruiuit ei fedissimis uo-
luptatibus: suáq; ipe senteriam uite prauitate dissoluit. Quod si aia ignis
est ut ostendimus: in celu debet emiti sicut ignis ne extinguatur. Hoc est ad
imortalitate que i celo e. Et sicut ardere ac niuere no pot ignis: nisi aliqua
pingui materia teneat in qua heat alimentu: sic aie materia & cibus e sola
iustitia: qua tenet ad uita. Post hec deus hoiem qua exposui roe generatum
posuit in paradiso: idest in orto secudissimo et amenissimo. que in partibus
orientis ommi genere ligni arboruq; conseruit. ut ex earu uariis fructibus
aleretur. Expersq; oim laboru deo pri summa deuotione seruiret. Tu dedit
ei certa madata que si obseruasset: imortalis maneret. si trascendisset: morte
afficeret. Id aut preceptu suit: ut ex arbore una que suit in medio paradisi
non gustaret. in qua posuerat intelligetiam boni & mali. Tu crimiator ille
inuidens opibus dei: oes fallacias & calliditates suas ad decipiendu hoiez
intendit. ut ei adimeret immortalitatem. Et pmo mulierem dolo illexit. ut
uetitu cibum sumeret. et per ea ipi quoq; hoi persuasit: ut transcenderet dei
legem. Percepta igit scia boni et mali: pudere eum nuditatis sue coepit. ab-
scoditq; se a facie dei: qd antea no solebat. Tum deus snia i peccatores lata
eiecit hoiem de paradiso. ut uictum sibi labore cogreret: ipmq; paradisum
igni circuuallauit: ne homo posset accedere. donec summu iudiciu faciat in
terra. et iustos uiros cultores suos i eudem locu reuocet morte sublata. sicut
sacre littere docet. et Sibilla erithrea cum dicit. Οἱ δὲ θεὸν αἴμωντες
ἀλίθιμον ἀεμμάον τε ζωὴν κληρομομονσί τον αἴωμος χρό-
μον αὐτοὶ οἰκοῦντες παραδεῖσον ὅμως ἐρίθηλεα κῆπον.
Qui aut deu honorat ueru: sempiterna utiq; uita hereditario iure possidet
seculi tpus ipi habitates ad paradisum similiter floretissimu ortu. Veru qm
hec extrema sunt: tota in extrema opis huius pte tractabimus. Nunc ea
que pma sunt explicemus. Mors itaq; sequuta est hoiem secudu dei sniam.
quod etiam Sibilla in carmine suo docet dicens. Άμθρωπον πεπλα-
σθαι θεοῦ παλάμαις ὁν καὶ πλάμηςεμ ὀφις δολιῶς ἐπὶ
μοίραμ ἀμελθειμτοῦ θαμάτου γμωσιμδε λαβειμ αγαθον
τε καλοῦ τε. idest. hoiem fictu dei maibus que et seduxit serpes dolose
ad fatu ascendere mortis: notioneq; boni et mali hoiem plasmatu dei ipius
palmis. que dolis fefellit serpes: ut uim mortis incurreret: et sciam accipet
boni & mali. Sic facta hois uita est tparia: sed tn longa. que in mille annos
ppagaret. qd diuinis lris, pditu est. et per oem sciam publicatu. cu Varro
no ignoraret argumetari nisus e: cur, putarent antiq mille anos uictitasse.

print in 1465, or possibly a year earlier, an edition of Donatus, no copy of which has survived. They next produced two books: Cicero's *De Oratore* and an edition of the works of Lactantius, which latter, in addition to being a very handsome volume, is distinguished by being the first book in which Greek type appears. A page of this volume is here reproduced. The type, it will be observed, is a condensed roman of considerable color, retaining many of the characteristics of the rounded gothics. This type has served as the model for the private type cut by the Ashendene Press and used in its books.

This is the story of the introduction of printing into Italy as it has been told for the last century. Recently, Professor Haebler has propounded a new theory, based on study of the fragments of an edition of the *Sieben Leiden vom Christi*. He believes they were printed about 1462 in Italy, in an Italian dialect, by an itinerant printer who came, found the field unpromising, and returned to Germany. It is not possible here to discuss the detailed evidence on which Professor Haebler's contention is based but the weight of his opinion in this field is very great. It will at least afford a variant on the commonly accepted version of Italian typographic origins.

To return to firm ground and the pair of German printers at the Subiaco monastery, we find they did not tarry there long. In the latter part of 1467 they moved on to Rome. Whether the first printing in that city was done by them or by Ulrich Han, another German who set up a press there, cannot be stated with certainty.

The first printer at Venice was Johann of Speyer, still

another German, whose first book appeared in 1469. He obtained a five-year exclusive patent or privilege for printing in Venice, destined to be the queen city, typographically, of Italy. But this monopoly was short lived, for he died the following year, and his brother, Wendelin of Speyer who took over the business, did not fall heir to the special privilege, as the authorities held that Johann's patent had lapsed with his death. The field was thus open to all comers, and the entrants were many. Wendelin's special distinction is that he was the first to print with a type of purely roman character—that is the round letter we use today in contradistinction to the gothic black letter used by the first German typographers.

It is not known just when printing began at Basel, in territory now within the political boundaries of Switzerland but which was still, in the fifteenth century, German domain. The first printer in that city was undoubtedly Berthold Ruppel, whose name was mentioned as one of Gutenberg's servants in the legal process initiated by Fust in 1455. His first *dated* book appeared in 1474 but a record of purchase in 1468 of a copy of his *Moralia in Job* makes it clear that he was printing in that year and perhaps earlier. The next printer to set up at Basel was Michael Wenssler.

The next country into which typography was introduced was France. The story of its coming reveals to us the zeal of two enthusiasts regarding the service of printing to the cause of learning: Jean Heynlin, who had been rector of the Sorbonne, and Guillaume Fichet, professor of rhetoric at the same institution. On their initiative, three German printers were brought to Paris: Ulrich Gering—generally regarded as the ranking member of the group and in consequence looked upon as the Caxton of France—Michael Friburger, and Martin Crantz. They set up their press within the confines of the Sorbonne and there, in the space of two years, printed nearly a score of books, all of them, it may be noted, in a very fair roman type, and all addressed to an academic circle of readers.

In 1473, these three pioneers, being deprived of their professional patronage, moved to the Rue Saint Jacques —a street destined to be the haven of printers for centuries to come—at the sign of the "Soleil d'Or." Their undisputed control of the field, however, was not long to continue, and we soon find two competitors at work: Pieter de Keysere and Johann Stoll in association, and the printers at the sign of the "Soufflet Vert."

The first printer at Lyons was Guillaume Leroy, who was brought thither by a Lyonnese citizen, Barthélemi Buyer, by whom he was employed. His first book, a volume made up of miscellaneous religious essays intended for popular reading, appeared in the latter part of 1473. The majority of the early books printed at Lyons were similarly popular in character but in the last decade of the century the output became more catholic in its range.

Printing was established in nearly forty towns and cities in France during the fifteenth century, but in most of them the functioning of the press was ephemeral. In only about four cities was printing established on a solid and permanent basis. Most of the French incunabula

[112]

were, as we might expect, printed at Paris, but the history of the first printers in the provincial towns offers an intriguing field of research—an opportunity embraced by the late Anatole Claudin, who issued a series of monographs on the genesis of printing in many of these communities. He had planned a general history of printing in France but this commendable project was unhappily cut short by his death.

We have already discussed in the chapter on the invention of printing the question of when and where the first printing was done in Holland. The earliest Dutch books which are signed and dated by a printer were produced by Gerardus Leempt and Nicholaus Ketalaer at Utrecht in 1473. The irrepressible art raised its head in 1477 at Delft (Jacob Jacobszoen and Maurice Yemantszoen), and at Gouda (Gerard Leeu). Printing began at Deventer in 1477, Zwolle in 1479, and Leiden in 1483, in addition to several other less important towns into which the press had meanwhile been introduced. Not until 1483, and December of that year, do we find issued at Haarlem a book ascribed to a specific printer, in the person of Jacob Bellaert.

We next come to a district, in its typographical history, of extraordinary interest to people of the English tongue, for here was the cradle of the first book printed in our language. This district was the southern portion of the Low Countries comprising approximately what is the territory of present-day Belgium. The first printing here was done in the town of Alost in 1473 by Johann of Paderbon, otherwise known as John of Westphalia, who in 1474 moved to the city of Louvain, famed for the treasures of its university library which was so regretably destroyed in the World War. Here he found a competitor, Jan Veldener, already at work, but managed to dispose of him by fair means or foul.

We now stand at the gates of Bruges, and it behooves us as members of the English-speaking fraternity, reverently to doff our hats. For here was produced in 1476 the first printed book in the English language: the *Recuyell of the Histories of Troy*, the printers being Colard Mansion and William Caxton. To Caxton and his work a chapter will presently be devoted, so we will not here discuss his activities at Bruges in more detail. After Caxton left for England, Mansion continued to print in this city until 1484.

Until recent years early Spanish printing was the *terra incognita* of bibliographers, but now, thanks to the labors of Dr. Haebler in the public, monastic, and private libraries of the Iberian peninsula, we have a far wider knowledge of the work of the typographic pioneers in Spain. A small volume of poems laudatory of the Blessed Virgin was the first product of the press, printed at Valencia by Lambert Palmart in 1474. From a colophon in a later book we learn that he was, like so many of the other pioneer printers, an *Alemanus*, which it is thought in this instance to mean that he was Flemish.

Matthaeus, another native of Flanders, carried the art to Saragossa in 1475. The total output of the press at Tortosa consisted of one book printed there in 1477. In the same year printing began at Seville—a city which was soon to be an important book printing center—disciples of Gutenberg in this instance being Antonio Martinez, Alonso del Puerto and Bartolome Segura. In 1478, Nicolaus Spindeler and Pedro Brun, who had been the transient printers at Tortosa, set up a press in Barcelona. In one of their books appears the date of MCCCCLXVIII, from which one X has obviously been omitted.

The earliest printing in Spain was, as in France, in roman type. Later the gothic came into use, particularly for books for liturgical use.

The last important country of Europe to receive the benefits of the printing press was England. Of its coming into Anglo-Saxon domain we will deal in the next chapter.

During the fifteenth century, however, printing was introduced in many of the lesser countries of Europe, the art becoming much more widespread than is generally realized. In addition to the countries already mentioned, it is surprising to realize that the first known printing was done in Czecho-Slovakia in 1468, at Pilsen by the "Printer of the Guido della Colonna"; in Poland in 1473, at Cracow by Caspar Hochfeder; in Hungary in 1473, at Budapest by Andreas Hess; in the Balearic Islands in 1480, at Valdemosa by Nicolaus Calafat; in Austria in 1482, at Vienna by Stephan Koblinger; in Denmark in 1482, at Odensee by Johann Snell; in Sweden in 1483, at Stockholm by the same Johann Snell; in Portugal in 1489, at Libson by Rabbi Elieser; in Montenegro in 1493, at Rieka by the Monk Makario;

and—finally—in Turkey in 1494, at Constantinople by David and Samuel ihn Nachmias.

By all of which it will appear that the new art of typography turned out to be a lusty infant.

X. *The Venetian Masters*

THE ordinary printer of today, even though he knows almost nothing of the history of his craft, is quite certain to have in his technical vocabulary the names of three printers of the fifteenth century, Gutenberg, Jenson, and Aldus. Mention of the first of these is generally recognized as a reference to the traditional inventor of the printing art. The historical significance of the other two names is more often unknown though the words themselves appear in numerous combinations. A certain group of type faces is widely recognized as the Jenson family, while many brands of paper and the like take as their distinctive trade name the adjective Aldine. There is a certain historical justice in the survival of these three names, for the men thus honored stand out in a group by themselves as the three great benefactors of modern civilization by their typographical achievements. If the German, Johann Gutenberg, invented the process of printing by movable types, a Frenchman, Nicholas Jenson, raised it to its highest artistic level, while Aldus

[117]

Manutius, an Italian, showed the way in which its benefits could best be disseminated to the greatest number. Since Gutenberg's contribution has already been described, we are concerned here only with the accomplishments of the other two.

The first of these, Nicholas Jenson, was certainly the world's first great type designer, perhaps the greatest in all typographical history. Of his life and personality we do not possess extensive information though what we do know is of the highest interest. The date of his birth is not recorded though from his own statements it is clear that he was born at Sommevoire (in the Department of the Aube) in southeastern France. He had a brother, named Albert who entered the priesthood. When Nicholas died, in 1480, the mother, Zanetta (Jeanette) as well as Albert, was still living, as were his three daughters, and his wastrel son, the last then resident at Lyons. For all of these relatives Jenson made ample provision, besides numerous bequests to charity, a circumstance indicating that he was a man of commercial as well as artistic ability.

When and why he emigrated to Italy are matters of uncertainty no less than the place and circumstance of his learning the new art. A tradition of the late seventeenth century pretends to explain this but the facts it cites are unsupported by other evidence and in themselves seem to be altogether improbable. According to this tradition Jenson after an apprenticeship to the art of die-making for coinage became Master of the Royal mint, first at Troyes and then at Paris. Here his skill came to the notice of the King Louis XI who had somehow heard of the new invention at Mainz and sent young Jenson there on a secret mission to learn the process and bring it back to France. If this story be true it leaves unexplained his appearance in Italy and his failure to establish himself under the auspices of royal favor at home. It is therefore much more probable that Jenson never visited Germany at all but went to Italy and became a goldsmith. In that capacity he might easily have been employed by the first German printers there to cut their punches and thus have learned the process.

Since Jenson's fame is derived chiefly from the beauty of his roman types we must understand clearly the historic origin of that form of letter. During the later Renaissance students of the humanities came to use almost exclusively a form of writing which is consequently known as the humanistic hand, and gradually the convention arose, primarily in Italy, but to a certain extent elsewhere, that manuscripts of the ancient classics, poetry, and belles lettres generally, should be written in this humanistic form of calligraphy while law, medicine, theology, and logical treatises should appear in the more conservative dress of the gothic letter. This was certainly the convention in Italy, where, moreover, the influence of the humanists being so great, there was a tendency to simplify the angularity of the gothic to the more graceful roman form. Thus the first printing in Italy (at Subiaco, see p. 108) was done in what must be called semi-gothic, a letter that has a distinct resemblance to the roman type in which this book is printed no less than to the true gothic black-letter. We are tempted to describe it as such a modified gothic as one who admired the roman letters might produce in copying a German black-letter model.

The next types produced in Italy were definitely roman in form and they take their name from the city in which they were cast. These, curiously enough, are not as well done as were the types of this design already cut in Germany. Similarly the first Venetian types, those of John of Spire which come next in the chronological series, were, though infinitely more beautiful in design than their immediate predecessors at Rome, extremely unsatisfactory in their irregular alignment. It is not until Jenson printed with his own letter in 1470 that we have a successful combination of a pure letter of great beauty in design accurately placed on the type body where it would harmonize perfectly with the other characters which precede and follow it. What is more natural then than to suppose that the craftsman who achieved this result had learned by the process of trial and error, or in other words that he had entered the service of one of these earlier printers and had perfected his technique in another man's workshop? To suppose that his first efforts should meet with immediate success is altogether improbable. Whether or not we can assume that Jenson worked with Sweynheym and Pannartz at Rome is not to be decided hastily. That John of Spire, with his brother Wendelin, had done so before he set up for himself in Venice, seems quite definitely established, while the hypothesis that Nicholas Jenson left Han's workshop to

Meminit quippe illius ĩ protagora illũ pro periãdro cõstituens. Dicebat autẽ nõ ex uerbis res: sed ex rebus uerba esse inqrenda: neqʒ propter uerba res perfici: sed rerũ gratia uerba consumari. Defunctus est autẽ ætatis anno.lxxyii.

Epimenides.

e Pimenides ut ait Theopompus: aliiqʒ complures patrẽ habuit Phæstium: alii Dosiadẽ: alii Agesarchum tradũt Cretensis genere: gnoso uico orĩdus effigiẽ immutasse perhibetur. Missus enim aliqñ a patre ut ouem rure deferret: meridiano tẽpore diuertit ex itinere: atqʒ ĩ spelunca ubi se iactarat: quinquaginta & septẽ aṅnos perpétuo sopore acquieuit. Dehinc somno excitatuſ quæsiuit ouẽ: putabat se enim parũ obdormisse: quam cũ nõ ĩuenisset: in agrũ reuertit. Cum uero rerũ omniũ faciem immutatã cerneret: agrũqʒ in alterius ius cõcessisse: stupore attonitus: & cunctabũdus rediit in oppidũ: ibi cũ domum suã uellet ingredi: quisnã esset interrogatuſ uixqʒ agnitus a iuniore fratre iam uetulo omnẽ ex illo didicit rei ueritatẽ. Porro illius fama per græciam uolante deo esse carissimus existimatus est. Vnde & Atheniéses cum aliquãdo peste laborarent: responso a Pythia accepto urbem expiari oporte re: Niciam nicerati filiũ misere epimenidemqʒ ex creta ad uocarũt: profectus autẽ olympiade.xxvii. lustrauit urbem pestéqʒ repressit hoc modo. Sumpsit oues nigro & candido uelere: duxitqʒ in ariũ pagũ: atqʒ inde quo uellét abire per misit: his qui illas sequebãtur mandãs ubicũqʒ illæ accubuissent: singulas mactare propicio deo: atqʒ in hũc modũ q euit lues. Ex eo iã hodie qʒ per atheniensiũ pagos aras sine noĩe ĩueniri certũ est: In eius quæ tũc facta est expiationis memoriã. Alii cãm dixisse pestis celonĩum scelus: liberatio nemqʒ signasse: atqʒ ideo mortuos duos adolescẽtes cratinũ & lysiniũ: sicqʒ cladẽ quieuisse Athenienses ea pnicie liberi

join the new establishment at Venice is quite within the range of probability. The fact that Jenson was able to produce a whole series of editions dated 1470 implies that he was already in Venice and had done considerable work on the new type before John's death late in 1469.

These early editions of Jenson were largely classical texts for which his new letter was perfectly adapted. Gradually however he diversified his output so that of the ninety-eight works published by him nearly every phase of the intellectual activity of his day was included, though theology in twenty-nine editions and the classics in twenty-five were preponderant. A few medical and legal works were included as well as several Italian translations and finally one work of pure literature, Boccaccio's *Fiametta*. For the production of legal and theological texts Jenson conformed to the convention which demanded a gothic letter, and from 1473 on used a face of this character in various sizes.

By 1475 Jenson enlarged his organization and formed a company, but this was probably concerned only with the selling and not with production. As legal custom required at that time this company could be formed only for a definite term of years, and the organization terminated in 1480. It had, however, been so profitable that a new company was immediately established and the number of partners increased. By this time, however, Jenson was evidently planning to take a less prominent part in business affairs, perhaps his health was already broken, for the new corporation instead of being titled "Nicholas Jenson and Company" as the first one had been, now bore the name "John of Cologne, Nicholas Jenson and Company." Their articles of incorporation were drawn up on the first of June, 1480, for a term of five years, but the new business was scarcely launched before Jenson was taken by death.

His will, which was drawn on his death bed, is dated September, 1480. It is a complicated document replete with interesting details but the outstanding features of historical significance are three: (1) the great wealth accumulated by the testator which seems to have been acquired solely through his activity as printer and publisher, (2) the complexity of his business relations, and (3) the fact that he seemed to value more than anything else his set of type punches. The disposal of these he hedges around with numerous provisions but he evidently desired his best friend, Peter Uglheimer, to have them. Evidently this transfer took place for Jenson type continued in use for many years afterward.

That Jenson's judgment was well founded in regarding his type design as his most precious possession is born out by the high esteem in which those letters have been held by every succeeding generation which has had any regard for the quality of its typography. As early as 1483 Andreas Torresanus boasts of printing with "the illustrious equipment and famous types of the late great master in this art, Nicholas Jenson, the Frenchman" and from that day to this the masters of typography have harked back to these types as a standard for beauty and balance in the design of typographical letters.

The third member of our triad, Aldus Manutius, was

also a printer at Venice in the late years of the fifteenth century. In contrast with Jenson his enduring fame rests not upon the beauty of his craftsmanship but upon his success as a publisher. Aldus began printing with his main interest focused upon the buyer and user of his books. Himself a profound scholar, imbued with the spirit of the Renaissance, he never lost his sense of awareness that books are made to be read, or his missionary zeal to put what he considered the best books into the hands of the largest number of readers. The ingenuity with which he developed methods for achieving these results and the success that he won by them set him apart as the first great publisher who built up a demand for an entirely new form of book publication.

He was born in the Papal States in the year 1450 and after an excellent education became tutor to the sons of the Prince of Capri. This proved an important connection for the eldest of these pupils later supplied him with funds to embark on his career as a printer. When he finally did this in 1490, his fortieth year, he had elaborated a careful scheme of action which he set in operation by assembling a group of the capable Greek scholars as well as the technical assistants necessary for equipping an ample printing establishment. Aldus' first purpose was to get into print all the important classics of ancient Greece which had so far remained unpublished, and also to issue in revised texts those which had appeared only in corrupt versions. He was thus primarily an enthusiast for the treasures of classical antiquity. But he was more than this; he was also gifted with a sense of practical values and he intended that these books should be not the expensive playthings of a learned amateur but marketable merchandise. For these books to sell, their price must not be too high in scale, and Aldus met this problem as a practical executive by reducing the cost of production. He was not himself a printer but he was evidently capable of grasping the essential points of a technical problem. Realizing that to print Greek with its polysyllabic endings in the way one printed Latin, consumed an appalling amount of paper, he devised as his first economy the reduction of this waste by supplying with his Greek alphabet a whole series of types for tied letters or ligatures. These were conventional signs developed by professional scribes for writing rapidly and each one represented from two to five letters in a space no larger than that required for a single character in ordinary script. By the standards of typographical aesthetic these Greek ligatures of Aldus are hideous monstrosities serving only to disfigure the pages on which they appear, but by them Aldus was able to do what he had set out to accomplish, to print Greek books cheaply enough for profitable sale.

Up to the time of his death in 1515 Aldus continued to print the Greek classics, but this was only one side of his ambition. The other was to do a similar work for the surviving texts of Roman antiquity, and also the best of contemporary vernacular. Again he secured a vast extension of his market by printing more cheaply than any one else. Here, however, instead of securing economy of paper by the use of contractions and ligatures he turned to a form of letter which had not yet been utilized by

M uralis saxi, tum toto corpore vulnus.
Q uem postquam aspexit geminatus gaudia ductor
Sidonius, fuge Varro, inquit, fuge Varro superstes,
D um iaceat Paulus: patribus Fabioq3 sedenti
E t populo, Consul totas edissere Cannas.
C oncedam hanc iterum, si lucis tanta cupido est,
C oncedam tibi Varro fugam. at cui fortia, & hoste
M e digna, haud paruo caluerunt corda vigore,
F unere supremo, & tumuli decoretur honore.
Q uantus Paule iaces? qui tot mihi millibus vnus
M aior letitiæ causa es: cum fata vocabunt,
T ale precor nobis salua Carthagine lethum.
H æc ait, & socium mandari corpora terræ
P ostera cum thalamis aurora rubebit apertis
I mperat: armorúmq3 iubet consurgere aceruos
A rsuros Gradiue tibi. tum munera iussa
D efessi quanquam accelerant, sparsósq3 propinquos
A gmine prosternunt lucos, sonat acta bipenni
F rondosis sylua alta iugis, hinc ornus, & altæ
P opulus alba comæ validis accisa lacertis
S cinditur, hinc ilex proauorum condita seclo,
D euoluunt quercus, & amantem littora pinum.
A t ferale decus, mœstas ad busta cupressos,
F unereas tum deinde pyras certamine texunt.
O fficium infelix, & munus inane peremptis.
D onec anhelantes stagna in Tartessia Phœbus
M ersit equos, fugiénsq3 polo Titania cæcam
O rbita nigranti traxit caligine noctem.
P ost vbi fulserunt primis phaetontia frena
                                        r·j.

THE ITALIC OF ALDUS

type designers, the cursive script in use by the Italian humanists.

We have already mentioned two forms of the writing of the period, the gothic style which was currently used for the books of the professional classes, and the humanistic style, or roman, applied only to literary and poetical volumes, but both of these were formal book hands used by professional scribes. There was also a third form of writing in common use for ordinary purposes and this was no more than a simplified roman in which for speed the pen was seldom raised from the paper in the body of the word. This was, in other words, the ordinary cursive Italian script of that period though it was much closer to the roman book hand than our own handwriting is to the letter form of our printed volumes. By copying in type this cursive humanistic hand Aldus found he could make an economy of space for his non-Greek printing comparable to the one secured by his Greek ligatures. There was one great mechanical difficulty, however, that his typefounders had to meet, which arose from the fact that an essential feature of this cursive writing was a marked forward slant of its letters. These problems were not solved until 1501 when a Dante in this new type brought into the world a book printed in *Italic* letter. A long series of compact editions of the Latin classics followed which Mr. Winship has well called the "Everyman's Library" of its day. These books, of handy pocket size, were sold at a price approximately equivalent to fifty cents in our present money.

The magnitude of Aldus' success was shown by the

immediate appearance of counterfeit Aldine editions, most of them printed at Lyons but many in Venice itself. Aldus complained bitterly of the damage he suffered from these piratical forgeries, but in spite of them, his financial success was enormous.

The significance of his achievements as a publisher are often forgotten, though as we have said, Aldus' name is yet current in the technical vocabulary of the printer, and similarly his device is still frequently used for various purposes. This familiar anchor with a dolphin entwined on its shaft appears frequently in typographical decoration though its significance as an emblem of the motto "Make haste slowly" is not always considered: the dolphin is a symbol of speed and activity, as the anchor is of stability and firmness.

Long after the death of Aldus Manutius in 1515 the business was carried on by his family, and it continued to function in one form or another until it finally ended with the year 1597. The later productions of the press, however, are of little interest by reason of either content or printing. But the early record of the family is writ on a "bright particular page" in the history of typography and bookmaking.

XI. *Early Illustrated Books*

T THE time of the invention of printing with movable types in Europe, the art of wood engraving was already fairly well developed, as we have already seen. Al-almost coincident with Gutenberg's invention there began the practice of cutting relief printing blocks on soft metal. The technique was similar to that of the wood engraver; the material alone was different. There has been preserved such an engraving on metal dated 1454. The art of copperplate engraving was also known at this period. There is, for example, a series of copperplate engravings of 1446 that were manifestly designed to appear in book form.

With type-printed books, however, the natural form of illustrations would be relief blocks, which could be printed at the same time as the type blocks. Since these could be cut more easily on wood than on metal, woodcuts became the medium of illustration for the first illustrated books printed from type.

We say such blocks could be printed in the same form with the type, but this does not appear to have been easy. The second illustrated type-printed book, produced by

Albrecht Pfister at Bamberg, was Boner's *Edelstein*, issued in 1461. In this book, the cuts were printed subsequent to the printing of the text. On the other hand, in the first illustrated book printed at Augsburg (the *Heiligenleben*, by G. Zainer) the blocks were printed first as in some instances the type is printed over them. The difficulties were, however, soon overcome and, in most of the fifteenth century books we find type and cuts printed together with entirely satisfactory results.

The earliest illustrated book was in all probability the first edition of Ackermann von Böhmen, printed by Pfister at Bamberg about 1460, as has been demonstrated by Zedler and confirmed by Schramm. The only known copy of this edition, preserved in the library at Wolfenbüttel, unfortunately lacks the wood cuts, but these appear in the second edition which appeared later.

Leadership in the field of book illustration, however, soon shifted from Bamberg to Augsburg. Here were issued many interesting volumes. Most of the woodcuts were rather primitive in character but this gave them a quaintness and naiveté which was attractive. Then too, many of the woodcuts harmonized excellently in color and style with the type used for the books and because of their character printed well on the paper used—two of the primary desiderata in book illustration.

For the earliest of these books, the woodcuts were designed especially for their illustration. There soon grew up, however, the pernicious habit of using any sundry woodcuts that chanced to be around the office and—to make matters worse—using them several times. This

WOODCUT IN EDELSTEIN, MAINZ, 1461

made nondescript scrapbooks rather than illustrated books. A rather startling example of this casual manner of illustration may be seen in the *Seelenwurzgarten* printed by Conrad Dinckmut. At first glance, this book appears to be profusely illustrated. Out of the 133 woodcuts, however, but seventeen are different, and one is used over and over again thirty-seven times!

We can here mention briefly only a few outstanding illustrated books, and most of these appeared in the later decades of the century after the art reached a higher state of development.

The first great example of book illustration was the *Perigrinationes in Montem Syon*, by Canon Bernhard von Breydenbach. This volume was printed in one of Schoeffer's types and was illustrated by Erhard Reuwich. According to the preface, the illustrator was taken along on this expedition to the Holy Land in order that the pictorial record might be authoritative. Many of the woodblocks show views of the cities through which the travelers passed, but there are some drawings showing the human aspects of life in the Near East that set a new mark in that they add definitely to the descriptive value of the text. The technique, also, was excellent, and we find in the blocks, the use of cross-hatching for the first time.

The best known woodcut in this celebrated volume is the frontispiece, which we here reproduce. It depicts a woman—possibly symbolizing the city of Mainz, as is suggested by Pollard—surrounded by the arms of Breydenbach and two of his companions on the "peri-

THE BREYDENBACH FRONTISPIECE WOODCUT

grination," and surmounted by a trellis in which children are climbing. The whole has a rare decorative quality, and gives us the impression of being, in artistry, a quarter century ahead of its time.

Supremacy in book illustration now shifts to Nürnberg. Here the *Schatzbehalter* was issued in 1491 with wood engravings by Michael Wolgemut and probably by assistants. The original plan of the book was most ambitious, for in the first half there are ninety-two full page plates; in the second half but two. Some of the illustrations are very fine but of many it would be a kindness to call them mediocre. While this is one of the celebrated illustrated books of the fifteenth century, it cannot in all aspects be considered a fine book from beginning to end.

Another book illustrated by Wolgemut with the help of his stepson, Wilhelm Pleydenwurff, is the "Nürnberg Chronicle" or, more accurately, the *Liber Chronicarum* by Hartmann Schedel, which was printed by Anton Koberger in 1493. For this book, plans were laid more carefully, but the reprehensible system of repeating cuts and using the same block to represent different persons or places is much in evidence. This is particularly flagrant in the case of portraits of celebrities, royal, religious, or otherwise. Nearly six hundred different individuals are portrayed by the use of less than a hundred blocks, so that each engraving had perforce to serve, on the average, for six different individuals. In all, over eighteen hundred pictures are printed from 645 blocks. The *Chronicle* was, however, a remarkable volume and

WOODCUT FROM THE SCHATZBEHALTER

must be regarded as one of the most important illustrated books of the period.

The first illustrated type-printed book to appear in Italy was issued by Ulrich Han at Rome in 1468: the *Meditationes* of Cardinal Turrecremata. The woodcuts, however, were not well executed, and the volume cannot be numbered among the outstanding examples of book illustration.

The great Italian illustrated book of the incunabula period is the *Hypnerotomachia Poliphili*, printed by Aldus at Venice in 1499. Not only are the illustrations spirited, varied, well drawn, and well cut, but in color and weight of line they harmonize extraordinarily well with the type of the text—a principle all too often violated in the designing of illustrated books. In turning the leaves of this book it is difficult to select a single page for reproduction, but the one shown later in our chapter on book illustration has been selected because it shows a woodcut, text, and decorative initial—all on a single page in harmonious combination.

The *Hypnerotomachia* has a fine flavor of romance about it. We find from an acrostic made up by the initial letters of the successive chapters that the author was Francesco Colonna, a Dominican monk, who is identified as Poliphilo, the hero of this fervid love story. Polia, whom he so ardently loved, was in real life Lucretia Lelio of Treviso, who after an attack of the plague, had taken her vows and entered a convent. In the story Polia takes refuge in a temple from which she is banished by reason of the attentions of Poliphilo. But the lovers are

CUnqz suggerente diabolo in forma ser/
pentis pthoparêtes mandatuz dei trãs/
gressi fuissent:maledixit eis deus: et ait
serpenti. Maledict⁹ eris inter omnia animãtia
z bestias terre:super pectus tuum gradieris: et
terram comedes cunctis diebus vite tue.Muli/
eri quoqz dixit.Multiplicabo erûnas tuas:z cõ/
ceptus tuos:in dolore paries filios z sb viri po
testate eris:z ipe dõiabitur tibi. Ade vo dixit
Maledicta terra in opere tuo i laboribus come
des ex ea:spinas z tribulos germinabit tibi:in
sudore vultus tui vesceris pane tuo:donec reuer
taris in terram de qua sumptus es.Et cu fecissz
eis deus tunicas pelliceas eiecit eos de paradi/
so collocans ante illum cherubin cum flammeo
gladio:vt viam ligni vite custodiat.

NAam primus homo formatus de limo
terre triginta annoru apparens imposi/
to nomine Eua vxori sue. Cuz de fructu
ligni vetiti oblato abvxore sua comedisset:eie
cti sunt de paradiso voluptaS: in terram maledi
ctionis vt iuxta imprecationez dominu dei. Adã
in sudore vultus sui operaretur terram:et pane
suo vesceretur.Eua quoqz in erûnis viueret fili
os quoqz pareret in dolore. quam incompabili
splendore decorauit. eã felicitatis sue inuid⁹ ho
stis decepit:cu leuitate feminea fructus arboris
temerario ausu degustauit: z viru suu,in sentêti
am suam traxit.Deinde perizomatibus foliozu
susceptis ex delitiaz orto in agro ebron vna cuz
viro pulsa exul venit. Tandem cuz partus dolo
res sepius expta fuisset cuz laboribus in senu z
tande in mortez sibi a domino predictã deuenit.

finally united and our scenario ends on a happy note.

Outside of Venice, the only other Italian city at all active in book illustration was Florence. Here we find a large output of fairly high standard, most of it so similar in character that it has been regarded by some as the work of a single artist. A sounder opinion, however, is that it was the product of a wood-cutting shop, which rendered the work of varied designers. Many of the blocks have attractive narrow borders of simple conventional pattern, which contribute materially to their charm when appearing in a book page.

It took more than ten years for the early printers in France to produce an illustrated book, the first such volume being issued in 1481 by Jean du Pré (in partnership with Didier Huym). In this missal, for such it was, there appeared a large wood block of the Crucifixion, of rather mediocre quality artistically. In another missal, following soon after, is a metal cut of much finer execution and several smaller blocks.

The first French illustrated book, not religious in character, appeared in 1483-1484, also from the press of Du Pré. It was an edition of Boccaccio's *De la Ruine des Nobles Hommes*. The woodcuts which illustrated it were later acquired by Richard Pynson, one of the earliest printers of Great Britain, and used by him in an English version of the same book. Before the origin of these blocks was known, they were considered excellent examples of English wood engraving. And for a number of years Du Pré continued production of illustrated books on a major scale.

ILLUSTRATED BOOKS

The best known French publisher of illustrated books in the fifteenth century, however, was Antoine Vérard. His work has usually been over-rated for on close examination, it does not measure up to the best standards of book illustration. We find him prodigal with the number of illustrations appearing in a book, but we also find, in the first place, that many of them do not illustrate the text at all and, in the second place, that many of them are repeated. In this we find him following the commercial practice of the Nürnberg printers.

In the last decades of the century began the production of illustrated and decorated editions of "Hours of the Blessed Virgin" or *Horae*, which kept the Paris printers busy. Many of these are very charming, but as some of the best of them appeared after the close of the fifteenth century, we will deal with them later.

XII. *The First Book in English*

THAT the first printed book in the English language is one of the great landmarks in Anglo-Saxon cultural history will hardly be denied. Strange to say, it was not printed in England but on the continent. And the manner of its printing was thus.

William Caxton was born about 1422 "in the weald of Kent" and, in 1436, was apprenticed to a prominent London merchant, a member of the Mercers Company, who soon thereafter was made Lord Mayor of London. His master died five years later and Caxton went to Burgundy where the English cloth merchants carried on an active business. He prospered there and in 1462 or 1463 we find him filling the post of "governor" of the Merchant Adventurers at Bruges, an accredited representative of the English king. William Obray had been named for this position for the years 1462-1463, but a record recently discovered shows he was discharged in June, 1462, for malfeasance in office. Though we have no record of his appointment it is probable Caxton was designated as his successor. The functions of this post were approximately similar to those of a consul at the present time. He was commissioned by the English government to negotiate, in conjunction with Sir Richard Whitehill, a diplomat of some eminence sent from home, a renewal of the commercial treaty between England and Burgundy which was due to expire in 1465. The mission reached an apparently successful conclusion, but Philip the Good, Duke of Burgundy, yielding to insistent internal demands for protection of home industries, ordered the exclusion of English cloth from his dominions.

The English merchants therefore withdrew from Bruges and moved in a body to Utrecht, which city received them eagerly. Full protection for their persons and goods was formally issued to William Caxton as "Governor of the English Nation" on November 24, 1464. During their stay in Utrecht, according to Crotch, who has made the most recent contribution to our knowledge of Caxton's record on the continent, the governor was empowered to control the merchants, regulate trade, and settle disputes, save that the town reserved the right to deal with cases involving life and limb.

In 1465 the House of Commons recommended to the King that he should retaliate for the Burgundian embargo by excluding from his realm all merchandise except food of the "growing, working, or making" of Burgundy. But in 1466 we find under way a negotiation of more peaceful character, plans being matured for the marriage of Margaret of York, sister of Edward IV, and Charles, son of the Duke of Burgundy. Charles was antagonistic to this plan but when it became apparent that such a marriage alone could bring about a protective alliance against his enemy, France, he was won over to the project.

Meanwhile Philip the Good died, and Charles succeeded to the throne. In November, 1467, was effected a commercial treaty with England to endure for thirty years. This was ratified early in 1468 and the marriage of Margaret and Charles was solemnized in June or July of that year. No longer, however, was Charles reluctant for his first glimpse of Edward's sister "had so enchanted him that he was in all haste to return and claim the kisses she was not loath to bestow."

The merchants now returned to Bruges. How long Caxton continued as Governor we cannot say with certainty but he must have relinquished the office sometime in the neighborhood of 1470. We know from his own account that he was in the service of the new Duchess of Burgundy in the early part of 1471.

In March, 1469, Caxton, "having no great charge of occupation," had undertaken the translation into English of the *Recueil des histoires de Troies*, "to eschew sloth and idleness and to put myself into virtuous occupation and business." The text he selected was one which was very popular at the time—a compilation from Latin sources by Raoul le Fevre. When he had completed five or six quires of the manuscript he laid it aside until "on a tyme hit fortuned" that he showed them to the Duchess who commanded him to revise his English and carry the task to completion. So the translation begun at Bruges was continued at Ghent and completed at Cologne in 1471.

WILLIAM CAXTON

The magnitude of the task is noted by Caxton in the epilogue to the third and last part of the tale: "Forasmuch as in the writing of the same my pen is worn, mine hand weary & not steadfast, mine eyen dimmed with over much looking on the white paper, and my courage not so prone and ready to labour as hit hath been, and that age creepeth on me dayly and feebleth all my body and also because I have promised to diverse gentlemen and to my friends to address to hem as hastily as I might this said book, therefore I have practised and lerned at my great charge & dispense to ordeyne this said book in print after the manner and form as ye may here see, and is not written with pen and ink as other books ben, to thende that every man may have them at ones, for all the books of this story named the Recule of the historyes of Troyes thus emprinted as ye here see were begonne in one day & also finished in one day."

In the quaint English of this passage we find the clear statement that Caxton learned the printing art in order that he might produce copies of the translation in book form and make possible its general circulation. It is thought that Caxton became familiar with the printing process during his stay at Cologne, to which city there is reason to believe he went in a voluntary and protective exile due to the insurrection of his native county of Kent. The Register of Aliens shows him to have been in Cologne on July 17, 1471, permission being that day extended to *Will. Caxton uyss Engelant* to reside in the city until August 16—a permission thrice extended, the final extension valid to December, 1472.

The hypothesis regarding Caxton's instruction in the printing art during his stay at Cologne is reinforced by a statement by Wynkyn de Worde, the successor to his printing business in London, in *De Proprietatibus Rerum* by Bartholomaeus Anglicus, printed about 1405.

And also of your charyte call to remembraunce
The soule of William Caxton first prynter of this boke
In Laten tonge at Coleyn hymself to avaunce
That every well disposed man may theron loke.

As Winship points out, an obscure edition of Bartholomaeus Anglicus, printed sometime about 1471, in the typography and style of Cologne printing of that period, indicates the probability that in the production of this volume Caxton learned the printing processes.

On his return to Bruges, Caxton presented his translation to Margaret who "well accepted hit and largely rewarded" him. He now undertook in earnest the establishment of a printing office, enlisting as an associate a talented calligrapher by name Colard Mansion, who had in his early youth been given a position in the library of the Duke of Burgundy. The first production of the press was the *Recuyell of the Histories of Troye* which Caxton had translated, a small folio of 351 leaves, the first of which, containing the prologue, was printed in red. This first book printed in English appeared somewhere in the neighborhood of 1475.

The most interesting example of this book is the Chatsworth copy in which is bound a slip on which it is noted in a fifteenth century hand that the volume belonged to Elizabeth, the wife of Edward IV and thus sister-in-law to Margaret, Duchess of Burgundy, for whom the translation was completed. But the outstanding feature of the book, as Winship tells us, is that "it has contained for at least a hundred years the only probable portrait of Caxton, and that not one of all the book lovers who have handled the volume with ever increasing reverence and interest during all that period paid any serious attention to this picture until the year 1895. Not until 1905 was its real importance to students of the history of English bookmaking fully appreciated. From the days of Dibdin and his friends of the Roxburghe Club to those of Blades, Bradshaw, and Gordon Duff, each of the bibliographical scholars who has examined this choicest of treasures, an almost perfect copy of the first English printed book, has been so interested in the thing he knew all about that he passed over the other, which was something that they all wanted to find more than anything else in the bibliographical world—Caxton's portrait—because it seemed to be merely an old engraving which was not apparently a part of the original volume. It is an old engraving, of unquestioned genuineness, showing convincing evidence that its designer intended it for Margaret of Burgundy. It represents a middle-aged man in plain citizen's garb, who kneels to present two bound volumes to the central figure, a lady attended by her women. Neither face nor figure is all that the imagination would like to ask for in picturing England's prototypographer, but it may be that it represents the kind of man who accomplishes desirable ends quite as often as do those who more satisfactorily look the part."

The next book to be issued at Bruges was *The Game and Pleye of the Chesse* which, contrary to general belief, is not a treatise on the rules of the game, but a "morality" with the characters presented in the guise of chessmen. One other book in French, for which a new type was cut, probably completed Caxton's product as a printer on Burgundian soil. Mansion continued the press, the first book bearing his own name, Boccaccio's *De la Ruine des Nobles Hommes et Femmes*, being dated 1476.

Caxton left for England, taking with him the new type recently cut. About Michaelmas, 1476, Caxton became the tenant of a shop in the Almonry, near Westminster Abbey, marked by a sign with a red pale or band across it. The *Dictes or Sayengis of the Philosophers* was the first dated book printed in England, the Epilogue being dated 1477 and in one copy November 18. Though this was the first *dated* book it was not certainly the first issue of the press, Caxton's translation of *Jason* and a few other publications of slight extent having probably preceded it.

The next publication of importance was an edition of Chaucer's *Canterbury Tales*, a very considerable volume of 374 leaves, appearing in 1478. Typography was now firmly established in Great Britain.

Most of Caxton's early publications were of a popular character and are, in consequence of the usage they received, very rare. He printed most of Chaucer's other works, Gower's *Confessio Amantis*, Malory's *Morte*

¶ How the land of Englond was fyrst named Albyon / And by what encheson it was so named

In the noble land of Sirrie / ther was a noble kyng & myghty & a man of grete renome / that me callid Dioclisian / that well & worthely hym gouerned & ruled thurgh his noble chyualrye / so that he coquerd all the londes about hym / so that almost al the kynges of the world to him were entendant / Hit befel thus that this dyoclisian spoused a gentil damisel / that was woder fayr that was his emes doughter Labana / and she loued hym as reson wold / so that he gate vpon hir xxxiij doughters / of the which the eldest me callid Albyne / & these damisels whan they come vnto age bicome so fair that it was woder / Wherfor that this dyoclisia anon lete make a somenyng / & comauded by his lres / that all the kynges that helden of him shold come at a certayn day as in his lres were conteyned to make a ryal feste / At whiche daye thider they comen / & brought with hem amyrals prynces & dukes & nable chyualrye / The feste was ryally arayed / & ther they lyued in ioye & myrthe ynough / that it was wonder to wyt / And it befel thus that this dyoclisian thought to marye his doughters amonge alle tho kynges that tho were at that solempnyte / & so they spaken and dide that albyne his eldest doughter / & al hir sustres richely were maried vnto xxxiij kynges / that were lordes of grete honour and of power at this solempnyte / And whan the solempnite was done / euery kynge toke his wyf & lad hem in to her owne countrey / & ther made hem quenes / And it befel thus afterward / that this dame Albyne bycome so stoute & so sterne / that she tolde lytel prys of her lord / & of hym had scorne & despyte / & wold not done hys wyll / but she wold haue hir owne wyll in dyuerse maters / and all hir other sustres euerychone bere hem so euyl ayenst hir lordes that it was wonder to wytte / & for as moch as hem thought that hir husbondes were nought of so hye parage comen as hir fader / But tho kynges that were hir lordes wold haue chastysed hem with fayr speche & behestes / and also by yeftes / & warned hem in fair maner vpon al loue & frendship that they shold amende her lither condicions / but al was for nought / for they dyden her owne wyll in all thynge / that hem lyked / & had of power / Wherfore tho / xxxiij / kynges vpon a tyme & oftymes beten theyr wyues for they wende that they wolde haue amended her tatches / & hyr wicked thewes / but of suche condicions they were / that for fayre speche & warnynge / they dyden al the wers / and for betynges

A 2

d'Arthur, the *Chronicles of England* (a page of which is here reproduced), Higden's *Polychronicon*, and the *Golden Legend*. Poems by Lydgate, translations of French romances, the *Fifteen Oes* (fifteen prayers), and many other publications to a total of one hundred (in which are included several indulgences), issued from his press. An excellent census of extant copies has been compiled by De Ricci. In all Caxton made use of eight different types.

Caxton could not by any stretch of the imagination be regarded as a fine printer. He was more interested in the textual content of books than in their appearance, and his work was, both technically and artistically, below the standards of his continental contemporaries.

The first English printer died in 1491, his business being continued by his foreman, Wynkyn de Worde, who had worked for him since 1480. The latter's output of books was large. In his edition of Higden's *Polychronicon*, dated April 13, 1495, a page of which is here reproduced, appeared the first music printed in England.

Printing was introduced at Oxford in 1478 by Theodoric Rood of Cologne. In 1479 or 1480, the anonymous "schoolmaster-printer" began work at St. Albans, issuing eight books up until 1486. He apparently borrowed some type from Caxton and it was probably with the latter's consent that he reprinted the Caxton version of the *Chronicles of England*, adding to it an appendix entitled *Fructus Temporum*. In Wynkyn de Worde's 1497 reprint of this edition we have our only hint of the printer's identity, it being stated that it was "compiled in a

de of twelue/the thyrde of eyght/the
fourth of .ir. as this fygure sheweth.

Whan these
accordes were
foūdeŋ pictago
ras paf heŋ na
mes. And so þ
he called iŋ nō
bre double / he
called iŋ sow
nes Dyapasoŋ
And þ he called
iŋ nōbre other
halfe he called
iŋ sowne Dya
pente. And þ þ
iŋ nōbre is cal
led all ⁊ þ thyr
de dele/hete iŋ sones Dyatesseroŋ/⁊
that þ iŋ nombres is called all ⁊ the
eyghteth dele / hete iŋ tewnes double
Dyapasoŋ.As iŋ melodye of one strē
ge/yf the strynge be streyned enlonge
vpoŋ the holownesse of a tree / ⁊ de
parted eueŋ a two by a brydge sette
there vnder iŋ eyther parte of þ stren
ge/the sowne shall be Dyapasoŋ/yf
the streng be streyned ⁊ touched.And
yf the streng be departed eueŋ iŋ thre
⁊ the brydge sette vnder/so that it de
parte bytwene the twey deles ⁊ þ thyr
de/thaŋ the lenger dele of the streng
yf it be touched shall yeue a sowne cal
led Dyatesseroŋ.And yf it be depar
ted iŋ nyne/and the brydge sette vn
der bytwene the last parte and the o
ther dele / thaŋ the lenger dele of the
strenge yf it be touched shall yeue a
sowne/that hete Tonus/for nyne cō
teyneth eyght/and the eyght parte of
eyght as iŋ this fygure that foloweth

Ie/
ronim⁹   Anno   A
Transmi.
Ab vrbe.

contra Ruf.Many of pictagoras dyf
cyples kepte her maystres heestes iŋ
mynde and vsed her wytte and myn
de iŋ studye of bookes / and taught
that many suche prouerbes shall hyt
te and departe sorowe from the bo
dye/vnconnynge from the wytte/le
cherye from the wombe/tresoŋ oute
of the cyte / stryfe out of the hous:
Incontynence and hastynesse oute of
all thynges.Also all that frendes ha
ue shall be comyŋ. A frende is the o
ther of tweyne. We must take hede
of tymes. After god sothnesse shall
be worshypped that maketh meŋ be
next god. Ysydorus libro octauo ca
pitulo sexto.

Capliŋ   .rii.

The name of phylosophres
hadde begynnynge of picta
goras.for olde Grekes cal
led hym selfe sophistris that is wyse/
But pictagoras whaŋ me axed what
maŋ he was/he answerde and sayde
that he was a phylosopher / that is a
louer of wytte and of wysedome for
to calle hym selfe a wyse maŋ/it wol
de seme grete boost ⁊ pryde.Afterwar
other philosophres hadden her names
of her auctours.And so they that hel
de pictagoras loore/were called pic
tagoraci. And they that heldeŋ pla
toos loore / were called platonici.
Pol.libro prīo.Some phylosophres
haddeŋ names of contrees / ⁊ so they
þ heldeŋ pictagoras loore were called

PAGE FROM THE POLYCHRONICON, DE WORDE, 1495

booke and also emprynted by one sometyme scolemayster of saynt Albons, on whose soule God haue mercy."

John Lettou, or John of Lithuania, began to print in London City proper in 1480. In the opinion of Gordon Duff he learned to print at Rome, bringing his punches to England with him, his type being very similar to that used at Rome by a printer whose name—strange to state —was John Bulle, though he hailed from Bremen. Lettou was joined in 1482 by William Machlinia, the latter being the Latinized form of the name of the Belgian city of Malines. After printing five law books in partnership, Lettou disappeared and Machlinia continued the business alone. By 1490 he too had dropped out of sight and his stock of books appears to have been acquired by Richard Pynson, a Norman, who began printing in 1491 or 1492.

Julian Notary was the last printer to begin work in England during the fifteenth century. He started in 1496 with two partners, an I. B. who was Jean Barbier and an I. H. who in all probability was Jean Huvin of Rouen. In 1498, Huvin had left the firm and Notary and Barbier were at Westminster. It will have been noted that all these printers, with the exception of Caxton and the printer at St. Albans, were foreigners.

The most important of the fifteenth century English printers was Caxton, not only because he was the first, but also because of his consequential contributions to English literature. He was the translator of more than twenty of the books he printed, and many others he provided with prologues or epilogues of rare good humor and charm. He also did yeoman's service in crystallizing and establishing the forms of English speech, our mother tongue being in a fluid state, to say the least, at the time his labors began.

Before we leave this great figure in English literary history it may be interesting to achieve a more intimate acquaintance with his work. With reference to the chaotic state of the English language he writes in the prologue to his translation of the *Eneydos* [Aeneid]: "I confess me not lerned nor knowing the arte of rethoryke, ne of suche gaye termes [the slang of his day] as now be sayd in these dayes and used." He later writes "having noe werke in hande, I sittyng in my studye where as laye many dyvers paunflettis & bookys, happened that to my hande came a lyttyl booke in Frenche, which late was translated out of Latyn by some noble clerke of France . . . whiche booke I sawe over and redde therin . . . In whiche booke I had grete plsyr, by cause of the fayr and honest terms and wordes in Frenche, which I never sawe tofore lyke, ne none so playsaunt ne so well ordred . . . And whan I had advysed me in this sayd boke, I delybrered & concluded to translate it in to Englysshe. And forthwyth toke a penne & ynke and wrote a leef or tweyne, whyche I oversawe agayn to correcte it. And whan I sawe the fayr and straunge termes therin I doubted that it sholde not please some gentylmen whiche late blamed me, sayeng that in my translacyons I had over curyous termes whiche coude not be understande of comyn peple, & desired me to use olde and homely termes in my translacyons. And fayn wolde I satisfye every man,

and so to do toke an olde boke and redde therin, and certaynly the Englysshe was so rude and broad that I coude
not wele understande it. And also my Lorde Abbot of
Westmynster ded do shewe me late certayn evydences
wryton in olde Englysshe for to reduce it in to our Englysshe now usid, and certaynly it was wreton in suche wyse
that it was more lyke to Dutche than Englysshe. I coude
not reduce ne brnge it to be understonden. And certaynly
our language now used varyeth ferre from that whiche
was used & spoken whan I was borne. For we Englysshe
men ben borne under the domynacyon of the moon,
whyche is never stedfast but ever waverynge, waxynge one
season and waneth and decreaseth another season. And
that comyn Englysshe that is spoken in one shyre varyeth
from another. Insomuch that in my dayes happened that
certayne marchauntes were in a ship in Tamyse for to
have sayled over the see into Zelande, & for lacke of
wynde they taryed at Foreland, & went to lande for to
refreshe them. And one of theym named Sheffelde a mer-
cer came in to an howse & axed for mete, & specyally he
axed after eggys. And the goodewyf answerde, that she
coude speke no Frenche. And the marchaunt was angry,
for he also could speke no Frenche, but wolde have hadde
egges & she understode hym not. And thenne at laste
another sayd that he wolde have eyren, then the good wyf
sayd that she understod hym wel. Loo what sholde a man
in thyse dayes now wryte, egges or eyren? Certaynly it is
harde to playse every man bycause of dyversite & chaunge
of langage. For in these dayes every man that is in ony
reputacyon in his countre, wyll utter his communycacyon

and matters in suche manners and termes, that fewe men shall understonde theym. And som honest & grete clerkes have ben wyth me and desired me to wryte the most curyous termes that I coude fynde. And thus bytwene playn, rude, and curyous I stand abashed. But in my judgemente the comyn termes that be dayly used ben lyghter to be understonde that the old & auncyent Englysshe."

Finally, let us enjoy the humor of his comment on the relative virtues of Greek women and English women. The Queen's brother, Earl Rivers, had translated the *Dictes and Sayengis of the Philosophers* which, as we have already noted, was the first dated book issued from his press. In comparing it with the original, Caxton found the Earl had omitted portions of the text which comprised "certayne and dyverse conclusions touchyng women. Wherof I mervaylle that my sayd Lord hath not wreton them, ne what hath movyd hym so to do ne what cause he hadde at that tyme. But I suppose that some fayr lady hath desired hym to leve it out of his booke, or ellys he was amerous on some noble lady, for whos love he wold not sette yt in hys book, or ellys for the very affeccyon, love & good wylle that he hath unto alle ladyes and gentyl women, he thought that Socrates spared the sothe and wrote of women more than trouthe.

"But I appercyve that my sayd Lord knoweth veryly that suche defautes ben not had ne founden in the women born and dewllyng in these partyes ne regyons of the world. Socrates was a Greke. I wote well that of whatsomever condicion women ben in Grece, the women of this contre ben right good, wyse, playsant, humble, discrete, sobre, chaste, obediente to their husbondes [it is supposed that Caxton married not long before he settled down at Westminster] trewe, secret, stedfast, ever busy and never ydle, attemperat in speking, and vertuous in alle their werkis, or atte leste sholde be so, for whiche causes so evydent my sayd Lord as I suppose thoughte it was not of necessite to sette in his book the saiengs of his auctor Socrates touchyng women. Therefore in accomplisshing his commandement to correcte & amende where as I sholde fynde fawte and other fynde I none . . . for as muche as I am not in certayn whether it was in my Lordis copye or not or ellis peraventure that the wynde had blowe over the leef at the tyme of translacion, I purpose to wryte the same sayings of that Greke Socrates, which wrote of the women of Grece & nothyng of them of this Royame, whom I suppose he never knewe."

Among the typographers of the past, we may well consider William Caxton one of the leaders in weight of contribution to the advancement of culture. First English printer and first English editor, he must be ranked with the great names in English literary history.

XIII. *The Study of the Incunabula*

FTEENTH century books, now so highly prized, were for a long time esteemed of little value. The intellectual and religious upheaval of the sixteenth century rendered a considerable portion of them of little interest to readers, and later editions were more convenient than their quaint, cumbersome predecessors. Incunabula, then, received almost no attention until 1640, when was celebrated the second centenary, as it was considered, of the invention of printing. Thereafter fifteenth century books were collected for their own sake, as curiosities and examples of typography.

This desire to collect incunabula—then an inexpensive hobby—called forth bibliographies to serve as guides for purchasers. The first one of any note is Cornelius Beughem's *Incunabula Typographiae* (1688), a small work which, though it gives short accounts of the authors of the books, omits the names of the printers and publishers. More pretentious is the *Annales Typographici* (1719-1741) of the classical scholar, Michael Maittaire, but

[155]

not until the appearance of Georg W. F. Panzer's large work of the same title (1793-1803) does the interest become definitely typographical. Here the books are arranged chronologically under the towns in which they were printed. In sharp contrast to Panzer's *Annales* stands the gossipy, pedantic, inaccurate, but interesting *Bibliotheca Spenceriana* (1814-1823), the catalogue which the Reverend Thomas Frognall Dibdin made of the great library of his patron, the Earl of Spencer.

Modern incunabula bibliography may be said to begin with Ludwig Hain. In his *Repertorium Bibliographicum* (1826-1834) he describes, usually in detail, over 16,000 editions. So successful was Hain that his work is to this day probably the most frequently cited catalogue of fifteenth century books. Two later works, the *Supplement* (1895-1902) of the versatile lawyer, theologian, musician and antiquarian, Walter A. Copinger, and the *Appendices* (1905-1911) of the German scholar, Dietrich Reichling, rectify, to some extent, the errors and omissions of Hain. The task of Copinger and Reichling was made easier because of the labors of Mlle. Marie Pellechet who, after compiling catalogues of the early printed books of several French libraries, prepared her *Catalogue Général des Incunabules des Bibliothèques Publiques de France* (1897 ff.) She died during the publication of her great work and the French Ministry of Public Instruction has printed but one third of her manuscript.

The bibliographies mentioned above contain much material of value to the student of printing. With the exception of Panzer's *Annales*, however, they are all arranged alphabetically by authors, a feature which makes them primarily guides for collectors. Progress in the study of early typography was for a long time seriously hampered by the fact that a large proportion of the books printed in the fifteenth century bear no indication of place, date, or printer. A method of determining the press by comparing the types of books of unknown origin with those whose printers are known was developed by Henry Bradshaw and was used with great success by Robert Proctor in his *Early Printed Books in the British Museum with Notes of those in the Bodleian Library* (1898-1906). In this work, which revolutionized the study of early printing, the books are classified chronologically by printer, town and country. Proctor's method of identifying incunabula of unknown origin was systematized by Konrad Haebler in his *Typenrepertorium der Wiegendrucke* (1905-1910). The great possibilities of bibliographical scholarship are in a large measure realized in a work which is following and perfecting Proctor's scheme of identification and arrangement, the *Catalogue of Books Printed in the XV th Century now in the British Museum* (1908 ff.), by all odds the most valuable work to date for the student of typographic history.

These titles, however, represent but a few of the productions of the many able and industrious men who have been attracted to the study of early printed books. Bibliographies of rare books such as Graesse's *Trésor*, or Brunet's *Manuel de Libraire* often contain notices of incunabula, while almost every large library has published a catalogue of its fifteenth century books.

A bibliography of incunabula may attempt, like Campbell's *Annales de la Typographie Néerlandaise au XVe Siècle*, to describe the fifteenth century books printed in one country, or like Voulliéme's *Der Buchdruck Kölns*, those printed in a certain town. Again, it may confine itself, as does Blades' *Caxton*, to the output of a single press. Of late years bibliographers, like Osler in his *Incunabula Medica*, have been dealing with fifteenth century books which treat particular subjects. Information about early printed books then must be sought for in many places. Robert A. Peddie, for example, in his unfinished *Conspectus Incunabulorum* (1910 ff.) a concordance to bibliographies of incunabula, cites descriptions from over two hundred reference works.

To meet the need of an inclusive bibliography of fifteenth century books, the Prussian Commission of Education in 1904 appointed a commission to make "a complete catalogue of all known incunabula." With the assistance of almost all the large libraries of the world and of many private collectors full descriptions of about 38,000 different editions of books printed before the year 1501 have been gathered and are now being published in the *Gesamtkatalog der Wiegendrucke* (1925 ff.), which it is expected to complete in twelve large quarto volumes.

As a result of these two-hundred and fifty years of bibliographical scholarship, fifteenth century books, in spite of the great difficulties which they present, have been more minutely and successfully studied than the books printed in any other period. The literary taste of the half century in which they were published can now be studied in great detail, and an intimate glimpse may be had into the practices of the early printers, whose number and activity has been proven far greater than any but the boldest could have conjectured.

XIV. *Subjects of the Incunabula*

YPOGRAPHY was born in an age of change and trouble. The glories of the middle ages which came to their culmination in the great thirteenth century were past. Europe was swept by devastating plagues and menaced by the Turk who in 1453 stormed Constantinople and early in the next century stood before the walls of Vienna. The old order of society, the feudal system, though still strong, was declining under the rising power of commercialism and absolutism, while craftsmen and merchants in whose ranks printers and booksellers took their place were growing in wealth and influence.

Intellectually, Europe was being swept by two forces which were to transform civilization. The first, which crystallized in Germany, was a religious movement among the lower and middle classes, personal and pietistic in temper, which to a large extent found expression outside of formal worship. Huss at the beginning and Savonarola at the end of the century are representative of the extreme form of this religious awakening which later culminated in the Reformation.

[160]

SUBJECTS OF INCUNABULA

The other great movement was Humanism. For more than a century Byzantine-Greek refugees from the advancing Moslem armies sought shelter in Italy, bringing with them manuscripts of the Greek classics, and opening schools in Italian cities. They were welcomed by scholars like Petrarch and soon old monastic libraries were being ransacked for codices of classic authors. Under the influence of the rediscovered literature of Greece and Rome human vision was broadened and in place of the narrow mediaeval conception of life as a sombre preparation for the next world there arose a new striving for culture and beauty, while faith, the ideal of the middle ages was slowly supplanted by free inquiry, the ideal of the Renaissance.

At a time, then, when the mighty forces which were to transform civilization were gathering strength, typography was born. How it hastened the process of change by making possible the wide dissemination of knowledge is well known. The books which the printing press produced during the first fifty years of its existence, however, were for the most part the classics of the middle ages, the theology and liturgy of the church, the law of the sixth century and the science of the twelfth. Yet along with these mediaeval classics appeared tracts of popular devotion and the writings of the philosophers of pagan Greece and Rome, forerunners of a great religious and intellectual upheaval in which the printing press should have an ever enlarging share.

Almost half of the books printed in the fifteenth century are religious in subject matter. This is not surprising when we remember that a large proportion of the literate population were ecclesiastics. Ample funds, too, for the purchase of such books had been afforded the monasteries by the bequests of benefactors who had died in the recent plagues. Even among the laity, especially in the northern countries, the religious awakening created a demand for devotional works.

The Bible may be justly termed the favorite book of the fifteenth century, for, despite its great size, which rendered it expensive to buy and difficult to print, it was issued more frequently than any other single work. The popularity of the Latin Vulgate version of the Bible is evidenced by the fact that at least 133 editions of it are known to have been printed in the fifteenth century and that after 1475 not a year elapsed without the production of at least one edition. Vernacular versions were sought by laymen. In the different dialects of German were issued fifteen editions of the Bible; in Italian, thirteen; in French, eleven; in Bohemian, two, and one each in Spanish and Dutch.

The writings of the church fathers also were much read. Of these St. Augustine was the favorite, with Jerome, Chrysostom, and Gregory as his closest rivals.

Theology, too, was in great demand. In the doctrinal aspect of the subject St. Thomas Aquinas, with over three hundred editions of his separate works, was preeminent. Disputation on such doubtful points of theology as we find collected in the *Sentences* of Peter Lombard was an intellectual exercise of which mediaeval scholars were extremely fond and numerous works of this nature by writers like Duns Scotus (usually in the form of small tracts) made their way into print.

Parish priests sought from the early printing press books which would aid them in the performance of their duties. Manuals such as Gregory's *Pastoral Care* and Nider's *Instructions to Confessors* found a ready market as did also compilations of the lives of the saints, like Jacobus de Voragine's *Golden Legend* which contained stories that a mediaeval audience delighted to hear. Many fifteenth century priests, it would seem, were in full accord with the sentiment which Addison's character, Sir Roger de Coverly later expressed, that it was better that a congregation should have read to them a discourse of a famous preacher than that they should hear a mediocre one composed by their pastor. This probably explains the great demand for the sermons of such men as Caraccioli, Meffreth, and of that master of eloquence in an age which loved oratory, Savonarola.

The liturgy of the church called forth many of the most sumptuous products of the fifteenth century press. Besides missals and other service books for public worship private devotion made a ready market for the Books of Hours, which today are so eagerly sought because of their exquisite decoration.

Religious tracts designed to stir the reader to greater piety such as *The Art of Righteous Living and Dying* circulated widely among the middle classes, while meditation, an important spiritual exercise, called forth many mystical treatises, the most important of which is *The Imitation of Christ* by St. Thomas à Kempis.

[163]

Closely allied to theology is ecclesiastical or canon law. *The Decretals* of Gratian and of Pope Gregory IX with their many commentators were in great demand in the early years of printing.

Outside the Church, in Germany and the greater part of Italy, Roman legislation and procedure was still in force and even where it was not the law of the land, it was much studied and admired. For this reason the codes of Justinian, often with annotations, were frequently printed. Local ordinances and the decrees of kings, despite their limited appeal, were fairly numerous in book and pamphlet form. Textbooks on national law, also, such as—in England—those of Stratham and Lyttleton, found wide circulation among the lawyers.

Encyclopedias were popular in the middle ages, for when books were scarce it is but natural that a volume which could pretend to be an epitome of human knowledge would be greatly desired. Pliny's *Natural History*, Isidore's *Etymologies*, Vincent of Beauvais' ponderous *Mirrors* and especially *The Properties of Things* by Bartholomaeus Anglicus were eagerly bought by students.

Fifteenth century science was still thoroughly mediaeval. Works upon physics, for instance, were almost exclusively comments upon Aristotle. Important among these are the disquisitions of Averroes, Albertus Magnus, and St. Thomas Aquinas.

Medicine, in a time when the pestilence was sweeping Europe, was a subject frequently treated in books printed in the fifteenth century. The works of such classic writers as Galen and of Arabian physicians like Avicenna

[164]

along with those of fifteenth century writers on the plague were repeatedly issued. Herbals, also, which told of many marvelous and infallible cures for all the ills to which man is heir were read and believed in by many.

Little practical help, however, could be derived from the fifteenth century books which discussed two of the most important occupations of the time—war and agriculture. Treatises like the Roman Vegetius' *Management of an Army* or Columella's commentary on Vergil's *Georgics* were of great interest to antiquarians but of little value to soldiers or farmers.

Books on mathematics were then, as now, difficult to print, and for that reason their number is small, Euclid's *Elements of Geometry* being the most popular. Astronomy is more liberally represented by such works as Holywood's *Spheres* and Muller's *Calendar*.

Closely connected with astronomy was one of the occult sciences which, though frowned upon by the Church, still flourished—astrology. The *Times of Birth* by the Spanish Jew Aben-Ezra was a favorite treatise on this subject, while the dream books and alchemical manuals of Arnold of Villa Nova and numerous treatises on witchcraft, like Institor's *Malleus Maleficarum*, are representatives of the literature which centered around the forbidden arts.

Geography was an important branch of study in that century which began a great era of discovery. The classic writers, Strabo, Pomponius Mela, and Ptolomey were printed, often with additions of new knowledge made by their editors, while the marvelous tales of travel by such men as Marco Polo, Breydenbach, and that Prince of Liars, Sir John Mandeville, fired the imagination of many a fifteenth century boy whose name is now written in the annals of a continent then unknown.

Turning to literature, we find the Latin classics dominating the fifteenth century book market. Cicero, with over three hundred editions of his different works, was the favorite, German readers being attracted to his ethical discussions quite as much as were Italians to his literary style. Virgil follows with over one hundred and eighty editions. Ovid, Horace, Lucan, and the Roman historians, were frequently published.

The Greek authors, although they were greatly admired, were printed less frequently. The many-sided Aristotle unquestionably had the greatest appeal of any Greek writer and over a hundred and sixty editions of his separate works, both in Latin translation and in the original, appeared before the end of the century. Aesop, whose works had a great attraction for the common people, was his nearest rival, while the works of Homer, Herodotus, Plato, and Josephus disseminated by the fifteenth century press—either in Latin or in Greek—created a great impression upon the next generation.

Vernacular literature is less liberally represented in the products of the early press, yet among them are many distinguished names. Dante, Boccaccio, Petrarch, Villon, and Chaucer, were repeatedly published, as were also several of the prose and metrical romances.

The dramatic literature available in printed form to the fifteenth century is of especial interest to us, in view of the great activity in that field in the next century. Besides the classic dramatists like Aristophanes, Euripides, Plautus, Terence, and Seneca, there appeared also the comedies of the mediaeval nun, Hrosvitha, and some French mystery plays.

Principles and methods of education were much discussed in fifteenth century books. One of the most popular treatises on this subject was Aeneas Sylvius' *Training of Children*, a work of pronounced humanistic tendencies. Grammars such as Donatus' *Eight Parts of Speech* and disquisitions of a more philological nature like Lorenzo Valla's *Elegancies of the Latin Language* found many readers in an age which was becoming sophisticated and careful of good form.

Commercial printing was firmly established in the fifteenth century. In fact, the famous Mainz Indulgences of 1454 were printed forms, pieces of job printing. Advertising, especially of books, by means of printed posters, like Caxton's famous placard, was not an unusual procedure, and although the newspaper did not come into existence until the seventeenth century the printed epistle served as an effective carrier of news. *The Letters of Christopher Columbus Concerning the Newly Discovered Islands*, for instance, before the century had ended, had gone through fifteen editions in three languages.

Incunabula, then, treat a large variety of subjects. Adopting a rough and rather arbitrary division we may say that approximately forty-five per cent of them are concerned with religion, ten per cent with law, ten per cent with science, thirty per cent with literature, and

[167]

the remaining five per cent with miscellaneous subjects.

Before the invention of printing, students must have heard or read of countless books of which it was impossible to obtain a copy. The early printers for this reason found the old standard authors in great demand and for this reason, until 1485, issued them almost exclusively. After that date the works of contemporary writers were printed with increasing frequency until, when the end of the century is reached, they form fifteen per cent of the total number of incunabula. The most popular contemporary author was Aeneas Sylvius, afterwards Pope Pius II, whose novel, *Concerning Two Lovers*, was the outstanding best-seller of the fifteenth century fiction. Chronicles of past and current events such as those of Schedel and Rolevinck and the sermons of the fiery preacher, Savonarola, also attracted the attention of their contemporaries but only one work by a writer who saw his work appear in an early printed book is likely to prove immortal. That work is *The Imitation of Christ* by St. Thomas à Kempis.

The book production of Europe was by no means uniform. Germany's contribution was largely religious, and no consideration of the struggle of the early sixteenth century can ignore the literature with which the German youth had been saturated. It is very significant that the Bible and the works of St. Augustine, powerful weapons in the hands of the Reformers, were the favorites of the German book trade. Italy, on the other hand, produced the Latin and Greek classics. In fact, printing in the Greek language was confined, in the fifteenth century, exclusively to that country where the Greek refugees from Constantinople afforded a ready supply of compositors and proofreaders. From Italy came those powerful influences which, in the sixteenth century, redeemed Europe from her crudeness and superstition and called forth that matchless blossoming of the human spirit which we call the Renaissance.

We are prone to think of incunabula solely as objects of art or as monuments of the pioneer efforts of the printer's art and to forget that they were factors in a great intellectual struggle. Even in the fifteenth century the power of the press was a great power.

XV. *The Golden Age of Typography*

THE sixteenth century was an age of strife and glory. Europe was rapidly casting from her the shackles of the middle ages under the leadership of daring scholars who were fired with the renaissance ideal of free inquiry. It was the age of the Reformation when a philosphical justification was demanded for many beliefs which preceding generations had accepted without question, when the traditions of centuries were fiercely assailed and vigorously defended. It was a time when men had at last discovered the meaning of intellectual freedom and found it delicious but dangerous. It stimulated art, literature and learning till they reached heights seldom attained in human history. But the stake and the block stood as grim reminders to the sixteenth century scholar that those who upheld the mediaeval ideal of authority would suppress free inquiry by force.

Education was quickened by this intellectual and religious upheaval. Among all classes of society, except the very lowest, there arose an intense desire to learn to read.

[170]

Books, as a result, could no longer be considered the exclusive property of a small class. Instead, the popular demand for such widely circulated works as Luther's translation of the Bible was so great that to meet it mass production was introduced into the printing industry.

Paris, in the sixteenth century was favorably situated to have a leading part in any movement in typography. It was probably the largest and most important city of Europe. Far enough removed from the religious controversy which was raging in the north to escape its violence, it was at the same time quickened by the intellectual excitement which the conflict engendered. It was also fortunate in that the successive kings who resided in it were for the most part patrons both of letters and typography. It was the seat, too, of a university which although in a state of decline was still in the earlier decades of the sixteenth century the largest and most important institution of learning in Europe. Even if the University of Paris was extremely conservative and unduly fond of mediaeval traditions, the campaigns of Francis I in Italy had brought to Paris a realization of the highest ideals of renaissance scholarship. It was this happy combination, then, of material prosperity and intellectual stimulation which played an important part in making the first sixty years of the sixteenth century in Paris, the Golden Age of typography.

Prominent in this notable period was a family of scholar-printers, the House of Estienne, perhaps better known by the Latin form of the name, Stephanus. Henri Estienne, the first of the family, in 1502 took over the business of Jean Higman whose widow, Guyonne Viart, he had married in the previous year. Greek and Latin classics were the chief products of his press and the high scholarly character of his work is evidenced by the fact that he had among his editors Jacques Le Fébvre d'Etaples, the teacher of Calvin, and among his proofreaders Geofroy Tory. Despite the fact that during the eight years in which he printed he produced more than a hundred editions, many fine books, such as Valla's translation of Galen's *De Sectis Medicorum* (1518), show his skill in combining the best features of French and Italian typography. He died in 1520 and his widow promptly married Simon de Colines. The influence of Guyonne Viart as the wife of three and the mother of two of the city's best printers must remain an unwritten chapter in the history of Parisian typography.

Robert Estienne, the second son of Henri, put to good use the instruction of his step-father. In 1524, at the age of twenty-one he took over the paternal printing office, Colines having set up another shop close by, and soon after he married Perrette, the daughter of Jodocus Badius. His wife was a thorough scholar and they worked together editing the Greek and Latin classics which he often printed. Latin, in fact, was the language of the Estienne home, spoken even by the servants and the children.

Robert Estienne attained fame by compiling, with the assistance of others, dictionaries of the Latin, Greek and Hebrew languages, works which were adopted by most of the universities of Europe and which unfortunately

Obiliſſimi Principatus fundamenta feliciter Otho iecit, Vberti filius, qui ab Aſiatico Othone proauo nomen acceperat. Natus eſt Inuorio in pago ad Verbanum lacum, magnis quidem natalibus, ſed patrimonio tenui, & tum adeò afflictis totius familiæ fortunis, vt quatuor tantum & planè ignobilium vicorũ ditione, propinqui Proceres maiorum ſuorum nomen tuerétur. Hi fuere, Inuorium, Maſſinum, Vergantum, & Olegium: ſed fundos etiam peramplos Mediolani extra portam Iouiam à Sultano Vicecomite emptos conſtat. Frequentibus enim Barbarorum irruptionibus, & ciuili præſertim bello, cuncta apud Inſubres conturbata proſtratáque erant, vt non mirum ſit, tantas opes in publica calamitate corruiſſe. Sunt qui ex genitura, propter admirabiles ſiderũ concurſus, imperiũ ei à Mathematicis prænun tiatum fuiſſe aſſeuerent. Verùm ipſe repudiatis prorſus Aſtrologis, id vnum pro inſigni oſtento iocabun dus accepit, quòd Vicecomite Placentino, Mediolani Prætore (qui tum erat ſupremæ poteſtatis magiſtratus) & Othone Cæſare imperante, in luce eſſet editus. Enituit ſatis maturè in adoleſcente ingenium alacre, præaltũ, ardens, & quod mirabile erat, graui prudétia temperatum: acceſſerat corporis atque oris dignitas maximè excellens. ſtatura enim erat excelſa, & nexu neruorum longè firmiſſima: pectore autem lato atque extanti, & radioſis prægrandibuſque oculis. eloquentia verò illuſtri, exquiſitíſque literis, quũ oporteret, ad

were pirated by unscrupulous printers. His ability as a scholar was equalled by his success as a typographer. His books, many of them printed with types designed by Claude Garamond and with borders, initials and ornaments engraved by Geofroy Tory, are extremely beautiful. The happy combination of the efforts of these three artists may be seen in the page of Paulo Giovio's *Vitae Duodecim Vicecomitum Mediolani Principum* of 1549 reproduced on page 173. He strove for accuracy even more than for beauty. To attain this, so it is said, he was accustomed to hang up his proof sheets in the streets by his shop, and near the university, and to offer a reward to anyone who could discover an error in them. His typographic ability was recognized by the title, "Printer to the King for Hebrew, Greek and Latin."

Robert Estienne, then, during the twenty-six years in which he worked in Paris, produced many beautiful and scholarly books and this in spite of the fact that he was hampered by an irritating quarrel. During his lifetime the University of Paris, though the largest university in Europe, was steadily declining both in numbers and in learning. The faculty of the Sorbonne was gradually being filled by doctors who attempted to conceal their ignorance by attaining a reputation for orthodoxy. The Greek and Roman classics, for example, some of the doctors denounced as pagan while they stoutly maintained that "a knowledge of the Greek and Hebrew languages would operate to the destruction of all religion." Robert Estienne printed a number of editions of the Bible in Latin, in Greek and in Hebrew. Besides introducing the verse division which is still retained in the King James and Douai versions, Estienne employed the critical method to restore the text and made free use of the emendations and notes of the humanist scholars, especially those of Erasmus. This aroused the enmity of the doctors of the Sorbonne who thundered against him in their pulpits but who, when called upon to point out specific errors in Estienne's editions, were seldom able to prove anything but their own inability to translate Greek. With the aid of the King, Francis I, a patron of typography and renaissance learning, Robert Estienne was able to defy the faculty of the Sorbonne but on the death of his supporter he, fearing persecution, fled, in 1550, to Geneva which, ruled over by John Calvin, had become the refuge of many scholars. Here he set up his press and continued to issue books of the same high character until his death in 1559.

The two brothers of Robert played less important roles in the history of Parisian printing. His elder brother, François Estienne, was a publisher who sold the books of his step-father and brothers. François seems to have shared Robert's love of intellectual freedom for in 1542 he was ordered to surrender certain prohibited books found in his possession. He died in 1553. Charles Estienne, the younger brother of Robert, was born about 1504. After a thorough classical training he studied medicine and became a *docteur-regent* to the faculty of medicine of the University of Paris. Famous for his learning, he attracted many pupils. He compiled also, usually from material gathered from ancient authors, works on medicine, agriculture and pedagogy. After Robert's flight to Geneva, Charles in 1551 took charge of the printing office and was permitted to assume the title of "Printer-in-Ordinary to the King." He suffered business reverses, however, and in 1561 became bankrupt. He died, so it is said, in 1564, in prison where he was incarcerated either because of his religion or for debt.

The fortunes of the other members of the Estienne family are somewhat outside the scope of this chapter. Henri, the son of Robert (usually called Henri II) was a precocious child. After completing his education at an early age he travelled through Europe gathering manuscripts and conversing with learned men. At the death of his father he took charge of the printing press at Geneva and produced numerous editions of the classics often edited by himself with the help of newly discovered manuscripts. In 1572, after many years of labor, he produced his great *Thesaurus*, a dictionary of the Greek language which is still used by scholars. His satire, *An Apology for Herodotus, or, A Treatise on Ancient and Modern Marvels* was popular with readers but was little relished by the Consistory of Geneva. The publication in 1578 of his satirical *Dialogues* so aroused the Consistory that he decided to leave the country. He remained an exile and a wanderer until his death in 1598.

Besides Henri, Robert Estienne had two other sons. Robert II succeeded to the office of "Printer to the King" after the retirement of his uncle Charles. He died in 1571. François II, the remaining son, printed both at

TITLE PAGE BORDER BY GEOFROY TORY

Paris and Geneva and his descendants followed the printing trade until late in the seventeenth century.

Simon de Colines may in many respects be considered
a member of the Estienne family. An associate of Henri
Estienne, the husband of his widow and the instructor of
his son, he left his impress upon Estienne typography.
He is said to have designed the first good Greek type
with accents and a beautiful italic, both types appearing
in his books in 1528. The books which he printed are for
the most part small quarto and octavo editions of the
Greek and Latin classics, cheap in price but tasteful and
workmanlike in execution. In this and in his successful
use of roman type in books where more conservative
printers still employed black-letter, Colines was a typographic reformer bringing to Paris the best features of
the books of the Aldine Press. He was, on the other hand,
no servile imitator of the Venetian printers. There is a
certain delicacy of execution and a tendency to variety
in the books of Colines that is distinctly French in tone.
This may be seen by a comparison of the title pages of
Colines, sometimes plain, sometimes decorated with exquisite woodcut borders, with the set pattern of the
Aldine title page. Frequently his works are illustrated
with excellent wood-engravings, examples of which may
be found in his Books of Hours or in the *De Dissectione
Partium Humanae Corporis* by Charles Estienne (1545)
the author of which, it would seem, preferred to have his
step-father rather than his brother print his scientific
works. Simon de Colines continued the exercise of his
craft until his death in 1546.

[178]

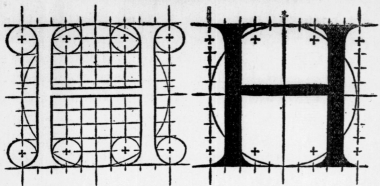

LA figure cy pres defignee & faicte de le I.auec huit cētres, eft de dix corps
en Quarre.Ceft a dire, auffi large que haulte. Les Grammairiens, & mef-
mement felon Prifcian en fon Premier liure ou il traicte De literarum poteſta-
te, difent quelle neſt pas lettre, mais la note & enfeigne pour monſtrer quant
quelque vocale, ou lune de fes quatre confones, C.P.R.T.doibt eſtre pronū-
cee graſſe & a plaine voix venant du profond de leſtomac. Iceluy Prifcian dit.   **Prifciatt.**

» H.autem afpirationis eſt nota, & nihil aliud habet literæ, nifi figuram, & quod
» in vfu fcribit inter alias lꝛas.Ceſt a dire.H,eſt la note de lafpiratiō, & na aultre
chofe deficace de lettre, fi non la figure, & auffi que par vfage elle eſt efcripte.

H.a fi peu de vertus auec les vocales, q̃ fi on len oſte, le fens ne fera point
diminue. mais ouy bien dauec leſſufdictes quatre confones. C.P.R.T.
Exemple des vocales.Erennius. Oratius.Exemple defdictes cōfones. Cremes
pour Chremes.Et a ceſte caufe comme dit Prifcian au fufdict lieu allegue, les   **Θ.Φ.X.Ρ**
Grecs ont faict ces fufdictes confones afpirees. Car pour Th, ilz ont faict Θ.
pour Ph.Φ.pour Ch.X.Le Rho na point eſte mue de fa figure, mais il prēt fus
luy vne demye croix en lettres maiufcules, ou vng point corbe en lettre courāt
qui denote la dicte afpiration. cōme on peult cleremēt veoir es impreſſions du   **Alde.**
feu bon imprimeur Alde, que Dieu abfoille.   **Aulus**
» Gellius.

» AVlus Gellius au.III.Chapiſtre du Segōd liure de fes nuyts Attiqués dit,
» que H.a eſte mife des Anciens & inferee es dictions pour leur bailler vng
» fon plus ferme & vigoreux quant il dit. H.litera, fiue illam fpiritu magis quam
» literam dici oportet, inferebant eam veteres noſtri plerifq; vocibus verború fir
» mandis roborādifq;, vt fonus earum eſſet viridior vegetiorq;.Atq; id videntur
» feciſſe ſtudio & exemplo linguæ Atticæ. Satis notum eſt Attiquos ιχθυν ηϱον.
» Multa itidē alia citra morē gentiū Græciæ cæterarū infpirātis primæ literæ di-
» xiſſe ſic, lachrymas, ſic fpechulū, ſic ahenū, ſic vehemēs, ſic ichoare, ſic helluā-
» ri, ſic hallucinari, ſic honera, ſic honuſtū dixerūt. In his verbis oībus literæ feu
» ſpūs iſti⁹ nulla ratio vifa eſt, nifi vt firmitas & vigor vocis quafi quibufdā ner-
» uis additis iutēderet.Ceſt a dire.La lꝛe H.ou ſil conuiēt myeulx la dire lefperit
· vocal, eſtoit fouuāt iferee des Anciēs Latins en beaucop de dictiōs pour les fir
· mer & roborer, afin q̃ leur fon fuſt pl⁹ vertueux & vigoureux. Iceulx Anciēs le
faifoiēt a limitatiō des Atheniēs, au lāgage defqlz ιχθυν ηϱον. & beaucop de fē
blables dictions eſtoiēt afpirees hors la coſtume des aultres Nations de Grece.
Aiſſi furēt afpirez Lachrymæ, fpechulū, ahenū, vehemēs, ichoare, hallucinari
honera, & honuſt⁹.En ces vocables fufefcripts lafpiratiō na eſte veue raifonna

                                                      I.ij.

Another printer who was influential in changing French typography from the ornate black letter to the magnificent roman of the Golden Age was Michael Vascosan, "Printer to the King." His books, such as the *Caesar* of 1543, are plainer and more Italianate than those of Colines, but his type is excellent and his maps and illustrations are noteworthy. He died in 1547.

No account of this period in French typography would be complete without a mention of Jodocus Badius Ascensius (1462-1533), the father-in-law of both Robert Estienne and Michael Vascosan. His typography, though excellent, does not compare with that of his sons-in-law and his reputation rests chiefly upon his scholarship. He edited with comment the editions of the classics which he printed and wrote a life of Saint Thomas à Kempis and a famous satire on the follies of women, *Navicula Stultarum Mulierum*. Today he is best known by the marks which appear on his title-pages showing scenes in an early printing office.

We now come to one who was perhaps the most versatile man ever associated with the craft of printing. Born about 1480, Geofroy Tory studied both at Bourges and in Italy and later became a professor of philosophy and an editor of the classics. His spare time he spent engraving ornamental letters, designs and borders at which he was so successful that about 1515 he gave up his professor's chair and devoted himself exclusively to graphic arts.

In 1523 he began a work which was an expression of two of his many interests. One of the manifestations of the spirit of nationalism which was growing strong in

the sixteenth century was a new concern for the vernacular tongue. Tory opposed those who were introducing
Latin words into French. He was also desirous of reducing French spelling into what he considered a logical

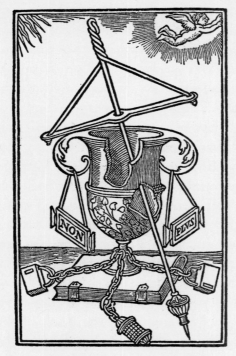

TORY'S MARK——THE BROKEN VASE

system. Among his permanent reforms were the introduction of the accent, apostrophe and cedilla into French
orthography. Again, Tory desired to improve type design. He believed that the shapes of all roman capital letters were derived from the different parts of the human
body and that the ideal letter must coincide with these

[181]

proportions. In 1529 Tory published his great work, the *Champfleury*. In the first of the three books into which the work is divided he extols the French language and suggests improvements in its spelling and in the second and third books he propounds, with the aid of magnificent woodcuts, his theories of letter design. A page from this celebrated volume is reproduced on page 179.

Tory was appointed in 1530 or 1531 "Printer to the King" and he continued in the exercise of his craft until his death in 1533. He is famous as a scholar, reformer of spelling, type-designer and printer but as a wood-engraver he is preeminent. The delicacy and exquisite taste of his woodcut borders and the beauty of his mark, the *Pot Cassé* (the broken vase), which commemorates the death of his brilliant ten-year-old daughter, are unsurpassed. His best woodcuts are found in the Books of Hours which he, Colines, and others printed. These will be discussed later in the chapter.

Unlike his versatile teacher, Geofroy Tory, Claude Garamond was the master of but one of the arts of the book, but in that art, type-designing, he has few rivals. His beautiful, clear and open roman character is probably based upon Jenson's celebrated letter, but it is less grave and simple and more conscious and elegant. The type of the Paulo Giovio, reproduced on page 173, to which we have previously referred affords an excellent example of the beauty and clarity of Garamond's design. The italic of Garamond is based upon that of Aldus but it is in effect much more free. His fine Greek types, the

Grecs du Roi, are based, like that of Aldus, upon the handwriting of a contemporary calligrapher but far surpass the Aldine letter in clearness and dignity, to such an extent, indeed, that for two centuries they served as models for designers of Greek types. Garamond, we are told, died in poverty in 1561, but his types were used and imitated in Italy, France, Holland, Germany and England, and to him may be justly assigned the honor of having dealt the death blow to black letter.

While Parisian printing during the early years of the sixteenth century tended to discard the gothic letter and to adopt a more Italianate style of printing, in the Books of Hours, a more conservative tone for a long time prevailed. The very success which met the efforts of the French printers of the late fifteenth century to copy and even to surpass the beautiful illuminated manuscript prayer-book rendered progress in the form difficult. The first period of fine Books of Hours was from the years 1490 to 1505. These *Horae* have certain marked characteristics. Printed in gothic type, often upon vellum, and resplendent with illustrations and borders, they closely resembled the manuscript Books of Hours. In their typography, then, the early Parisian *Horae* are of all books the most typical of the mediaeval spirit in art. In strange contrast to the religious nature of the pictures and text the borders contain figures as grotesque as the gargoyles which stared from the eaves of a mediaeval cathedral. The Parisian Books of Hours, then, such as were produced in the last decade of the fifteenth century by Philippe Pigouchet, had all the coarseness and incon-

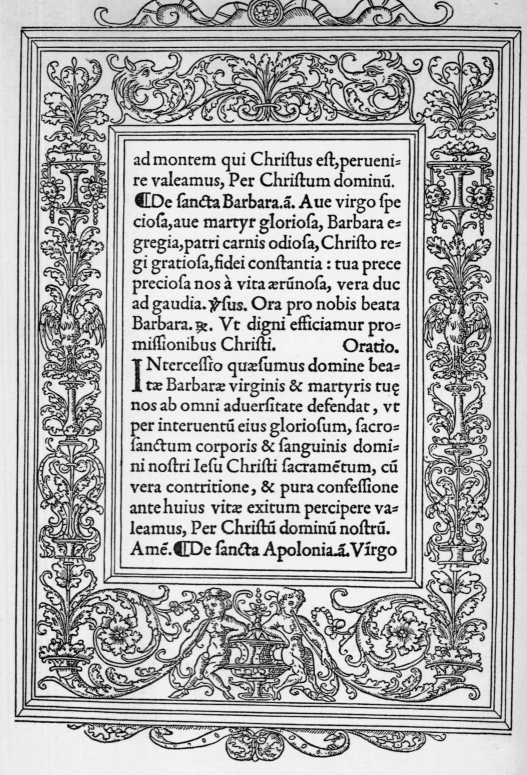

ad montem qui Christus est, peruenire valeamus, Per Christum dominū. ℂDe sancta Barbara.ā. Aue virgo speciosa, aue martyr gloriosa, Barbara egregia, patri carnis odiosa, Christo regi gratiosa, fidei constantia : tua prece preciosa nos à vita ærūnosa, vera duc ad gaudia. ℣sus. Ora pro nobis beata Barbara. ℟. Vt digni efficiamur promissionibus Christi.   Oratio.
INtercessio quæsumus domine beatæ Barbaræ virginis & martyris tuę nos ab omni aduersitate defendat, vt per interuentū eius gloriosum, sacrosanctum corporis & sanguinis domini nostri Iesu Christi sacramētum, cū vera contritione, & pura confessione ante huius vitæ exitum percipere valeamus, Per Christū dominū nostrū. Amē. ℂDe sancta Apolonia.ā. Vírgo

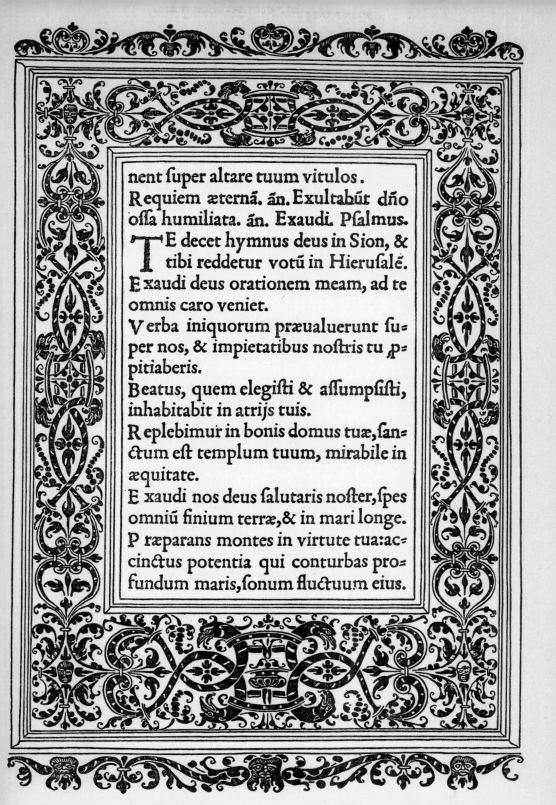

nent super altare tuum vitulos.

Requiem æternã. ãn. Exultabũt dño
ossa humiliata. ãn. Exaudi. Psalmus.

TE decet hymnus deus in Sion, &
tibi reddetur votũ in Hierusalẽ.

Exaudi deus orationem meam, ad te
omnis caro veniet.

Verba iniquorum præualuerunt super nos, & impietatibus nostris tu p͞=
pitiaberis.

Beatus, quem elegisti & assumpsisti,
inhabitabit in atrijs tuis.

Replebimur in bonis domus tuæ, san=
ctum est templum tuum, mirabile in
æquitate.

Exaudi nos deus salutaris noster, spes
omniũ finium terræ, & in mari longe.

Præparans montes in virtute tua: ac=
cinctus potentia qui conturbas pro-
fundum maris, sonum fluctuum eius.

THE BORDERS ON BOTH PAGES BY GEOFROY TORY

gruity and all the vigor and freshness which characterized mediaeval art and life.

After 1505 the beauty of the *Horae* steadily declined.
The Parisian wood-engravers began to imitate German
models and the borders and illustrations though not lacking in vigor became over-elaborate, unimaginative, and
stupidly realistic. The task of restoring the Book of
Hours to its former position of artistic merit was undertaken by Geofroy Tory. In 1524, he published a prayer-
book printed by Simon de Colines with borders, initials
and illustrations engraved by himself and this edition
was followed by four or five others. After his death, however, his engraved blocks were used by other printers who
carefully copied his typographic arrangement. His designs, too, were imitated by other engravers who were
illustrating *Horae* and as a result Tory's influence completely revolutionized the printing and decoration of the
Books of Hours.

Tory substituted for mediaeval ornament a renaissance
form of decoration. As may be seen by the reproduction
of the pages of the *Horae ad Usum Romanum*, printed
in 1543 by Simon de Colines (reproduced on pages 184
and 185), the borders of Geofroy Tory which appear in
them, are refined, balanced, restrained and somewhat
frigid. After attempting the use of black-letter type
Tory concluded that only roman could match the delicate
borders and his decision was approved by those who followed in his footsteps. The Books of Hours of Tory and
his school are infinitely superior to the elaborate *Horae* of
the 1520's and if they lack the vigor of the early prayer

[186]

book they compensate for that deficiency by their elegance and dignity.

The printers of Paris, then, who with the aid of Francis I made the first sixty years of the sixteenth century the Golden Age of typography were scholars as well as artists. In them may be found an expression of the renaissance ideal. They wrote books as well as printed them. They edited the classics which they issued from their presses. The art of the book, also, in the Golden Age was typically renaissance. In sharp contrast to the French book of the fifteenth century with its vigor, variety and naiveté, the book of the Golden Age displayed a chaste simplicity, a classical restraint and a delicate refinement which is typically renaissance in spirit.

The designers and printers of these books were not copying the styles of others, but were breaking new ground, and establishing styles of rare beauty and charm which have inspired the best book designers of the last three hundred years. If one traces back to its source the inspiration of many of the finest books produced today, he will find their designers under deep obligation to the French practitioners of the arts of the book during this properly styled Golden Age.

XVI. *Plantin of Antwerp*

 PRINTER of great achievements and great misfortunes was Christopher Plantin, the Frenchman who won a place in the typographic hall of fame by his work in the Flemish city of Antwerp. Born about 1514, he learned the art of printing and bookbinding at Caen. Due to limitations on religious freedom in France, Plantin left Paris in 1548 and settled in Antwerp.

There were many printers then at work in Antwerp and the prospects in this field did not look bright. So Plantin opened a shop where he sold prints and books, while his wife sold haberdashery "on the side." To employ his spare time he did bookbinding and decorated jewel boxes. He established an excellent reputation for work of this character but, just as fortune prepared to smile upon him, he had a tragic mishap. Mistaken on a dark night for someone else, a ruffian stabbed and so disabled him that he could not again handle gilding tools.

He thus had to make a new start in a somewhat different field, and determined to try his luck at publishing. Starting in 1555, in a very small way, the books he issued became more numerous each year and many were publications of considerable merit: among them a Bible in Latin, texts in Greek and Latin, and a quadrilingual dictionary. He had meanwhile begun to print as well as to publish.

Again Plantin was prospering but the old spectre of religious intolerance which he had fled France to escape again raised its head. In 1562 the authorities ordered search for the printer of an unorthodox prayer book and it was found the book had been produced in Plantin's office. Being forewarned, our unlucky printer decamped abruptly, going to Paris, in which city he remained for twenty months. When he finally returned he found his business ruined and even his household furnishings had been sold at auction for the benefit of creditors. In the words of the Salvation Army, Plantin was down but not out! Again he put his hand to the plough.

Four men backed him in the re-establishment of his printing office. This time he managed to ingratiate himself with both Church and State and was able to work without interruption. Perhaps he had found that heresy did not pay. The enterprise now prospered to a remarkable degree and Plantin was able to commission types from the most renowned punch-cutters in Europe. In three short years he gathered a fine typographical equipment as is evidenced by the specimen book which he issued in 1567.

Honors were now heaped on Plantin in quick succession. He became, by appointment, Printer to the King of Spain, and was called upon to print the liturgical

[189]

books used in that country. He was invited to Paris by the King of France and he was offered special inducements by the Duke of Savoy to establish a printing office at Turin. But he "stuck to his last" and not only he, but all the members of his family labored to build up the business. It is related that his youngest daughters were taught to read copy to the proof correctors at as early an age as twelve — often on books in foreign languages.

Plantin's ambition was to make his the greatest printing office in the world; and he certainly realized this ambition. By 1570 the institution was one of the show places of Europe. Twenty-two presses were working continually and as one writer recorded with considerable awe —2,200 crowns daily were paid as wages to the workmen. The plant outgrew the four houses it occupied and Plantin was soon under necessity of purchasing the property which has been preserved to the present day as the Plantin-Moretus Museum; a shrine to which printers from all parts of the world make pilgrimage.

The crowning glory of Plantin's printing career was the production of his Polyglot Bible. This was a project that he had long hoped to execute. The text was to run parallel in four different languages, Latin, Greek, Hebrew and Chaldaic. To make possible the production of the six projected volumes, Plantin sought a subvention from the King of Spain which, after much deliberation, was granted, the king making an advance of 6,000 ducats with the understanding that he was to receive equivalent value in copies of the book.

Like so many other projects when the printer has his

heart in the work, the project grew more ambitious as it went along. The six volumes became eight and the cost ran much higher than had been anticipated. The edition consisted of 1200 copies, divided up in much the manner of a French limited edition of the present day:

10 on grand imperial paper of Italy__price not stated
30 on grand imperial, at the price of____ 200 florins
200 on the fine royal paper of Lyons_____ 100 florins
960 on the fine royal paper of Troyes____ 70 florins

In addition, twelve copies on vellum were printed for the King of Spain.

Plantin's only troubles were not those involved in printing the book. The King of Spain would not permit its publication until the Pope expressed his approval, and this sanction was denied. Arias Montanus, who had edited the book, travelled to Rome to seek a revision of this fiat, but only when a new Pope was elevated to office was the necessary approval obtained.

Even then the book was under the shadow of suspicion, one authority having denounced it as heretical and Judaistic. The Inquisition undertook to examine its text but took many years to do so, and only in 1580 ruled that the book might properly be circulated. The strain of these delays on Plantin's finances can easily be imagined. The great Polyglot, therefore, on which a large share of his reputation was based was not a very great satisfaction to him at the time of its production.

The King of Spain, who was Plantin's royal patron, was ready with promises in the grand manner but very remiss in meeting his obligations. He was lax in paying his grants to Plantin and just about the time that worthy printer was most sorely pressed he would command him to print more service books for the church. But the King's financial derelictions had a direct effect even more disastrous. He committed the supreme error of neglecting to pay his soldiers, and as a result, the military threatened to plunder the city to obtain their compensation. In 1576, after Plantin was established in his new and handsome office, mutiny broke forth. In the sack of the city which ensued, eight thousand citizens were killed. The soldiers set fire to a thousand houses and six million florins worth of property was consumed. Everything that could be moved was stolen and hideous cruelties were perpetrated. When the smoke of the battle cleared away, Antwerp, one of the queen cities of Europe, was in ruins and never again recovered its former prosperity.

The effect on Plantin's business was disastrous. According to his own account "nine times did I have to pay ransom to save my property from destruction; it would have been cheaper to have abandoned it."

In the face of this last and greatest blow, Plantin still refused to admit he was beaten. He again vigorously attacked his work, but from that time to the end of his life he was severely cramped financially. To meet his most pressing obligations, he often had to sell books at sacrifice prices. Often he had to sell some of his equipment. In 1581 he sold his library in Paris for less than half its value. His predicament was, that although he had large resources in stock of books on hand, in printing plant equipment, and in accounts receivable, he had little ready cash with which to carry on his business. He was not, however, the first business man who has found himself in this position.

The political horizon again becoming threatening, Plantin turned over his office to his sons-in-law and went to Leyden in 1582. Here the authorities of the University received him with open arms and appointed him as their printer; which function he discharged for a period of almost three years. Political conditions in Antwerp having then become more favorable, he returned to that city. The zenith of his career, however, had passed and though he again went to work, the results obtained were not what they had been in the past. On July 1, 1589, Plantin passed to his heavenly reward which, let us sincerely hope, was more in consonance with his merits than that which had fallen to his lot this side of St. Peter's Gate.

We know more about Plantin than about most early printers, because not only his office and a great deal of its equipment but also his papers and records have been rather completely preserved. His correspondence, for example, has been published in a series of volumes and his manuscript records and accounts, which were kept with commendable neatness and thoroughness, are preserved today in the collection of the Plantin Museum. In 1850 the building was falling to decay, but some public spirited citizens of Antwerp, induced the public authorities to purchase the property, which purchase was accomplished in 1875. The Museum, for by this

[193]

name it is known, has been restored just as accurately as possible to the state in which it was in Plantin's day. It gives the visitor a vivid idea, which he can nowhere else obtain, of the atmosphere of a printing office of the sixteenth century.

From Plantin's records we gain a pretty clear idea of the industrial conditions of his time. In his office work began at five o'clock in the morning, but the quitting time was not stated. Every workman coming into the organization had to pay as initiation eight sous which were devoted to buying drinks for the other employees of the office. He was also required to contribute two sous to the poor-box. At the end of the month he had to put thirty sous in the poor-box and pay ten sous to his comrades.

From the typographical point of view, Plantin was not a great printer. He contributed little to type design or to book design but he was, in every sense of the word, a great publisher. And as a printer he was a thorough and conscientious craftsman.

He had imagination — more imagination than any of his contemporaries or near contemporaries, and he planned his books on a grand scale. He took as his printers' device, a compass describing a circle and guided by a hand emerging from the clouds. The device bore this motto: *Labore et Constantia* — "Labor and Constancy," and if any man's life ever typified a motto, Plantin's life was an example of the one which he adopted for his own.

As we have seen in this short sketch of his activities, on occasion after occasion, he started climbing the hill

CHRISTOPHER PLANTIN'S PRINTERS' MARK

toward success and every time some new disaster for
which he was in no way responsible, overwhelmed him
and cast him back. Each time, however, he returned
gamely to the struggle and, in the course of his continual
battle with circumstances, he produced books which have
made his name immortal in the annals of bookmaking.

XVII. *Master of Roman Type Design*

N England, at the beginning of the eighteenth century, an important opportunity awaited any competent typefounder. The efforts in this field of Nicholas Nicholls, Joseph Moxon, and others had been nothing short of pitiful. The James foundry had obtained matrices for most of its types from Holland but, even then, its casting was poor. It was, as one writer remarked, an era of "brown sheets and sorry letter." Judging by the books issued by the best publishers of the day, the type supply could not have been worse.

In 1716, William Caslon, who had been previously apprenticed to a London engraver of gun locks and barrels, set up a shop of his own in which he did similar work; also silver chasing and the cutting of binders' gilding tools and letter stamps. Under the patronage of William Bowyer, Caslon undertook typefounding, the first fount which we know he cut being an Arabic. Other faces were added and in 1734, when his first specimen

WILLIAM CASLON.

AN ENGRAVED PORTRAIT OF WILLIAM CASLON

sheet was issued, we find him with the equipment of a complete foundry. His types met with immediate success.

To the question: "What is the best type for all purposes which has been designed from the beginning of printing until the present day?" there can be no uncertain answer. The type is that designed and cut by William Caslon. As Mr. Henry L. Bullen, an authority on type history, once said to me in conversation: "The true test of a great type is whether you can set in it everything for which type is used; whether it can be used throughout a newspaper for headings and want 'ads,' display advertising and text."

Caslon is such a type. It can be used for years for all purposes without palling on the taste. One American printer who was among the first to establish a reputation for fine and forceful composition in the field of commercial printing, had for many years nothing in his cases but Caslon. And his work never lacked sparkle and spontaneity. The type is today, in spite of all the good types now available, still the dependable standby of advertising typographers.

Caslon is, too, the best book type so far produced. It is legible in the highest degree yet is not monotonous in color. In the exhibitions of the fifty best books of the year held annually by the American Institute of Graphic Arts, Caslon is always the type in which is set at least half the number of books selected to be shown, far outdistancing any other type. As interpreted on the linotype, it is the type in which this text is set, the title page showing the version produced by the Ludlow Typograph.

[199]

What is the reason for this undisputed supremacy? I think the secret lies in the stress placed comparatively, in the mind of the designer, on legibility and beauty. When we seek legibility only, we obtain a readable type which is stupid and monotonous; when we seek alone beauty of form, we obtain a type of great charm in individual letter forms but tiring in mass, because the element of design is too consciously apparent. In Caslon we have the product of a master designer, who made drawing the servant of readability rather than its master.

Caslon type could not be regarded as an entirely original creation on the part of its designer. It represented a synthesis of the best elements in letter designs of the Dutch founders. How good some of their types were is proved by the excellence of the Fell types, punches and matrices for which were procured in Holland late in the seventeenth century by the Oxford University Press — the types being still in use today by that great printing and publishing organization. But in adopting the best features of the Dutch types Caslon went further, putting into his design a spirit and virility that makes his types far greater than the models on which they were based. The reason for the difference is simple: William Caslon was a master of surpassing genius rather than a mere craftsman punch-cutter. That genius has left an influence on typography which seems destined never to be effaced.

The French Eighteenth Century

THE mid-point of the eighteenth century found a new style in book design in vogue in France. Much more attention was given to the illustration and decoration of books than to their typography. The decorative features were, in fact, overdone, but they were executed in so charming a manner that we can well forgive the excess of zeal on the part of the highly competent artists concerned.

The copper plate reigned supreme. It was either etched or engraved and often a combination of both processes was used; that is, the subject was first etched and then touched up with a burin. We find in the signature of some plates a definite statement of the cooperation of two artists in this manner, as for example, "Gravé à l'eau forte par C. Cochin, terminé au burin par P. Chenu."

A remarkable galaxy of talent was enlisted in the illustration and embellishment of books. Henri Cohen, the author of the standard bibliography of the illustrated books of this period, a sixth edition of which has been revised and edited by Seymour de Ricci, listed as the

[201]

masters Eisen, Moreau, Gravelot, Boucher, Cochin, Marillier and Choffard. As next in rank he enumerates Quéverdo, Monnet, Saint-Quentin, Le Barbier, and Duplessi-Bertaux.

In addition to the illustration these engravers conceived and executed a multitude of vignettes or decorations which were used throughout the books as headpieces or tailpieces. Every area throughout the books not occupied by type was filled in by a decoration of real charm and grace.

It is hard to choose among the books of the period a single volume for reproduction, but I believe *Les Baisers* by Dorat, published at Paris in 1770 by Lambert is representative. Two pages, which in the original volume face each other, are here shown. The engraved headpiece and tailpiece were designed by Eisen.

Among other books of note may be mentioned the *Oeuvres de Molière* of 1734, illustrated by Boucher; the *Fables de La Fontaine* of 1755, illustrated by J. B. Oudry, interpreted by Cochin and others; the *Décameron de Boccace* of 1757, illustrated by Gravelot, Boucher, and Eisen; and the *Oeuvres de J. J. Rousseau* of 1774-1783, illustrated by Moreau le jeune.

The subjects of the illustrations of this period ran largely, it would appear, to illicit lovemaking. We see charming ladies either in a state of extreme deshabille or wearing invisible garments obviously less dainty than those which are visible, which exerted on their waistlines a degree of compression so exquisite that we wonder how they kept their minds on the particular intrigue in

112 *LES BAISERS.*

Avec toi croîtra mon amour :
Puissent tes feuilles quelque jour
Se voir tresser pour sa couronne !
Oui ; qu'elle r'envie à son tour,
Que ta verdure s'épaississe ;
Et que ta tige s'arrondisse,
Pour l'ombrager à son retour !

XVIII BAISER.

XVIII. BAISER.

L'IMMORTALITÉ.

De quels charmes tu m'environnes !
Que je sens près de toi d'amoureuses fureurs !
Comme ils sont parfumés les baisers que tu donnes !
En les cueillant, je crois cueillir des fleurs,
Telles que les vergers d'Hymette
En fournissent de le matin
A ces filles de l'air qui sur la violette
Et l'œillet et le lis vont chercher leur butin.

H

TWO FACING PAGES FROM DORAT'S LES BAISERS

hand at the time. The scenes are laid almost invariably in a boudoir or in a formal garden, the latter *milieu* being rendered with much charm. Another characteristic of these illustrations is the decorative border in which many of them are framed.

We have recently had a typographical by-product of the work of these French eighteenth century engravers. Under many of their plates they caused to be engraved the title, often accompanied by explanatory matter. This lettering, being engraved with a burin, took on a character all its own. Within the last decade a French foundry brought out a series of types based on this engraved lettering, naming the series for Charles Nicolas Cochin, one of the most brilliant of the eighteenth century engravers. Furthermore, on closer observation of the heading type shown in one page of *Les Baisers*, we will recognize another letter recently revived.

The florid style of the engravers exerted its influence on the typefounders and we find all the founders competing with one another in the production of type ornaments or *fleurons*, which at this period reached their zenith in fecundity of output as well as in charm. The picturesque Paris typefounder, Simon Pierre Fournier did not invent these ornaments but they are usually associated with his name, because of his enthusiasm not only in their design but also in their use. These little ornaments with their limitless possibilities of combination, did much to enhance the grace of the printing of the period and—in a modern reincarnation—are performing a like service for printers of the present day.

[203]

To return to the engravers—we have seen that illustrations and vignettes on almost every page had relegated the type of the text to a position of comparative insignificance. In the next stage of development it was destined to be completely overwhelmed, for we find appearing books in which text as well as illustrations were engraved, the entire volume being printed from engraved plates. The best-known example of such a book, representing the last word in ultra-elegance as it was then conceived, was Pine's *Horace*, issued at London in 1733.

This example was, as might have been expected, emulated by the French engravers, an example of a book so producd being *Le Temple de Gnide*, illustrated after designs by Eisen, which appeared in 1772.

For every swing of the pendulum in one direction, we may expect a swing in the other direction. And thus it was with French bookmaking, for the super-elegant volumes of 1775 were destined to be succeeded within a generation in the favor of bibliophiles by the severely classical volumes soon to be issued by a new dynasty of bookmakers.

XIX. *The Writing Master's Disciples*

O YOU remember the japanned trays, hairpin holders and knick-knacks that were popular in the days of your youth? The profits on the manufacture of such japanned ware paid for the issue of some of the finest books ever produced. It came about this way. John Baskerville's first position was that of servant in a clergyman's household, in Birmingham, England. His employer found that he had more than ordinary skill in penmanship and enlisted his services in the instruction of poor boys in the parish in the art of writing. He soon secured an appointment as writing-master in a local school. He also applied his skill in letter formation to cutting inscriptions on grave stones.

To make more money, Baskerville took up the production of japanned ware of high quality and with a superior type of decoration. At this business he made a great success and within a few years amassed a considerable fortune. He took a place in the outskirts of the city, which he called "Easy Hill" and there built a handsome dwelling. Alexander Carlyle in his *Autobiography*

describes it thus: "Baskerville's house was a quarter mile from the town, and in its way handsome and elegant. What struck us most was his first kitchen, which was most completely furnished with everything that could be wanted. Kept as clean and bright as if it had come straight from the shop, for it was used, and the fineness of the kitchen was a great point in the family, for here they received their company, and there we were entertained with coffee and chocolate."

When Baskerville was fifty years old he took up the avocation that was to make his name famous: printing. He entered upon this work not as a business, but rather as a hobby. At this time printing as an art was still in eclipse in England. To be sure Caslon had, a generation earlier, provided some good types for the use of printers, but they were seldom put to good use. Baskerville determined to print a few books just as well as they could be printed, so he started in at the beginning of the printing process — with the making of types. From 1750 to 1752 he devoted himself to this task, taking the greatest care to have every letter perfect. At the same time his printing equipment was being set up. His press was of the same type as those commonly in use at the time, but it was made with greater precision. The paper available in the market did not suit his fastidious requirements, so he apparently had made to his own specifications the first wove paper — that is paper which does not show the laid lines of the screens of the molds. This type of paper has since come into almost general use so that now laid paper is the exception, rather than the rule.

[206]

PUBLII VIRGILII

MARONIS

BUCOLICA,

GEORGICA,

ET

AENEIS.

BIRMINGHAMIAE:

Typis JOHANNIS BASKERVILLE.

MDCCLVII.

TITLE PAGE OF BASKERVILLE'S VIRGIL

The printer's ink then made did not come up to his standards, so he entered upon the manufacture of this accessory, boiling his own oil and burning his own lampblack. As fast as the sheets of dampened paper were printed, they were placed between hot copper plates. The sheets were thus dried, the ink set, and the printed pages given a burnished appearance not found in any other printing of the period. In short, Baskerville's process of printing was original in many features, and each step was carried out with infinite care.

Seven years elapsed between the inception of the printing enterprise and the issue of the first book from the Baskerville press, the intervening period being occupied with the perfection of the materials and equipment. Again and again, the publication date of the Virgil—the initial issue of the press—was postponed, in order that it might be just as perfect, in Baskerville's judgment, as human effort could make it. When the book finally appeared its reception by the world of booklovers in Europe, justified its printer's expectations. It was highly praised on all sides and, overnight, Baskerville became a famous printer.

Baskerville's aim is well set forth in the preface to his second book, Milton's *Paradise Lost*—the only preface he ever wrote. In this he tells us:

Amongst the several mechanic Arts that have engaged my attention, there is no one which I have pursued with so much steadiness and pleasure, as that of *Letter-Founding*. Having been an early admirer of the beauty of Letters, I became insensibly desirous of contributing to the perfection of them.

I formed to myself ideas of greater accuracy than had yet appeared, and have endeavoured to produce a *Set* of *Types* according to what I conceived to be their true proportion.

Mr. Caslon is an Artist, to whom the Republic of Learning has great obligations; his ingenuity has left a fairer copy for my emulation, than any other master. In his great variety of *Characters* I intend not to follow him; the *Roman* and *Italic* are all I have hitherto attempted; if in these he has left room for improvement, it is probably more owing to that variety which divided his attention, than to any other cause. I honor his merit, and only wish to derive some small share of Reputation, from an Art which proves accidentally to have been the object of our mutual pursuit.

After having spent many years, and not a little of my fortune in my endeavors to advance this art, I must own it gives me great satisfaction, to find that my edition of *Virgil* has been so favorably received. The improvement in the manufacture of the *Paper*, the *Colour* and *Firmness* of the *Ink*, were not overlooked; nor did the accuracy of the workmanship in general, pass unregarded. If the judicious found some imperfections in the *first attempt*, I hope the present work will show that a proper use has been made of their Criticisms: I am conscious of this at least, that I received them as I ever shall, with that degree of deference which every private man owes to the Opinion of the public.

It is not my desire to print many books; but such only, as are *books* of *Consequence*, of *intrinsic merit*, or *established Reputation*, and which the public may be pleased to see in an elegant dress, and to purchase at such a price, as will repay the extraordinary care and expense that must necessarily be bestowed upon them . . .

Though the issues of his press were well received, the financial returns were not such as "to repay the extra-

[209]

ordinary care and expense," and the printing venture operated always at a loss. Baskerville had not expected the enterprise to show a profit. He had, for example, written Robert Dodsley, his publishing representative in London, regarding the projected printing of a "pocket Classick" as follows: "nor should I be very sollicitous whether it paid me or not." But he had not expected the operating deficit to be as great as it turned out to be. At one time he became disheartened and gave up printing for several years. But he was spurred again into activity by the attempt of a local competitor to print a Bible.

Baskerville was not highly regarded by other printers, probably because of the superior attitude he assumed, and his work was subjected to many unfounded criticisms.

The Birmingham amateur printed many editions of classics, but his *chef d'oeuvre* was the folio Bible which he printed at Cambridge under the auspices of the University. The printing of this book, completed in 1763, gratified a long-cherished ambition. The Bible was a noble volume, but out of an edition of 1250 copies published at four guineas, he could sell less than half of them, and in 1768 he "remaindered" over five hundred at a sacrifice price to a London bookseller. That ardent bibliophile, Thomas Frognall Dibdin, called it "one of the most beautiful printed books in the world."

Baskerville also issued a Book of Common Prayer which he intended to be "as perfect as I can make it." He wisely planned the typography "for people who begin to want spectacles, but are ashamed to use them in Church." He also designed and cut a font of Greek type

CHRISTMAS-DAY.

The Epistle. Heb. i. 1.

GOD, who at fundry times, and in divers manners fpake in time paft unto the fathers by the prophets, hath in thefe laft days fpoken unto us by his Son, whom he hath appointed heir of all things, by whom alfo he made the worlds; Who being the brightnefs of his glory, and the exprefs image of his perfon, and upholding all things by the word of his power, when he had by himfelf purged our fins, fat down on the right hand of the Majefty on high: being made fo much better than the angels, as he hath by inheritance obtained a more excellent name than they. For unto which of the angels faid he at any time, Thou art my Son, this day have I begotten thee? And again, I will be to him a Father, and he fhall be to me a Son? And again, when he bringeth in the firft-begotten into the world, he faith, And let all the angels of God worfhip him. And of the Angels he faith, who maketh his angels fpirits, and his minifters a flame of fire. But unto the Son he faith, Thy throne, O God, is for ever and ever: a fcepter of righteoufnefs is the fcepter of thy kingdom: Thou haft loved righteoufnefs, and hated iniquity; therefore God, even thy God, hath anointed thee with the oil of gladnefs above thy fellows. And, Thou, Lord, in the beginning haft laid the foundation of the earth; and the heavens

are

for Oxford University, but this latter performance added nothing to his reputation.

In all, he printed about sixty-seven books—not a large total output for a printer. But Baskerville was always interested in quality rather than quantity. Judged by current standards, his books were expensive, and could be afforded only by collectors of means. Most of his books were delivered unbound, the purchasers having them bound up to suit their individual tastes.

All of his books are characterized by great simplicity of typography. Of ornament he used almost none. He depended on well cast type carefully set and spaced and rightly positioned on the page. The simplicity and perfection of Baskerville volumes made them stand out spectacularly among the ill-printed product of the contemporary English press.

Baskerville type was more than well executed mechanically. It represented a real departure in type design. His is generally considered as the first real "modern" type face in contradistinction to the "old style" types which had hitherto been in vogue. An *old style* type is one in which the various elements in the letters are of fairly uniform weight; in other words, the design is of approximately the same color throughout. A *modern* type varies in the weight of its elements, some strokes being relatively thick and others relatively thin. One other feature of *old style* type is that the *serifs* or terminals of the main strokes are club shaped and rounded at their extremities, while the extremities of the serifs in a *modern* type are pointed.

[212]

The sharp pointed serifs which printed well on Baskerville's smooth finish paper, gave the printing an effect of brilliance never before seen. This effect was claimed by many contemporary critics to be dazzling and hard on the eyes. This criticism was seized upon and propagated by the printers with whom Baskerville was unpopular, due to his rather insolent attitude of superiority.

Benjamin Franklin, who was a subscriber to Baskerville's editions and a regular correspondent of the Birmingham printer, wrote him regarding an amusing instance of this prejudice:

Let me give you a pleasant instance of the prejudice some have entertained against your work. Soon after I returned, discoursing with a gentleman concerning the artists of Birmingham, he said you would be the means of blinding all the readers of the nation, for the strokes of your letters being too thin and narrow, hurt the eye, and he could never read a line of them without pain. "I thought," said I, "you were going to complain of the gloss on the paper some object to." "No, no," said he, "I have heard that mentioned, but it is not that; it is in the form and cut of the letters themselves, they have not that height and thickness of the stroke which makes the common printing so much more comfortable to the eye." You see this gentleman was a connoisseur. In vain I endeavoured to support your character against the charge; he knew what he felt, and could see the reason of it, and several other gentlemen among his friends had made the same observation, etc. Yesterday he called to visit me, when mischievously bent to try his judgment, I stepped into my closet, tore off the top of Mr. Caslon's Specimen, and produced it to him as yours, brought with me from Birmingham saying, I had been examining it, since he spoke to me, and could not for my life perceive the disproportion he mentioned, desiring him to point it out to me. He readily undertook it and went over the several founts showing me everywhere what he thought instances of that disproportion; and declared that he could not then read the specimen without feeling very strongly the pain he had mentioned to me, I spared him the confusion of being told, that these were the types he had been reading all his life, with so much ease to his eyes; the types his adored Newton is printed with, on which he has pored not a little; nay the very types his own book is printed with (for he himself is an author), and yet never discovered the painful disproportion in them, till he thought they were yours.

John Baskerville was personally a most interesting character. In dress, he was fastidious to a degree, verging on foppishness. He drove an elegant coach, with a pair of cream-colored horses, which was one of the marvels of Birmingham. He was vain and eccentric.

A Mrs. Eaves went to live at Easy Hill about 1750, probably in the role of housekeeper. She had been left destitute by her husband, who had been forced to flee the kingdom, with two daughters and a son on her hands. Soon after she and Baskerville were living together and, though her husband was still living, she passed everywhere as Mrs. Baskerville. One is happy to report that his social position in Birmingham does not appear to have been prejudiced by this relation. Baskerville was very fond of her and, upon the death of Eaves, married her in 1764. To her he bequeathed most of his property. She bore him one son, who died in infancy to the great grief of the father.

Baskerville was a sincere unbeliever and he stated his convictions regarding theology in his will:

"My further will and pleasure is and I Hearby Declare that the Device of Goods and Chattles as Above is upon this Express Condition that my Wife in Concert with my Exors do Cause my Body to Be Buried in a Conical Building in my own premises, Heretofore used as a mill which I have lately Raised Higher and painted and in a vault which I have prepared for It. This Doubtless to many may appear a Whim perhaps It is so—But is a whim for many years Resolv'd upon as I have a Hearty Contempt of all Superstition the Farce of a Consecrated Ground the Irish Barbarism of Sure and Certain Hopes &c. I also consider Revelation as It is call'd Exclusive of the Scraps of Morality casually intermixt with It to be the most Impudent Abuse of Common Sense which Ever was Invented to Befool Mankind. I Expect some srewd Remark will be made on this my Declaration by the Ignorant and Bigotted who cannot Distinguish between Religion and Superstition and are Taught to Believe that morality (by which I understand all the Duties a man ows to God and his fellow Creatures) is not Sufficient to entitle him to Divine favour with professing to believe as they Call It Certain Absurd Doctrines and mysteries of which they have no more Conception than a Horse. This Morality Alone I profess to have been my Religion and the [Rule] of my Actions to which I appeal how far my profession and practice have Been Consistant."

And finally he gave to his executors each "6 Guineas

Keepsake." To some questions of friends, regarding the manner in which he wished to be buried, he said they could "bury him sitting, standing or lying, but he did not think they could bury him flying." Baskerville died in 1795 and was interred in the vault as he had specified.

The name of John Baskerville will be immortal in the annals of printing—and rightly so, for he was one of the all-too-few idealists in the field of typography. Personally, I confess to a great admiration for him and for his work, and "in witness whereof," have named my youngest son after him. The basis of Baskerville's fame is well outlined by Josiah Benton, at the conclusion of his excellent biographical essay:

"What is it that makes the life and work of this middle-aged, vain and silly Birmingham Englishman interesting to us? Why do we collect his imprints, and why do we talk about him? I think it is because he had the true artistic vision and courage. He conceived the idea of a perfect book, such as had not been printed in England. He did not grow into it. He did not make one book, and then a better one, until at last he achieved the beautiful book. He conceived the book as an artist conceives a statue before he strikes a blow with his chisel into the marble. It was wonderful that he should have done so. He had grown up in a manufacturing and mercantile business, making japan work for sale, and profiting by its sale. Most men never get out of the work and of the ideas of the work which they do until they are fifty years of age. He did. Why was it? I think, as I have said, it was because he had an artistic perception and conceived the thing which he was to do, and adhered to his conception. Everything shows that he wrought in the true artistic spirit: having conceived the thing to be done, he proceeded to do it. All his work was executed upon a hand-press. His printing-office was what we should call a private printing-office in his house. He cut the type; he made the ink and improved the press; he devised the paper; and from start to finish the work was his. Everybody who will do better work than anybody else must have this spirit and conception of the work he proposes, and must adhere to it, or he will not produce perfect work. It is this that makes Baskerville interesting to us, and makes the productions of his little private press treasures in the world of art."

Even more important than Baskerville's own work was the influence of that work on the development of typography in Europe. This became apparent first in the work of the Didots—the famous family of French printers. The Didot types reflected the *modern* character of the Baskerville types, their *papier velin* imitated the paper he introduced, and their "classic" style of composition likewise showed evidence of his example. Partly direct, and partly through the Didots, the work of Baskerville exerted a great influence on Giambattista Bodoni, the eminent Italian printer who attained eminence during the last quarter of the eighteenth century.

The most celebrated of European printers thus became, in a sense, disciples of the English writing master who entered upon printing as an avocation.

[217]

The name of Didot is a familiar one in French typographic history: for several reasons. The Didot family contributed a long line of illustrious printers and typefounders; from one the Didot point system (which is today the system of typographic mensuration in use throughout Europe) took its name, for another was named a type design which has exerted a consequential influence on the appearance of French printing up until the present time. The name, however, strange to relate, is not well known and would mean nothing to the present-day printer of average intelligence. Even the French have not properly appreciated the services of the Didots to their national typography. There is no book dealing adequately with their work and information regarding them is far to seek.

The founder of the line is usually considered to be François Didot born in 1689. One of his sons, François Ambroise Didot, was a typefounder of ability who brought out the first "Didot" types in the early seventeen seventies or possibly before—types which bore a startling resemblance to those produced in or about the same period by Bodoni in Italy.

The question of precedence in the creation of the design has not been given the study it deserves for the point is one of considerable importance if we are to give credit where credit is due. From the information I have been able to gather it would seem that Bodoni, who was copying the designs and the composition style of Fournier, found that typography was being superseded by the types and style of the Didots, and thereupon copied their types and adopted their style. We cannot, however, disparage the ability of the Italian, for he was an apt pupil and developed the inspiration perhaps thus gained in a splendid manner indeed.

François Ambroise, by the way, was the member of the family who instructed Franklin's grandson, Benjamin Franklin Bache, in the mysteries of typefounding. Young Bache referred to him in his diary as "the best printer of this age and even the best that has ever been seen," but added on the same page the very human entry: "The meals are frugal." The subject of this comment had two sons, Pierre *l'ainé* (born 1761) and Firmin (born 1764), the former succeeding to the printing office, the latter to the paternal typefoundry. Pierre issued some fine monumental editions in a very severe style, one of them, the *Racine*, receiving an official award as the finest book ever printed! It is a very impressive volume, but I have always had a failing for the Didot Bible, a copy of which on vellum is one of the most remarkable achievements in perfection of printing technique it has ever been my pleasure to see. The title page of this edition is here reproduced in slight reduction.

Firmin applied himself to typefounding and was responsible for the point system already mentioned. He did what no typefounder ever did before or since: cut one design in a series of types a half a point apart in size. Most founders are content with a two-point step in progression of type sizes, but Didot divided this by four. There was, for example, a ten point, a ten and a half point, an eleven point, and so on.

BIBLIORUM
SACRORUM
VULGATAE VERSIONIS
EDITIO.
TOMUS PRIMUS.

———

JUSSU CHRISTIANISSIMI REGIS
AD INSTITUTIONEM
SERENISSIMI DELPHINI.

PARISIIS,
EXCUDEBAT FR. AMB. DIDOT NATU MAJ.
M. DCC. LXXXV.

TITLE PAGE OF THE DIDOT BIBLE

There were many other members of the family all of whom did distinguished work in one or more fields. As Mr. Updike remarked, their family reunions must have resembled a meeting of the Royal Society!

Before discussing further the printing of the Didots we will turn for a moment to Giambattista Bodoni and his work, which ran parallel in so many ways with theirs.

Giambattista (John Baptist) Bodoni, born at Saluzzo in Italy in 1740, was the son of a printer and mastered in early life the principles of the paternal trade. While still a boy he cut some woodblocks of much merit, and the young printer was soon planning to go to Rome for further training in this art. He was especially interested in a visit to the great press of the Propaganda at Rome, which printed religious texts in a multitude of languages in order to further the evangelistic work of the Church. The director of this press was so impressed by the enthusiasm of Bodoni that he offered him a job as compositor—an offer immediately accepted.

Bodoni specialized in the typography of the Oriental languages and was soon able to put in order many of the ancient punches and matrices, some of which had been cut by Guillaume le Bé and Claude Garamond. These had fallen into utter confusion but Bodoni managed to clean and sort them, and make them again ready for use. His interest in Oriental typography, acquired during this period, never deserted him, as is attested by the second volume of his *Manuale Tipografico* which is entirely given over to types for non-roman alphabets. This work

MANUALE

TIPOGRAFICO

DEL CAVALIERE

GIAMBATTISTA BODONI

VOLUME PRIMO.

PARMA

PRESSO LA VEDOVA

MDCCCXVIII.

TITLE PAGE OF BODONI'S MANUAL

with punches and matrices also led him to undertake
punch-cutting on his own account.

At the age of twenty-eight, Bodoni was appointed director of the ducal press at Parma, established by Fer-
dinand I, Duke of Parma. He bought his first supply of
types and ornaments from Simon Pierre Fournier, the
Paris typefounder, better known as Fournier le jeune.
At this period Bodoni was strongly under the influence
of Fournier, copying almost slavishly some of his models.

The period was one of classical influences and the
tendency was to simplify and regularize all forms of
artistic expression. The florid style of the French eighteenth century was giving place to a colder and more
formalistic manner. Garlands of flowers were being
supplanted, so to speak, by icicles. These tendencies had
their effect on Bodoni who interpreted them typographically not only in the design of his types but also
in their use. In the production of types of pointed serifs
with a wide difference in color between the thick and
thin strokes, Bodoni out-Baskervilled Baskerville—if
we may be permitted the use of this cumbrous expression.

The Didots and Bodoni were active competitors working in much the same style and on much the same type
of material. Both concentrated their attention on monumental volumes of regal magnificence, though the
Didots issued also charming little volumes for the general
reader. Both used the "classical" types printed on plate
finish wove paper. The presswork of both was well-nigh
flawless. The Didots claimed a higher degree of ac-

curacy in their editions of the classics and this claim could undoubtedly be sustained. Bodoni on the other hand can be credited with a greater inventiveness in type arrangement and make-up.

Both cut good types. As the new style swept over Europe, however, the design was generally credited to Didot. We find the German founders, for example, speaking often of "Didotsche Lettern."

The tradition of modern types and plate finish paper initiated by the writing master of Birmingham was thus carried forward in good hands in both France and Italy. My object in discussing together the work of Bodoni and the Didots was by way of slight tribute to the memory of a great family of French printers who have gone down in typographic history, comparatively speaking, "unwept, unhonored, and unsung." Bodoni has received his meed of merited praise, in which I most cordially join, but he had contemporaries in France of stature fully equal to his own.

XX. *In the Track of Columbus*

NE OF THE most astonishing facts in the history of printing is that a printing press crossed the Atlantic Ocean not later than 1539. At this date typography was still being introduced in European cities of considerable importance, yet a printer and his assistant took the long trip to the viceroyalty of New Spain and there began to print in Mexico City. The enterprise had the hearty encouragement of the archbishop, Zumarraga and the viceroy, Mendoza. The motive in establishing the press in Mexico was, however, predominantly religious—a motive that has almost always resulted in the printer following close on the steps of the explorer.

Confining ourselves first to facts established beyond dispute, we know that Juan Cromberger, one of the leading printers of Seville, Spain, decided to start a printing office in Mexico, to be operated as a branch of his main office. With this end in view he entered into a contract, on June 12, 1539, with Juan Pablos, a printer of Seville, to go to Mexico and there establish the shop. Fortunately, the original notarial record of this contract has recently been discovered. The conditions imposed by the master printer could hardly have been more rigorous.

Pablos was to act as compositor and manager of the office, but Cromberger reserved the right of placing a representative beside him to check up on all the transactions. Neither Pablos nor his wife (who was to do the housekeeping for the printer and his assistant) were to draw any salary, nor were they to spend a cent of the income in excess of bare living expenses.

He was to print three thousand sheets daily. And he was to be held responsible for errors in original composition or the correction of proofs. He was to seek out and obtain the personnel requisite to the organization of the office, but at first must content himself with a pressman and negro as helpers. He was prohibited from entering into partnership for any business whatsoever, and any emoluments he might receive personally were to go into the common fund. He was obliged to act as agent for the sale of books and merchandise sent over by his principal, and was entitled to no commission on such sales.

Pablos, on the other hand, supplied no capital at all. The traveling expenses of himself, his wife and his pressman were defrayed by Cromberger, as well as the cost of shipping the printing press, materials, and equipment. The partnership was to last ten years, counting from the day of the execution of the contract, and at its expiration accounts were to be settled. After salaries, transportation costs, house rent, the personal expenses of Pablos and his wife, and depreciation of the equipment were deducted from the income of the office, Pablos was to receive one fifth of the net profits. Accounts were to be settled in Spain, to which country Pablos was to return for this purpose.

According to other clauses in the contract, it was stipulated that worn-out type should be melted rather than sold, so that competition by other printers might not be encouraged. Before undertaking the printing of books, manuscripts of which were brought to his press, he was to obtain permission of the Bishop of Mexico, and obtain all the usual licenses. On all the books he printed was to appear the imprint "In the House of Juan Cromberger."

On the same day Cromberger made a contract with Gil Barbero, a pressman, to exercise that function in the new office overseas.

We know little of Pablos. He was a native of Brescia in Lombardy, Italy. At the time of his departure for New Spain he was married to Jeronima Gutierrez, probably an Andalusian. We have no knowledge as to whether he worked at the printing trade in his native country nor as to how long he had been in Spain. At the time the contract was made, it is most probable he was employed in Cromberger's Seville shop, so that the master printer was taking no chances on the ability and reliability of his typographic emissary.

Before discussing the early printed Mexican books which are known to us, it should be stated that José Toribio Medina, the greatest authority on Spanish American printing, believes there was a printer at work in Mexico City from 1535 to 1538—prior to the arrival of

Pablos—and that his name was Esteban Martin. He adduces considerable evidence in support of this contention. Martin is supposed to have printed the "Escala Spiritual," of S. Juan Climaco, but no copy of this or any other books printed by him have come down to us.

Evidence of vital importance in Martin's claim to priority is provided by a passage in a letter from Archbishop Zumarraga, to the Emperor, under date of May 6, 1538: "Little progress can be made in the matter of printing on account of the scarcity of paper, a difficulty in the way of many works which are ready here [to be printed] and of others which will have to be reprinted, because there is a scarcity of those most needed, and few are coming from overseas." We have further to consider a statement made in 1599, by Davila Padilla, the earliest historian to mention the early printing in Mexico, telling us the first book written in the New World and the first for which the printing press was used there was by S. Juan Climaco, translated from Latin into Spanish by Fray Juan de Estrada. He further says this was the first book printed by Juan Pablos but does not specify the date of printing.

Fray Alonso Fernandez, writing in 1611, apparently from independent sources, names the same book as the first work printed in Mexico, does not mention the printer, but fixes the date as 1535. Medina believes Davila Padilla was right about the book but in error as to the identity of the printer, because there was no imprint on the title, and named Pablos because his was the only name appearing on other known early Mexican books. He accepts as correct the date mentioned by Alonso Fernandez: 1535. Then again there is no reason to doubt the date of 1537 given by Beristain de Sousa as the date of printing the "Catecismo Mexicano."

Who was the printer at work in Mexico City before 1539? In the records of the Cabildo of Mexico is found the following entry: "On Friday the fifth of September, 1539. On this day, being in meeting assembled . . . the aforesaid gentlemen received as resident Esteban Martin, a printer, and that he give security and, until he gives it, shall not enjoy . . ."

As Pablos is known to have left Spain in June, 1539, as he had as assistants only Gil Barbero and a negro, and as a reasonable period of time almost invariably elapsed between arrival of a stranger and admission to citizenship, Medina concludes that Esteban Martin was responsible for the earlier printing activities recorded by various chroniclers, and must therefore be regarded as the first typographer on the American continent. Though the theory has not gained universal acceptance by Spanish American bibliographers, the fact that it is advanced by so thorough a scholar as Señor Medina entitles it to very serious consideration.

The first work for Pablos' press was undoubtedly the production of "cartillas" or primers, for the education of the youth, but none of these have survived. The earliest printed book of which we have perfect clear record was the "Breve y mas compendiosa doctrina christiana," Mexico, 1539. A description of this book was published in 1877 in the "Cartas de Indias," but unfortunately

[229]

this precious ancestor of books in the New World cannot now be located.

The next book regarding the printing of which we have definite evidence, is the *Manual de Adultos*, issued December 13, 1540. Of this there has survived only a fragment consisting of the last two leaves of the book discovered in a volume of miscellaneous papers in the Biblioteca Provincial at Toledo, Spain. The printer's note tells us that the book was printed "in the great city of Mexico by order of the very reverend bishops of New Spain, and at their expense, in the house of Juan Cromberger." That is to say the volume was published by the Church. Two out of three pages are given over to errata, correcting mistakes by the "Typographers." The fact that the last correction relates to the 36th sheet, page 1, line 4, shows that the book was one of consequential proportions.

In 1541, appeared a book on Guatemala by the notary Rodriguez, and from this time on volumes appear with varying regularity, or perhaps we might better say with varying luck as to preservation, for many volumes may have been printed about which we know nothing. During this period, the types were exclusively gothic in character, four sizes being in regular use. The printing office was evidently supplied with just two type ornaments, one a maltese cross and the other a unit of a vine pattern, both being used regularly in the adornment of title pages. Pablos also had a miscellaneous lot of woodcut borders which he cut up and used indiscriminately in the weirdest of combinations. There was also a

TITLE PAGE OF THE DOCTRINA OF 1543

woodcut design in the nature of a canopy with tassels hanging at the sides (as in the illustration on page 231) which was apparently a favorite, being used on the title pages of at least five books and perhaps more.

It appears that Cromberger, the principal in the operation of this Mexican printing office, died about September, 1540. After some interruption of operation, the office was taken over by Juan Pablos and continued under his own name. On February 17, 1542, he was admitted to citizenship in Mexico City, and on May 8 of the following year the district of San Pablo granted him a lot on which to build his house.

In 1554 there comes a change in the character in the books printed by Pablos, which has not received adequate notice at the hands of the bibliographers. During this year, appeared three books in folio format, the *Diálogos* by Cervantes de Salazar, the *Recognitio Summularum*, and the *Dialectica Resolutio*. In them we find the first use of roman and italic type in Mexico, we find a new style in the composition of title pages, we encounter two or three new type ornaments, and we see used some effective woodcuts, one of which, a title page border, had been used a few years previous in London. Why the radical change in typographic style?

This question has but recently been considered and the answer was published first in June, 1927, by the present writer. The "answer" was the arrival in Mexico City of Antonio Espinosa, an expert type-cutter who brought with him a typefounder, both having contracted to enter the employ of Juan Pablos, thus putting that printer in position to augment his type equipment at will, without recourse to the distant European sources of supply. Judging by his own later work as a printer Espinosa was a typographer of taste and he did much to improve the output of the Pablos press.

The manner of his affiliation with Pablos was in this wise. The Mexican printer in 1550 sent a commercial envoy to Spain, with power of attorney to transact for him various items of business. One of the commissions with which he was entrusted was the employment of a typefounder. According to a document but recently discovered in the notarial archives of the Spanish city of Seville, the envoy contracted with Espinosa and an assistant to come to Mexico City and work for Pablos, "cutting and casting type" for a period of three years. It was thus that the typography of the first Mexican press was rejuvenated.

During the succeeding years some fine books came from the Pablos press. In 1559 came his first competition in the person of his associate Espinosa, who had gone to Spain and there obtained, on the plea that the prices charged for books printed by Pablos were prohibitive of their purchase by persons of moderate means, the privilege to operate a second printing office in Mexico City. He was undoubtedly a finer craftsman than his former master and some fine volumes issued from his press.

In 1560, Juan Pablos the pioneer typographer, brought out his last and most notable work: the *Manuale Sacramentorum*. But he was nearing the end of his career. His health must have been failing for in that year

[233]

he drew his will, and before August 21, 1561, he had printed his last sheet. On that date we find his widow administering his estate.

The name of Pablos is little known in the English-speaking countries of the New World. Yet he is entitled to rank among the great pioneers in the development of civilization in the Americas.

As to other cities of Mexico, printing was introduced at Oaxaca in 1720 by a woman, Doña Francisca Flores, but was soon discontinued for reasons unknown, and printing was not resumed in that city until 1812. Mariano Valdés Tellez Giron began to print at Guadalajara toward the end of 1792; at Vera Cruz, Manuel Lopez Bueno established a press in 1794, while the first printing was done at Mérida in 1813 by Francisco Bates.

As we cannot trace here the further history of printing in Mexico, suffice it to say that the next country on the American continent to which type and printers' ink were to penetrate was Peru. There in 1584, the first printing was done at Lima, "the City of the Kings" by Antonio Ricardo. This typographer, a native of Turin, Italy, had been printing in Mexico, but finding the competition there quite keen, and hearing of the riches of Peru, emigrated to that country. The only known copy of the earliest known specimen of Peruvian printing was discovered by an American, Mr. George Parker Winship, and is now preserved as one of the treasures of the John Carter Brown Library at Providence, R. I. It is an edict of Pope Gregory, initiating the Gregorian calendar.

XXI. *The Press Comes to Massachusetts*

PRINTING types and printing presses move with the pioneers in opening up new frontiers. When we investigate the coming of typography to English-speaking North America, that is, to the territory which is now the United States, we find that there was no exception to the general rule. In 1619 the Pilgrims landed on Plymouth Rock. In 1638, the first printing press arrived in Massachusetts. In its coming there was much of romance. In its operation there was much of import to the development, intellectual and spiritual, of the infant colony.

Reverend Jose Glover of Sutton, England, was a clergyman of some wealth who for non-conformity with the principles of the church had been suspended from his pastorate. He decided to go to New England, and probably sailed in his own ship, the *Planter*, early in 1634. He apparently liked the new country and decided to make it his home. He secured two pieces of property and ordered the erection of a house on one of them, in order to have ready accommodations for the members of his family when he brought them from England. The land records of Boston show that he was an inhabitant of that town, and a householder, in 1635.

At this time the American colonists were beginning to take an interest in education. Schools were started and the establishment of a college was discussed. Mr. Glover became interested in this project and returned to England to raise funds for the enterprise. For several reasons it seems probable he had ambitions to be president of the institution. While there he permanently resigned the pastorate at Sutton from which he had been suspended.

It was evidently planned that a printing plant should be an important adjunct to the educational and religious work of the college. Mr. Glover bought a press with his own funds and a supply of type with money contributed by friends of the college. He also purchased supplies of paper, ink and other accessories to take along when he and his family sailed for the new world in July or August, 1638.

Prior to his departure he contracted with Stephen Day (whose name is sometimes spelled Daye) his two sons, and another workman to go with him. Stephen Day was a locksmith and a resident of Cambridge, England. It does not appear that he was a printer, but it seems his two sons (who had not yet reached their majority) were probably apprentices in a Cambridge printing office. There is later evidence that Mr. Glover was counting principally on Matthew Day to do the composition.

Unfortunately, Jose Glover, who may properly be regarded as the "father of printing in the United States," never reached the shores of that country on this second trip, for, during the voyage, he fell ill and died—probably of smallpox. In Winthrop's *Journal* is this entry:

> 1639, Mo. 1. A printing house was begun at Cambridge by one Daye, at the charge of Mr. Glover, who died on seas hitherward.

We thus learn that in March, 1639, the printing plant was in operation. Meanwhile the college (which it was decided to name Harvard College) had been organized. In 1640, Henry Dunster became its president.

Mrs. Glover and the workmen her husband had engaged arrived in Boston about the middle of September, 1638. In Cambridge she promptly arranged first for the renting and then for the purchase of property to serve for a printing office, and as a residence for the printers. Stephen Day, as has already been noted, was probably not a printer, but his son Matthew, in 1639 nineteen years of age, evidently had printing experience. His father, being a skilled locksmith, was qualified to erect the press and assist in the mechanical end of the work. He also undertook the business direction of the office.

The first piece of work produced at the press was the "Freeman's Oath" printed on a half sheet of small paper. Another item issued in 1639 was "An Almanac for 1639, calculated for New England, by Mr. William Pierce, Mariner." No copies of either of these publications have been preserved.

In 1640 appeared the first publication, copies of which are known to us: "The Whole Booke of Psalmes,

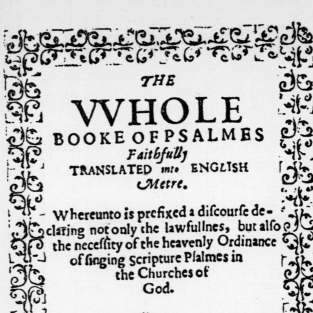

THE
VVHOLE
BOOKE OF PSALMES
Faithfully
TRANSLATED *into* ENGLISH
Metre.

Whereunto is prefixed a difcourfe de-
claring not only the lawfullnes, but alfo
the neceffity of the heavenly Ordinance
of finging Scripture Pfalmes in
the Churches of
God.

Coll. III.
*Let the word of God dwell plenteoufly in
you, in all wifdome, teaching and exhorting one another in Pfalmes, Himnes, and
fpirituall Songs, finging to the Lord with
grace in your hearts.*

Iames V.
*If any be afflicted, let him pray, and if
any be merry let him fing pfalmes.*

Imprinted
1640

TITLE PAGE OF THE PSALMES, CAMBRIDGE, 1640

faithfully Translated into English Metre . . . Imprinted 1640." This was a volume of 147 unnumbered leaves, the title page of which is shown on the opposite page. This is generally referred to as the "Bay Psalm Book." There are ten copies of this American incunable known to be in existence, six of which are imperfect. It was far from an elegant piece of printing, but it served its purpose well.

This first existing book printed in what is now the United States must always have a well-nigh sacred interest to any cultivated American. A perfect copy, should it come up for public sale, would bring a fabulous figure —and properly so. For it stands to American printing in the same relation as does the "Gutenberg Bible" to the printing of Europe.

About four other publications are supposed to have appeared before the printing of the next extant item, a *List of Theses* at the Harvard College Commencement in 1643, which showed considerable improvement in typography and presswork.

In 1647 appeared the first and only book bearing the imprint of Matthew Day. Stephen Day had retired from active connection with the press and was devoting his time to other pursuits. His son took it over and conducted it until his death on May 10, 1649, printing a number of other books, in the imprints of which, however, his name does not appear.

The widow of Jose Glover had married Henry Dunster who thus, as president of the college (which owned some of the type) and as representative of the Glover

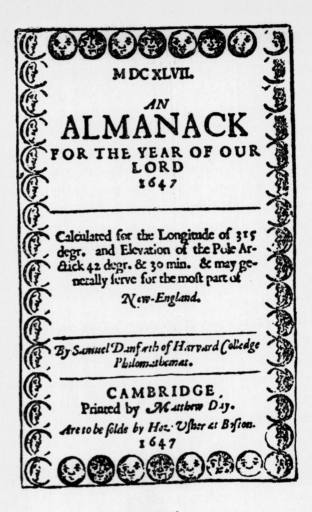

TITLE PAGE OF THE 1647 ALMANAC

estate, had a double interest in the direction of the press. On her death, however, the estate had to be settled and the house originally bought for the Day family and the press was sold. The press was thereupon removed to the newly-built "President's House" and Matthew Day bought a residence.

After Matthew Day's death, Samuel Green was chosen to take over the office. He had no training as a printer, but stepped into the breach and was several years later doing creditable work. The first known work bearing his name in the imprint is "A Platform of Church Discipline . . . Printed by S. G. at Cambridge in New England and are to be sold at Cambridge and Boston Anno Dom: 1649." He continued to print actively until he retired in 1692, the year in which his name last appears in an imprint.

The next factor of importance in the development of printing in the United States was the work of Rev. John Eliot, the missionary to the Indians. He spent a number of years learning their language and finally formulated it so that it could be reduced to print. He next became convinced of the necessity of some evangelistic and educational literature in the Indian tongue. Acting on suggestions from the new Colony, Parliament provided in 1649 for the creation of "A Corporation for the Promoting and Propagating the Gospel of Jesus Christ in New England." This organization helped Mr. Eliot's work in many ways, not the least of which was the contribution of money and materials to make possible the printing of texts in the Indian language.

Samuel Green was called on to print these books, the *Catechism* appearing before September 1654, the *Book of Genesis* in 1655, the *Psalms in Metre* in 1658, and *Pierson's Catechism*, 1658-1659. Eliot had been working for some time on his translation of the whole Bible into the Indian tongue, and he found the typographic facilities in Cambridge insufficient to its printing. On December 28, 1658, in a letter to the Corporation in London regarding this question, he wrote: "I proposed this expedient for the more easy prosecution of this work, viz., that yourselves might be moved to hire some honest young man, who hath skill to compose, (and the more skill in other parts of the work the better) send him over as your servant, pay him there to his content, or engage payment, let him serve you here in New England at the press in Harvard College, and work under the College printer, in impressing the Bible in the Indian language, and with him send a convenient stock of paper to begin withal."

Meanwhile Hezekiah Usher had been in London, and purchased for the printing office a press, type and other materials. These were placed in the Indian College to which the printing office had been moved, when its chief concern had come to be the production of books for the Indians, and consigned to the care of Samuel Green.

On April 21, 1660, the Corporation in London records its action on Mr. Eliot's suggestion. It had contracted with Marmaduke Johnson, a skilled master printer of London, to go to New England for a period of three years. He was to receive £40 per annum in ad-

MAMUSSE
WUNNEETUPANATAMWE
UP-BIBLUM GOD
NANEESWE
NUKKONE TESTAMENT
KAH WONK
WUSKU TESTAMENT.

Ne quoſhkinnumuk naſhpe Wuttinneumoh *CHRIST*
noh aſoowefit

JOHN ELIOT.

CAMBRIDGE:
Printcuoop naſhpe *Samuel Green* kah *Marmaduke Johnſon.*
1 6 6 3.

TITLE PAGE OF THE INDIAN BIBLE OF 1663

dition to board, lodging, and washing. In announcing Johnson's departure the Corporation requests "for his encouragement" that his name be mentioned in the imprint.

Marmaduke Johnson arrived in Boston in June 1660, and immediately began working with Green on the Bible, which by the way, was the first edition of the Scriptures in any language to be printed in the United States. The title page of the volume, which was completed in 1663, is reproduced herewith.

This Indian Bible involved many typographical difficulties, and its execution was a great credit to the Cambridge printers. The New Testament was finished first and was issued with a separate title page dated 1661, and was then combined and issued with the Old Testament when that part of the work was finished. The volume was without doubt the most important production of the early press in the United States.

A copy of this Bible, which would today command a king's ransom, was purchased for Isaiah Thomas in 1791 for the large sum of seven dollars, the copy being now in the collection of the American Antiquarian Society. Eben T. Andrews, Thomas' partner in Boston, wrote him under date of September 6 of that year (in a letter not heretofore published or referred to) as follows:

Mr. Harris was here today, and mentioned that he had procured an Indian Bible, which he had heard you express a wish to possess, and that you might have it if you please, as he supposes he can procure another for himself out of the College

Library. He gave 7 dollars for the copy which he has, which he says is very good, excepting the binding, which is flattened. I enclose you some of his proposals.

Since the publication of any existing treatise on the early Massachusetts press, there have been made three very important finds. One was the discovery of a copy of the Indian version of Richard Baxter's *Call to the Unconverted*, which was known to have been printed, but no copy was thought to be extant. It turned up in the sale of non-scientific works from the library of the Royal Society which were sold at auction in London on May 4, 1925, and was purchased for the Henry E. Huntington Library at a price of approximately $38,000.00. Like the Bible it was printed by Samuel Green and Marmaduke Johnson.

In 1661, Marmaduke Johnson fell in love with Green's daughter and the latter objected to his attentions on the ground that he had a wife still living in England. Johnson failing to desist Green took the matter to the courts and Johnson was ordered to leave the country. Because of the value of his work on the Bible, however, the order was not then enforced, but his further relations with his associate must have been rather strained. In 1664 at the end of his period of employment, however, he returned to England.

The Corporation, however, transferred its printing equipment in Cambridge to the care of Mr. Eliot, who was very friendly to Johnson, and sent the latter back to New England with a new supply of type. He also brought with him a press of his own, and planned to set up in Boston where there would be more patronage than in Cambridge. This prospect was not at all pleasing to the authorities of the College press, to Green, and his friends. So purely to hamper Johnson, the legislature or "General Court" issued an order on May 27, 1665, providing that no printing press should be erected in any town in the colony except Cambridge, and that any text to be printed must first be approved by a board of licensers. The result was that Johnson was forced to locate in Cambridge, which is across the river from Boston. The first book issued from the new office and bearing the imprint of Marmaduke Johnson alone was the *Communion of Churches* by John Eliot, Cambridge, 1665.

In 1674 Johnson succeeded in having lifted the ban on printing in any other town but Cambridge, so he immediately made plans to remove to Boston where he considered he could do more business. On July 18 of that year he bought a house on what is now known as Hanover Street, but the realization of his ambition was destined to be short lived, for he passed to his reward on Christmas day, 1674.

Though there is no publication of Johnson's with a Boston imprint it was the belief of Mr. Littlefield that the later signatures of Torrey's *An Exhortation Unto Reformation* were printed after the removal of his office, thus constituting the first printing done in the city of Boston. After Johnson's death his equipment was bought and his office continued by John Foster.

To complete the record of early printing in Cambridge, it remains only to record that Samuel Green, who continued printing there, in 1691 took into partnership his son Bartholomew. Their joint imprint appeared in 1692 on *Ornaments for the Daughters of Zion,* which was the last book with which Samuel Green was associated. In that year he is supposed to have retired. No more printing was done in Cambridge for over a hundred years, with the exception of a brief period during the Revolutionary War when Boston was occupied by British troops. His service in charge of the college press for over forty years entitles him to a position of distinction among American colonial printers, but perhaps his main claim to fame is that he was the father of a long line of printers who carried the typographic art into many communities of the new world, members of the family being identified as pioneers in American printing for a period of well over a hundred years.

It is a matter of regret that space forbids a full description of the spread of printing through the other colonies of English-speaking America, and indeed, to the states west of the Atlantic seaboard after the Revolution, for there is no story more interesting.

Pennsylvania was the second colony to extend hospitality to the printing press, William Bradford beginning to print there in 1685. Getting into trouble with the Quaker authorities, he moved to New York in 1693, thus becoming the first printer in that colony as well. Meanwhile William Nuthead had in 1682 established a press at Jamestown, Virginia, but before he got well under way its operation was forbidden by the authorities. In 1685, we find him established at St. Mary's City, Maryland.

Printing came to Connecticut in the person of Thomas Short, who began printing at New London in 1709. He was succeeded four years later by Timothy Green, son of the Samuel Green with whom we are already well acquainted.

In all probability the first printing in New Jersey was done by William Bradford at Perth Amboy in 1723, followed by Samuel Keimer at Burlington in 1728. In 1755 James Parker established a press in his home town of Woodbridge. Typography invaded Rhode Island in 1727, the pioneer printer being the James Franklin to whom young Benjamin Franklin had been apprenticed, as we shall learn in the following chapter.

The earliest printing in South Carolina took place about 1731 at Charleston, the printer being Eleazer Phillips, Jr., and in North Carolina in 1749 at Newbern, the first typographer in that state being James Davis. New Hampshire was late, the first printing being done at Portsmouth in 1756 by Daniel Fowle. James Adams began to print at Wilmington, Delaware, in 1761.

In 1763 printing began in Georgia, James Johnston starting in that year the issue at Savannah of the *Georgia Gazette* and various individual acts of the assembly. In 1768 or earlier, Denis Braud began to print at New Orleans for the French authorities and doubtless continued to serve the incoming Spanish administration. The first printing on territory now within the state of Vermont was done in 1780 at Westminster by Judah Paddock Spooner and Timothy Green.

Immediately following the Revolution we find the

pioneers starting west, with the printing press following hard on the heels of the leaders. The part played by printers in the winning of the west makes a thrilling story of hardships and difficulties encountered and overcome. And as always, we find that wherever civilization obtained even a toehold, the press did yeoman's service in making that hold secure.

XXII. *The Precocious Apprentice*

CITIZEN of Boston returned from England about 1717 with an equipment of type and press and set up as a printer in his native city. At this time, his younger brother was casting about for a suitable trade to choose as his life work. A hard bargain was driven, and a nine-year apprenticeship contract was drawn, the father paying the fifty dollar fee required.

In those days an apprentice was paid nothing except during the last year of his term of indenture, but he was lodged, fed, and clothed by his master. In this case, however, the master, being unmarried, did not keep house, so both he and his apprentice boarded with another family. The younger brother was a great reader and, although he was able to borrow many of the books he desired, there were others he wanted to buy. So he proposed that his brother pay him in cash one half the sum then being paid for his board, allowing him to provide his own meals. Out of this meagre allowance he was able to save nearly a half, and with this income he began to acquire a small private library.

In the course of his business the older brother was commissioned to print for William Brooker, the postmaster at Boston, a weekly newspaper known as the *Boston Gazette*. But a new postmaster coming soon into office placed the job with a rival office, and our printer started a competitive sheet known as the *New England Courant*, the first newspaper in the United States not connected with a post office.

The first issue of the *Courant* appeared August 17, 1721. The enterprise was undertaken contrary to advice of father and friends. These critics agreed that there were already three papers being published in the American colonies, and two of them in Boston. Another could, therefore, hardly be expected to succeed. But advice was of no avail. The young publisher proposed to issue a newspaper different in character from the existing publications. The editorial policy was hostile to the clergy, attacked some prevailing opinions on religion, and opposed various fads.

Expression of these opinions brought criticism from many quarters, but the young publisher soon ventured criticism in the more dangerous field of politics. Pirates were active in New England waters, and there was an idea current that the governmental authorities had not been very vigilant or effective in their suppression. In one issue appeared this sarcastic news note, purporting to come from Newport, R. I.:

"We are advis'd from Boston that the government of Massachusetts are fitting out a ship to go after the pirates to be commanded by Captain Peter Papillon and it is thought he will sail sometime this month, wind and weather permitting."

[251]

The Governor and Council took this as an affront and promptly committed the publisher of the *Courant* to jail. A week's incarceration put the offender in a repentant frame of mind, and he duly apologized, entreated forgiveness, and sought his release.

Following release, however, the repentant spirit did not last long. Before long, a single issue of the *Courant* contained three articles, all objectionable to the authorities. After due consideration, the publisher was forbidden to print the *New England Courant* or any other similar publication, unless the copy was first approved by the Secretary of the Province.

The younger brother had meanwhile been learning the printing trade and making progress in other directions. He began to write short pieces and slip them at night under the printing office door. Many were printed, and there was considerable speculation among the editorial circle as to their authorship. We can imagine the thrill of the young apprentice as he heard the names of various well-known members of the community suggested as possible authors. Finally, the young apprentice revealed to his brother and friends, the identity of the mysterious contributor, thereupon rising considerably in their estimation.

The printing office now faced a crisis, as the publisher had been forbidden to print further issues of the paper without official censorship. This condition being unacceptable, the publisher conceived the subterfuge of issuing the paper under the name of his apprentice. The name of this apprentice was Benjamin Franklin.

THE APPRENTICE

So we find the eightieth number of the *New England Courant* for the week of February 4 to February 11 published with this imprint: "Boston: Printed and sold by Benjamin Franklin in Queen Street, where Advertisements are taken in." To make this possible it had been necessary to cancel publicly the bonds of apprenticeship between James Franklin and his brother, but the former, seeking to preserve the advantage of a good agreement executed secretly a new indenture, repeating the provisions of the original.

James Franklin was evidently an exacting master, ill natured and sullen, and his apprentice brother had always had a difficult time getting along with him. Finally, hard words were superseded by blows, and young Benjamin announced a termination of agreement, knowing James was not in position to enforce the secret contract. Being powerless to object to Benjamin's leaving his employ he persuaded the other Boston printers to refuse him employment. This boycott was serious, as there were only four printing offices in the colonies outside of Boston, in which he could obtain employment in the trade to which he had devoted four years of application. To reach either New London, New York or Philadelphia, the points at which possible employment might be found, required either a long and dangerous journey on foot or a passage by boat. The latter required passage money, and Benjamin had no funds available for this purpose.

He could not appeal to his father, who sided with the older brother in the dispute. In fact, he could not even disclose to his father his plan for leaving town for fear that he would be restrained. He was nevertheless determined to go through with the project. So he sold some of his books and secured passage on a sloop bound for New York City. He promptly presented himself at the only printing office in that town, conducted by William Bradford "at the Sign of the Bible" on Hanover Square.

The New York printer could offer him no employment, but suggested that he go on to Philadelphia where Bradford's son Andrew was engaged in the business and was, by reason of the death of one of his workmen, in need of help. So thence he immediately repaired, reaching the city with which he was afterwards so intimately associated, on a Sunday morning in October of 1723.

Purchasing three penny worth of bread in a bakery, he received much more than the same money would have purchased in Boston. Taking away with him three large rolls, he disposed one under each arm and was munching the third as he walked up Market Street. He wore his working garb, his "best clothes" having been shipped in his "chest" by another route. His pockets were stuffed with shirts and stockings and, all in all, he must have presented an uncouth figure indeed. So amusing did he appear, that Miss Deborah Read, standing on the stoop of her house, snickered audibly as he passed. For this indignity Franklin later retaliated by marrying the young lady.

Monday morning, he applied for employment at the shop of Andrew Bradford, and was surprised to find there Andrew's father, who had made a faster trip to Philadelphia than Franklin. Bradford had no work immediately available, so the young man next applied to Samuel Keimer, the other printer then established in that city.

Keimer soon after gave Franklin employment in his ill-equipped office. The new workman saved a good share of his wages and made many friends. Keimer was unmarried and could thus offer him no place to live, so Franklin had continued to board with Andrew Bradford, to whose house he had first moved. The idea of his assistant lodging with his competitor did not appeal to Keimer, so he arranged to have him board with a Mr. Read, father of the young lady hereinbefore mentioned.

One new acquaintance was Sir William Keith, the Governor of the Province of Pennsylvania. One day the Governor and a friend called on young Franklin at his place of business, and almost flabbergasted his employer. He invited Benjamin to dinner and talked with him regarding his plans. Keith deplored the poor workmanship of the Philadelphia printers and encouraged Franklin to set up in business for himself, promising him the public printing. He urged him to return to Boston and secure his father's financial backing, and gave him a letter to Josiah Franklin recommending the enterprise.

Franklin occasioned considerable surprise, particularly among the workmen in his brother's shop, by his return to Boston with money in his pockets and giving other evidences of prosperity. But his father was an ultra-conservative, and viewed the proposition with disfavor. He thought little of Governor Keith's judgment in advocating the setting up in business of an eighteen year old lad. So he replied courteously to the Governor, and Benjamin returned to Philadelphia with the parental blessing and a promise of assistance later on if he should continue to make satisfactory progress in the business, and save up some money of his own.

On his return, Keith expressed regret at the elder Franklin's conservatism and proposed backing the boy himself. He instructed Benjamin to prepare a schedule of necessary equipment and an estimate of its cost, and promised to send to London for the material. Later he suggested that Franklin himself go to London to select the equipment, so a passage was duly engaged. Keith was to provide him with letters of introduction to persons of consequence in London and letters of credit wherewith to make his purchases. When Franklin called on the Governor soon before sailing, to obtain these letters they were not ready, but according to the gubernatorial secretary they would be at Newcastle before the ship left that point. Keith was there, but was too busy to be seen, but the secretary assured him they would be sent on board before departure. The Governor's mail was brought on board in a pouch which the captain of the vessel refused to open until later. When the sack was opened there were no letters for the young printer.

Franklin was thus disappointed by the Governor and, had he discussed the project earlier with his friends, he would have learned this was just the outcome he might have expected in any dealings with Keith. So the dreams of setting up as a master printer faded into thin air. But the young printer faced the future undismayed.

THE APPRENTICE

Almost immediately upon his arrival in London, Franklin obtained employment with Samuel Palmer, a well known printer of that city, who was also the author of a history of printing, the first part only of which was ever completed. In Palmer's office, he was assigned to set type on the third edition of Wollaston's "Religion of Nature." Disagreeing personally with certain theses in this work, Franklin wrote in refutation "a little metaphysical piece" called "A Dissertation on Liberty and Necessity, Pleasure and Pain." This brought him favorably to the attention of his employer, but Franklin is said to have endeavored to suppress the edition, regretting its publication on account of the atheistic views expressed. Be that as it may, four copies have survived. Once again, we find the young printer facile with the pen.

After a period of satisfactory service with Palmer, Franklin accepted a job from John Watts at a higher wage. Soon came an opportunity to return to America. Denham, a Quaker merchant whom he had met on the voyage to England and with whom he had kept in touch, was going to Philadelphia with an extensive stock of merchandise, to open a store in that city. He offered Benjamin a position as clerk and bookkeeper at lower wages than he was then drawing as a compositor. At any rate, Franklin accepted, and sailed with Denham on July 23, 1726.

For six months all went well with Franklin in the Denham store. Then both master and clerk fell ill and the former did not recover. The store was taken over by his executors and Franklin had to look for another job.

He tried first to obtain a mercantile position, but finding no opening, became foreman of the shop of Samuel Keimer, his former employer, who now had a force of several men. For the purpose of training these men and bringing the shop up to the best London standards of efficiency, Keimer paid Franklin what was then a comparatively high wage. The job had another element of attractiveness, however, in that the shop was closed Saturdays and Sundays, thus giving Franklin ample opportunity for reading and study.

After the men in the shop began to show the results of training, Keimer started to fret and fume over Franklin's wages, finally demanding a readjustment downward. They finally, however, broke entirely over a trivial incident which is thus described by Franklin:

At length a trifle snapp'd our connections; for, a great noise happening near the Court-House, I put my head out of the window to see what was the matter. Keimer being in the street look'd up and saw me, call'd out to me in a loud voice and angry tone to mind my business, adding some reproachful Words, that nettl'd me the more for their publicity, all the Neighbors who were looking out on the same occasion, being Witnesses how I was treat'd. He came up immediately into the Printing-House, continu'd the Quarrel, high Words pass'd on both sides, he gave me the quarter's Warning we had stipulat'd, expressing a wish that he had not been obliged to so long a Warning. I told him his wish was unnecessary, for I would leave him that instant; and so, taking my Hat, walk'd out of doors, desiring Meredith, whom I saw below, to take care of some things I left, and bring them to my lodgings.

THE APPRENTICE

It was Franklin's idea to return to Boston, but he was stayed in this move by a visit from Hugh Meredith, the fellow printer just mentioned. Meredith proposed they go into business together, suggesting that his father might provide the necessary capital in consideration of Franklin's superior knowledge of the trade, the two partners to have an equal share in the profits. The father consenting, the equipment of a printing office was ordered from London.

There was, of course, a long wait to be contemplated before the equipment could arrive. Andrew Bradford could or would give Franklin no work, but Keimer, having a large job in prospect, soon re-employed him and sent him to Burlington, N. J., to print paper money for the Province of New Jersey.

When the type and press arrived from London, the new firm of Franklin & Meredith began business. Almost immediately they received an order to print forty sheets of a large book on the history of the Quakers, which Samuel Keimer, their former employer, had started but had failed to finish on time. Franklin undertook this at too low a price, as he soon found out, so he resolved to finish a sheet each day, even though this often took him till late at night. On this book he did the composition and Meredith the presswork.

The new firm made a good impression with the accuracy of their typesetting and the quality of their work, this being all the more noteworthy in comparison with the rather slipshod product of their two Philadelphia competitors. On one occasion, Bradford, who was the public printer, printed an address from the House to the Governor in a particularly careless manner. Franklin and Meredith promptly reprinted it accurately and well and sent a copy to each member of the House. Franklin writes: "They were sensible of the difference; it strengthened the hands of our friends in the House, and they voted us their printers for the year ensuing."

The firm facing a financial crisis, Meredith withdrew and Franklin raised from his friends the funds necessary to meet outstanding obligations. From then on the title under which the enterprise operated was "B. Franklin, Printer."

His business prospered. Keimer went into bankruptcy in 1729 and the apprentice who succeeded him soon retired from the field. This left Andrew Bradford as Franklin's sole competitor in Philadelphia, and as Bradford was likewise postmaster, the duties of that office diverted much of his attention from the concerns of printing and publishing.

Franklin now began to think of getting married. One projected match falling through, he renewed his acquaintance with Miss Deborah Read and on September 1, 1730, she became his wife. Concerning his conjugal relations Franklin wrote: "She proved a good and faithful helpmate, assisted me much by attending the Shop; we strove together, and have ever mutually endeavored to make each other happy."

One of Franklin's important ventures in publishing was the issue of the *Pennsylvania Gazette*. When he embarked on the printing business the only newspaper being published in Philadelphia was the *American Weekly Mercury*, founded in 1719 by Andrew Bradford and published regularly thereafter. Though not well edited, this paper had been profitable, and Franklin was sure there was room for a well edited competitive sheet. He confided his ideas to an English journeyman printer, George Webb, who promptly carried the news to Keimer. The latter appropriated the plan and lost no time in getting out the first issue of *The Universal Instructor in all Arts and Sciences; and Pennsylvania Gazette*. This paper limped along to its thirty-ninth number, when it went under, and its good will was purchased for a song by Franklin and Meredith, who abbreviated its title to *The Pennsylvania Gazette*. The paper contained much clever material and proved popular with the citizens.

All through the columns of the *Gazette* ran a vein of good humor which was sadly lacking in most American literature of the period. The editor was always ready with a quip. One correspondent asked: "I am courting a girl I have but little Acquaintance with. How shall I come to a Knowledge of her Faults and whether she has the Virtues I imagine she has." Franklin replied to the lovelorn inquirer: "Commend her among her female Acquaintances."

The second important publishing venture was the one with which Franklin's name is principally associated: *Poor Richard's Almanac*. Few know just how this name was derived.

At that period the annual publication of an almanac was a matter of great commercial importance to the

M. T. CICERO's

CATO MAJOR,

OR HIS

DISCOURSE

OF

OLD-AGE:

With Explanatory NOTES.

PHILADELPHIA:

Printed and Sold by B. FRANKLIN,

MDCCXLIV.

American Colonial printers. An almanac constituted the one item of printing that could be sold in quantity, for every household needed one, the booklet usually hanging by a string from a door jamb, available for ready reference. Almanacs also served as diaries or journals, and many important records have come down to us on the leaves or interleaves. The almanac was therefore a staple, and although a number were already published regularly in Philadelphia, Franklin was sure he could make profitable the issue of still another.

The chief expense of publication was for copy, the "philomaths" who compiled them, charging a stiff fee. Franklin decided to avoid this cost by writing the copy himself and as he did not wish to appear as both author and publisher, decided to issue it under a pseudonym. He borrowed a *nom de plume* from an English almanac by Richard Saunders. The fictitious author of the same name of the American almanac was therefore known as "Poor Richard."

Through the pages of the successive issues appeared the homely wisdom which has crystallized into Poor Richard's philosophy. The success of the publication was very great. The almanac for the first year was twice reprinted to meet the demand. Of the almanac Franklin says: "I reaped considerable profit from it, vending annually near ten thousand."

Franklin summed up the maxims of Poor Richard in the preface to the 1758 almanac. This summary is sometimes known as "Father Abraham's speech to the American People" and sometimes as "The Way to Wealth."

It has been reprinted again and again and translated into dozens of languages. Some sentences in it are better known than any other passages in American literature. We have only to recall:

Early to bed, Early to rise, makes a Man healthy, wealthy and wise.

God helps Them that help Themselves.

Keep thy shop, and thy shop will keep thee.

Diligence is the Mother of Good Luck.

Do you recall the name of that valiant ship of John Paul Jones: the *Bon Homme Richard?* How came it by that name? During the American Revolution, the French government had promised John Paul Jones a new ship. He waited at Brest month after month for it to arrive, but it did not come. He wrote to everyone concerned, from the King of France down, pleading for fulfillment of the promise. Still the ship did not come. One day he read in Poor Richard this maxim: "If you would have your Business done, go; if not, send." He acted on the precept. He went. He got the ship. He named it for his preceptor.

Franklin went to France in 1776 as one of the three commissioners to represent the Colonies. He took up his residence in the village of Passy, now swallowed up in the growth of the French capital. In his house there he established a little private press on which he printed a number of items in blithesome mood, mostly for the entertainment of his friends. Bagatelles, he called them. Until recently most of these were believed to be lost, but an almost complete set is now in the library of a distinguished American collector of Frankliniana.

Benjamin Franklin's history as a patriot statesman and diplomat, as a scientist, and as the most distinguished American citizen of his time, is too well known to require review here. The more we become familiar with his many-sided activities, the more we must come to admire him. There is one point, however, that those of us who are concerned in the making of books will never forget. Though he was a signer of the Declaration of Independence, though he had rendered to his country service of incalculable importance as the ambassador of the Colonies at the Court of France, though he had attained eminence in many branches of science—when he came to write his last will and testament, he began it this way:

"I, Benjamin Franklin, Printer . . ."

XXIII. *Printer—Historian—Educator*

HERE is one other personality which stands out among the printers of the American colonies. The name of Isaiah Thomas is not so well known as it deserves to be, perhaps because no undue political prominence nor picturesque incident has led to its inclusion in the popular accounts of American history. Yet Thomas, a competent and conscientious printer of Boston and Worcester, has rendered service of real importance in the building of these United States.

We are first introduced to young Isaiah at the tender age of six, when he was, in the early part of 1750, apprenticed to Zechariah Fowle, a Boston printer! The lad's indenture to his master contained explicit specifications regarding his education and training, but these were more honored in the breach than the observance for, aside from six weeks' schooling precedent to his apprenticeship, the printing office dictionary and Bible were his only instructors, outside of the trade which he was picking up. But typography, as Dr. Charles L. Nichols, the competent biographer of Isaiah Thomas, points out, exercises in itself an educative force of no mean importance. "One is apt to forget," he writes, "in our day of widespread schools and colleges, that books are not the only means of education; that many men have learned, and still do learn, more by turning the leaves of the book of experience in their chosen trade than they would gain in the formal institutions established for that end. This is particularly true of the art of printing, as the elements of good expression and the thoughts of the best intellects are forced upon the minds of those who work at the composing-case."

Fowle was ignorant and indolent, but was not a hard task-master. Young Thomas, however, took an earnest interest in his work and made some good friends. He is said to have set up his first book at the age of eight and to have engraved some rude illustrations on type metal at the age of thirteen.

After eleven years with Fowle, Thomas left with the intention of going to London, but only got as far as Halifax. In 1770 he was again in Boston and entered into partnership with his former master, the firm undertaking the publication of the *Massachusetts Spy*, the newspaper with which Thomas' name is so intimately associated. The business association not working out well, Thomas bought out his partner and continued the office as his individual enterprise.

The original aim of the *Massachusetts Spy* was to present impartially both sides of the argument between the Royalists and the Colonial patriots, but Thomas soon found that the path of an editor in those days was not strewn with rose leaves. Unless he chose definitely to espouse the Tory cause, he was in constant difficulty. Regardless of difficulties, however, he determined to cast his lot with the patriots.

Some further history is told in vivid form by a letter addressed by Thomas to Daniel Hopkins of the Massachusetts House of Assembly then sitting (precariously) at Watertown. This letter, which has never heretofore been published, is preserved among the Thomas papers in the collection of the American Antiquarian Society at Worcester. It reads:

Worcester, October 2d, 1775.

Sir:

I have the honor of receiving two Letters from you which you sent by order of the Hon. House, desiring me to send no more papers to them on the account of the Colony. In your last, Sir, you mention, "that it is thought highly improper to continue the papers if they were to be paid for, but that it was possible you had been misinformed and that the Printers intended those papers as a present as you 'till of late supposed." I will, agreeable to your request, inform you of the true state of the matter; and humbly submit it to consideration.

A few days before the late memorable Battle of Lexington, I applied at Concord, to a member of the Hon. Delegates, then sitting in Congress, among whom was the Hon. President, to ask their opinion, if it was not proper, as public matters then were, for me to remove my Printing-Office out of Boston, as I found the Liberty of the Press, in that devoted Capitol, daily declining, and myself growing more and more obnoxious to the Enemies of our once happy Constitution, and more particularly to our then *Military Masters,* (some of whom had carried their resentment so far as *Twice* to endeavor to assassinate me, for no other reason, as I humbly conceive, than doing the little in my power, in the way of my Profession towards supporting the Rights and Privileges of my Countrymen.) The Hon. Gentlemen informed me that they thought it was *highly requisite* I should *immediately* remove myself and printing materials out of Boston, as in a few days it might be too late. I accordingly went and, as soon as could be, packed up my Press and Types, and in the dead of night *stole* out of town. Two nights after this the Troops went to Lexington, and the next evening Boston was entirely shut up:—I escaped myself the day of the battle and left every thing my tools excepted behind me. Some of the Delegates, of the Hon. Congress, in a day or two after desired me to get my Press ready for Printing, as they had several things to be done. I informed them of my *unfortunate circumstances at that time*—fleeing from Boston, without any money to purchase stocks (I had just laboured through another year with my paper, and it being the custom for Subscribers to pay yearly, all that I should *at that time have possessed* was then, *and is now,* in the hands of my numerous Subscribers, now scattered throughout the Continent, to the amount of above *Three Thousand Dollars.*) The Hon. Committee of supplies were so kind as to order me paper for a present supply, as something was due me from the Province, and I was requested immediately to continue the publication of the Massachusetts Spy.—In a few days after this, I was ordered with my tools to Concord thither I directly went myself, but before my tools could possibly arrive, the Congress had adjourned to Watertown, and it was told me by several of that Hon. body, that it was best for me, to continue for the present at Worcester.— As none of the Boston Printers then published a paper or were like to do it, myself excepted, I was desired by many Gentlemen, both in the Congress, the different Committees and the army, to forward mine to them; and several who I imagined knew my circumstances, told me I should send a number to the Congress and to the head quarters:—I immediately established a Post to the army to bring me intelligence, and carry my Papers to the Hon. Congress and the Army.—As matters were then in much disorder, together with my residing at such a distance, added to the desire I ever have had of doing my Country *all the service in my power,* I did what my Superiors bade, without ever enquiring—*who was to reward me?*—And as it was thought I could serve my Country best in the capacity of a Printer, I went on publishing my paper, although *at that time,* I had not *200* subscribers exclusive of what I sent to the Hon. Congress, the Committees and Army.—I never meant to make any *great* profit by the Papers I have sent, and have only charged *One Penny* for each paper, which is hardly what it cost me for the stock and Labour, exclusive of *any emolument.* If the Hon. House, after this detail, (for the length of which I humbly crave your forgiveness, as I thought it best to be particular) should think I was *too forward* and do *not merit any pay,* either for the papers, or any part of the Postage, I shall content myself with their determination.

Your Candor, Sir, will excuse the inaccuracies of this letter, wrote in haste, as I have just now an opportunity of transmitting it to you.

I have the honour to be

Your obliged,

humble servant

Isa. Thomas.

P.S. I have sent weekly, since my publishing in this place, 100 papers to the Hon. Congress while they sat, and afterwards the same number to the Hon. House—80 to the Head Quarters in Cambridge—60 to Head Quarters in Roxbury—16 to the Hon. Council—16 to the Committee of Supplies—and 16 to The Committee of Safety—In the whole 288 papers weekly, for which I have only charged 6/- per week for postage.

288 papers, for twenty weeks @ 1d each, and 6/- per week postage.

$£31.10.$

I. T.

Thomas was, therefore, established as a printer at Worcester, and they were not prosperous days. Benjamin Russell, one of his apprentices, tells of sleeping on rags in the garret and eating with his master in the office bread and milk bought by the pennyworth.

After the conclusion of the war the business of Isaiah Thomas began to prosper. Not only did he build up his own office in Worcester to a commanding position, but he financed former apprentices to set up in business in other cities, forming partnerships with them. The firm of Thomas & Andrews in Boston built up an extensive and profitable business—a partnership with Eben T. Andrews. Then there was Thomas & Carlisle at Walpole, N. H., Thomas & Waldo at Brookfield, Mass., Thomas & Tappan at Portsmouth, N. H., Thomas & Merrifield at Windsor, Vt., and Thomas & Tinges (later Thomas & Whipple) at Newburyport, Mass. In 1794 was established in Baltimore the firm of Thomas, Andrews & Butler, and in 1796 in Albany the firm of Thomas, Andrews & Penniman. It is apparent from this that he directed what was almost—for those days—a printing "trust".

[271]

At the home office were printed large editions of school books, notably Perry's Spelling Book, which continued popular for forty years. We learn from the preface to the edition of 1804 that "fourteen editions (constituting at least 300,000 copies) of this useful book have issued from our Press at Worcester." At the same time his Boston office was printing still larger editions of Noah Webster's Spelling Book.

There were also issued many works of political character, Fourth of July orations, and Masonic orations, Thomas being an enthusiastic member of that order. Religious works formed another important class and the Bible was the best seller in this category. This was issued in all formats from folio to duodecimo. The text being so long it was impossible for the average printer to set all the text in type at one time, much less to tie up such an amount of type to keep the job standing. The usual method was to set up several forms and print off the quantity of sheets required for the edition in hand, then distribute the type, print some more forms, and repeat until the book was completed. This involved the expense of composition for each edition printed, as well as the likelihood of errors creeping in each time. Thomas conceived the idea of buying enough type to set the whole Bible at one time and keep it standing, thus making the printing of a new edition a simple matter. It was arranged for the Fry Foundry in London to supply the type and the pages were set in London and shipped to Worcester. The book was known as the "Standing Bible" and was the first edition of the Scriptures published on this plan in America.

The other important publishing enterprise was the issue of the books for children, patterned after those published in London by John Newbery.

Isaiah Thomas rapidly became one of the first citizens of Worcester, and there were few activities of a civic, social, or educational character in which he did not play an important part. Into these activities, however, we cannot enter in detail. There remain for us to discuss two accomplishments which have done much to make his name remembered.

The first was the *History of Printing in America*, which Thomas wrote and published in two volumes in 1810. With the preparation of such a history in view he had been for years corresponding with printers throughout the colonies and collecting and preserving specimens of their newspapers and other products of their presses. Based on this material, supplemented by study of historical records to acquaint himself with the work of American printers of earlier years, he compiled a record which, for the period in which it was written, is in many respects remarkable. But for his interest in the subject, record of the work of many pioneer American printers would have been lost.

While there have been published in recent years several monographs on the work of individual American printers, the Thomas book has remained to the present day the only general work on early printers and printing in the United States.

The first attempt at such a record could not, in the nature of things, be perfect, and no one realized this better than the author. No sooner was the book out than he began making notes and gathering material based on the correspondence he received, in preparation for a revised edition. At the beginning of his notes Thomas wrote: "If I should not live to fulfil my intention, and the books should be printed again, I hope that some friend will do it." This wish was carried out when the American Antiquarian Society, over a half century later, issued a revised edition of his *History of Printing in America.*

This historical interest on the part of Isaiah Thomas led to his second crowning achievement: the foundation of the American Antiquarian Society. To this organization he gave his library, his collection of early American newspapers, and his papers and records. At his death he bequeathed to the Society what was, in those days, a consequential fortune. Since its foundation the American Antiquarian Society has developed a library which constitutes now one of the most important sources for the study of American history anywhere to be found. Unlike many historical societies it is operated on enlightened principles, the aim being to render to students all assistance within its power, and to make its collection not a morgue for mummies but a laboratory for creative work. Perhaps, though, this is only a reflection of the spirit of its founder.

Starting with a good collection of early American newspapers, there have been constant additions of newspapers which constitute, after all, one of the fundamental sources of historical fact. The present librarian, Clarence S. Brigham, has made a census of American newspapers published before 1820 in all the libraries of the country, an invaluable contribution to American bibliography.

Regarding his aims in founding the American Antiquarian Society, his grandson, Judge Benjamin Franklin Thomas, wrote: "In his business as a printer and book seller; in gathering the materials for his history of printing, having a deep personal interest in the annals of a country whose course he had watched, not idly, from colonial dependence to national greatness, a lover and reader of books, touched early by the gentlest of infirmities—bibliomania—he had collected a library especially rich as to the fountains and springs of American history. His researches taught him the value of such a collection; his observation and experience had shown him how quickly the sources of our history were drying up, how rapidly the monuments of the past were crumbling and wasting away. He saw and understood—no man better— from what infinitely varied and minute sources the history of a nation's life was to be drawn; that the only safe rule was to gather up all the fragments, that nothing be lost. It was in the light of this experience and with a view to garner up and preserve the materials of our history that he conceived the plan of the American Antiquarian Society, of making his own library the basis of its collections, and of leaving to the cause of good letters a liberal share of the fortune he had acquired in their service."

Ardent patriot, able typographer, successful printer, erudite historian, founder of a great learned society, respected citizen—such was the career of the lad apprenticed to typesetting at the age of six.

XXIV. *A Typographical Messiah*

BRITISH printing standards were at their worst and ugliness ran riot in the field of typography, when an artistic genius of amazing versatility turned his interests to bookmaking. The results were spectacular. William Morris was, in 1888, a poet and writer of eminence. He had revived fine standards of artistry in the weaving of tapestries, the making of furniture, the printing of cotton and linen, and other crafts. He was a prominent advocate of socialism. He was over fifty—the age at which most men begin to think of retiring—when the design and printing of books came to be one of the major interests in his life. It came about in this wise.

When materials were being gathered for the first Arts and Crafts Exhibition, Morris found that there were none of the books which he had written or with which he had been otherwise concerned which were worthy, on the basis of their artistic merit, of inclusion among the exhibits. Among the arts and crafts in intimate contact with daily life printing was conspicuous as one to which he had made no contribution, and he now became aware of the importance of the omission.

His friend, Emery Walker, delivered at that Exhibition an illustrated lecture on "Printing." In preparing slides for this address, he discussed his material with Morris, and the two made a joint examination of incunabula as well as of manuscripts which might have served the first printers as models. This circumstance served to awaken his latent interest in bookmaking and Morris then resolved to design and cut a fount of type and re-establish long lost standards of craftsmanship in printing.

He thought of this entirely as an enterprise to be undertaken at his own cost and for his own gratification, having no thought of selling any volume or volumes to be produced. Though enthusiastic, his work was deliberate, for he spared no pains to attain perfection. The chronology of his early efforts was:

November, 1888. Emery Walker's lecture.
December, 1889. Type designing begun.
December, 1890. Last punches of the "Golden" type cut.
January, 1891. Proof of specimen page of "Glittering Plain."

The general model for the Golden type was the roman of Jenson and his contemporaries. The best obtainable examples of such letters were enlarged photographically and, with these before him, Morris drew the designs for the new type in large scale. These were next reduced photographically to the size in which the type was to be cut, and studied, in consultation with Emery Walker, in this scale. Each letter was revised and re-studied with unstinted pains and, when the designs met with the approval of the collaborators, they were turned over to

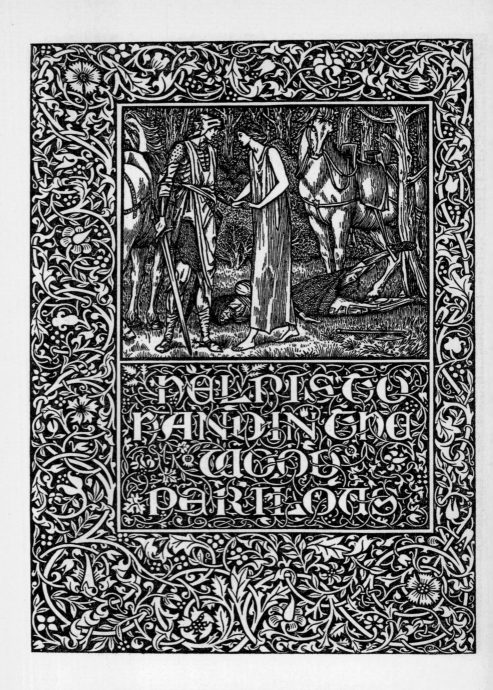

FROM "WELL AT THE WORLD'S END," 1890

THE WELL AT THE WORLD'S END
BOOK I. THE ROAD UNTO LOVE

Chapter I. The Sundering of the Ways

Long AGO there was a little land, over which ruled a regulus or kinglet, who was called King Peter, although his kingdom was but little. He had four sons whose names were Blaise, Hugh, Gregory, and Ralph. Of these Ralph was the youngest whereas he was but of twenty winters & one; and Blaise was the oldest and had seen thirty winters

NOW it came to this at the last, that to these young men the kingdom of their father seemed strait; and they longed to see the ways of other men, and to strive for life. For though they were king's sons, they had but little world's wealth; save and except good meat & drink, and enough or too much thereof; house-room of the best; fair friends to be merry with, and maidens to kiss, and these also as good as might be; freedom withal to come and go as they would; the heavens above them, the earth to bear them up, & the meadows and acres, the woods & the fair streams, & the little hills of Upmeads, for that was the name of their country and the kingdom of King Peter

So having nought but this little they longed for much; and that the more because, king's sons as they were, they had but scant dominion save over their horses & dogs: for the men of that country were stubborn & sturdy vavassors, and might not away with masterful doings, but were like to pay back a blow with a blow, and a foul word with a buffet. So that, all things considered, it was little wonder if King Peter's sons found themselves straitened in their little land: wherein was no great merchant city; nor no mighty castle, or noble abbey of monks: nought but fair little halls of yeomen, with here & there a franklin's court or a shield-knight's manor-house; with many a goodly church, & whiles a house of good canons, who knew not the road to Rome, or how to find the door

FROM "WELL AT THE WORLD'S END," 1890

Edward Prince for rendering in the form of steel punches. After cutting by this expert and sympathetic engraver, the punches were "smoked" and proofs drawn. These were likewise studied, again considered, and the punches altered when alteration was considered necessary by the ultra-exigent critics. The punches were now driven, types cast, and the specimen page above referred to was set up.

The results so far were encouraging to the apprentice printer now past the half century mark. The original idea was that Morris should have a small composing room and the presswork be done outside. As his study of the elements of bookmaking progressed, however, it became evident that all the processes must be done under one roof and one direction. A cottage was taken at Hammersmith, near his residence, and the equipment of a small press installed. So the Kelmscott Press, since become so celebrated in the annals of fine bookmaking, came into being. Its name was derived from Kelmscott Manor, near Lechdale on the Upper Thames, concerning which Morris wrote: "It has come to be the type of the pleasant places of earth, and of the homes of harmless, simple people not overburdened with the intricacies of life; and, as others love the race of man through their lovers or their children, so I love the Earth through that small space of it."

The first book was to have been Caxton's translation of the *Golden Legend* but this proved too lengthy for fairly prompt production, Morris being impatient to produce his first book. So a shorter composition of his own, the *Story of the Glittering Plain*, was selected and put into work at once. In the engraving of a border designed for this book by Morris, the services of William Harcourt Hooper, a retired wood engraver, were enlisted. The relation thus established continued throughout the life of the Press, it being Hooper who rendered on wood the great illustrative work of Sir Edward Burne-Jones and the inimitable book decorations from the hand of the Master of the Press.

The plan was to print twenty copies of the *Glittering Plain* for presentation to Morris' friends, the "adventure" being a purely private and personal one. But an unexpected announcement in the *Athenaeum* regarding the work of the Press gave rise to many urgent requests that copies be made available for purchase. After many misgivings, Morris decided to print what seemed to him the large number of two hundred copies of the *Glittering Plain*, twenty for presentation as originally contemplated, and one hundred and eighty for sale through his regular publishers, Reeves & Turner. The edition was promptly oversubscribed, before any price had been announced. The price when it was fixed represented only actual cost as indeed throughout the history of the Press, the books were sold only at rates calculated to save Morris from being out-of-pocket on the enterprise.

Other books followed and soon Morris projected an edition of Caxton's *Recuyell of the Historyes of Troye*, designing for this the "Troy" type, a letter of strongly Gothic character. A move was made to larger quarters, and a second press installed. On New Year's Day, 1895, still another move was made to afford larger space, and

[281]

Let bounteous Fates your spindles full
Fill, and wind up with whitest wool.
Let them not cut the thread
Of life until ye bid.
May death yet come at last,
And not with desp'rate haste;
But when ye both can say,
Come, let us now away.
Be ye to the barn then borne,
Two, like two ripe shocks of corn.

TO ELECTRA.

'LL come to thee in all those
shapes
As Jove did when he made his
rapes:
Only I'll not appear to thee
As he once did to Semele.
Thunder and lightning I'll lay by
To talk with thee familiarly.
Which done, then quickly we'll undress
To one and th' other's nakedness.
And, ravisht, plunge into the bed,
Bodies and souls commingled,
And kissing, so as none may hear,
We'll weary all the fables there.

50

TWO FACING PAGES IN HERRICK'S POEMS, 1895

HIS PROTESTATION TO PERILLA.

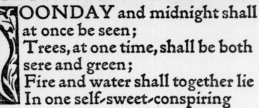OONDAY and midnight shall
at once be seen;
Trees, at one time, shall be both
sere and green;
Fire and water shall together lie
In one self-sweet-conspiring
sympathy;
Summer and winter shall at one time show
Ripe ears of corn, and up to th' ears in snow;.
Seas shall be sandless; fields devoid of grass;
Shapeless the world, as when all chaos was,
Before, my dear Perilla, I will be
False to my vow, or fall away from thee.

TEARS ARE TONGUES.

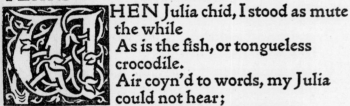HEN Julia chid, I stood as mute
the while
As is the fish, or tongueless
crocodile.
Air coyn'd to words, my Julia
could not hear;
But she could see each eye to stamp a tear:
By which my angry mistress might descry,
Tears are the noble language of the eye.
And when true love of words is destitute,
The eyes by tears speak, while the tongue
is mute.

at this time a third press was added to the equipment. And
the steady flow of fine books, mostly printed in editions
of about three hundred copies, continued to be taken up
by enthusiastic subscribers.

The third type, which was projected for the *Chaucer*,
the majestic volume destined to be the crowning glory of
the Press, and known as the "Chaucer" type, was simply
a re-cutting in smaller size of the Troy type. This type
was first used in the *Recuyell* above referred to, which
was published late in 1892.

The *Works of Geoffrey Chaucer*, which had been projected in 1891, was finally issued in large folio format
in 1896. It included no less than eighty-seven illustrations by Sir Edward Burne-Jones and many elaborate
borders, initial letters and initial words, as well as a decorative title page designed by Morris and engraved on
wood. There were 425 copies on paper issued at £20 and
13 on vellum issued at 120 guineas.

The earliest Kelmscott books were bound in "half
holland," that is board sides with a canvas back, but the
standard form of binding soon established was limp vellum with silk ties.

A word must be said about materials and processes of
production. William Morris felt that much of the degradation of standards in contemporary craftsmanship
was due to mechanical methods designed to promote
speed. In seeking high standards, therefore, he found his
inspiration in the work and methods of the early craftsmen who worked by hand. So his type punches were

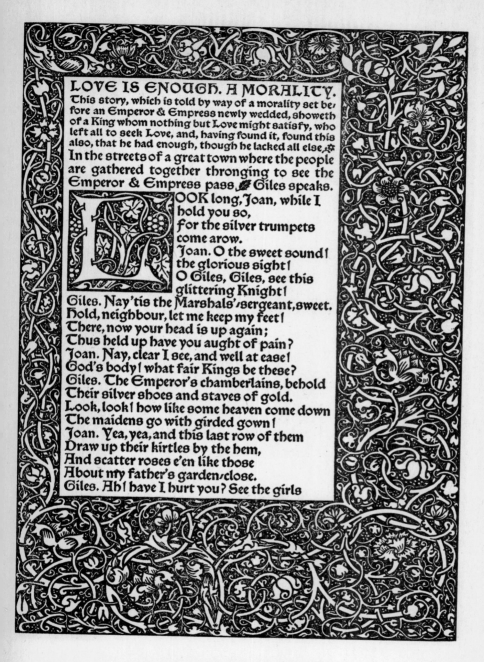

LOVE IS ENOUGH. A MORALITY.

This story, which is told by way of a morality set before an Emperor & Empress newly wedded, showeth of a King whom nothing but Love might satisfy, who left all to seek Love, and, having found it, found this also, that he had enough, though he lacked all else. In the streets of a great town where the people are gathered together thronging to see the Emperor & Empress pass. Giles speaks.

LOOK long, Joan, while I
hold you so,
For the silver trumpets
come arow.
Joan. O the sweet sound!
the glorious sight!
O Giles, Giles, see this
glittering Knight!
Giles. Nay 'tis the Marshals' sergeant, sweet.
Hold, neighbour, let me keep my feet!
There, now your head is up again;
Thus held up have you aught of pain?
Joan. Nay, clear I see, and well at ease!
God's body! what fair Kings be these?
Giles. The Emperor's chamberlains, behold
Their silver shoes and staves of gold.
Look, look! how like some heaven come down
The maidens go with girded gown!
Joan. Yea, yea, and this last row of them
Draw up their kirtles by the hem,
And scatter roses e'en like those
About my father's garden-close.
Giles. Ah! have I hurt you? See the girls

FRONTISPIECE OF "LOVE IS ENOUGH," 1897

produced in exactly the same manner as those produced by Claude Garamond centuries earlier by purely manual processes. Casting, however, was done by machine, as he found he could thus obtain better results than by the ancient method of "pour and jerk" with a hand mould.

With paper, however, he decided that hand fabrication could give him the only satisfactory product and, early in the career of the Kelmscott Press, he was fortunate in enlisting the enthusiastic cooperation of Joseph Batchelor of Little Chart, near Ashford in Kent, a paper-maker of high ideals and great skill. Three papers, each named from a watermark designed by Morris: the Flower, the Perch, and the Apple, were made for the Kelmscott Press at the Batchelor mill.

With vellum for the special copies, a product satisfactory to Morris was practically non-existent. The entire output of one Italian maker had been bespoken by the Vatican. A commercial maker of binding-vellum, drum heads, and so forth, was, however, interested in the quest and, after many experiments, produced an excellent vellum. It was made with special care from the skins of calves not yet six weeks old.

A source of good ink was another worry. The attitude of the English and American makers was, as Sparling tells us: "Take it or leave it; what's good enough for others is good enough for you!" Jaenecke, the celebrated ink-maker of Hanover, Germany, however, offered an ink said to be made of the old-fashioned pure materials, and this satisfied our fastidious printer.

The noteworthy characteristic of the Kelmscott publi-

[287]

cations was their rich decoration, as may be seen from the pages of the books reproduced in the present chapter. The illustrations, most of which were from drawings made originally in pencil by Burne-Jones, translated into line by R. Catterson-Smith, provided with borders by Morris, and the whole rendered in wood by Hooper, were also part of the decoration of the book, all the elements of which were planned in harmony.

The criticism leveled by competent critics against the Kelmscott books holds that the fundamental purpose of books is to be read, and that the Morris books are neither legible in their type matter nor convenient for handling in their format. They contend that they are, first, exercises in decorative design and, secondly, books intended for reading; that even if one endeavors to read them, the mind is distracted from the sense of the author by spots or masses in decoration so insistent in mass and color as to completely overshadow the text.

Even the most enthusiastic admirers of William Morris must admit that there is much of truth in these criticisms. They must further admit that the Kelmscott books are not to be handed to the neophyte in book design as models for him to emulate.

Why is it then that the Kelmscott books mark the beginning of the modern revival of fine printing, for such is unquestionably the case? In the first place, whether easy to read or not, they are things of great beauty and the work of a decorative artist of unparalleled genius. As such they will always be prized by the collectors and amateurs of fine bookmaking to whom they were ad-

[288]

traytour Calcas, whiche was traytour to the Troians,
and said, Ha, A, noble men, what thinke ye to doo
ayenste the comandement of the goddes; haue not
they promisid to yow the victorie, and will ye now
leue hit? Certes that shold be grete folye; take agayn
corage to you & fighte ye agaynst the Troians more
stronglye than ye haue doon to fore, and cesse ye not
tyll ye haue the victorie that the goddes haue promisid to yow. And than with the wordes of the said
Calcas the Grekes toke herte to hem, sayng verily
that they wold mayntene the warre ayenst the Troians whether Achilles helpe hem or not, and that for
him they wold not leue.
Of many bataylles that were made on that one side
and of that other or to their bothe grete domage, and
of certayn triews, & of the deth of the noble Troyllus that Achylles slewe ayenst his promys & drewe
hym at his horse tayll thurgh the oost, & how Achilles slewe the kynge Menon.

HAN the triews of two monethis
were passid they began to fighte
in bat.aylle right sharpely. There
did Troyllus meruaylles of armes
for to avenge the deth of his bro-
der; Dares saith in his book that
he slewe that daye a thousande
knyghtes; and the Grekes fledde
to fore hym and the bataylle endured to the nyght
that departed hem. The day folowyng, the four-
tenth bataylle began harde & sharpe; there dide Dyo-
medes meruaylles of armes, and slewe many Troians

dressed. Never again will be offered them a like orgy of beauty in the embellishment of books.

But in the second place, the Master of the Kelmscott Press is revered by succeeding generations, because he led printers back to the fundamental principles of fine craftsmanship. He taught them that when good types were not available for their use, the remedy was not dumbly to complain but to go forthwith and make them. He demonstrated that fine paper could still be made; that careful presswork was not a lost art. Above all, he taught them that infinite care and patience in the design of the book as a whole, and infinite pains in its execution, are not only still possible, but profitable as well.

Other presses which owed their existence to Morris' example and the success of his pioneer enterprise, printed books conceived in a mood of far greater simplicity, and undoubtedly better exemplars of the principles of fine bookmaking. But they all builded on principles which he evolved single-handed in the midst of difficulties apparently insuperable. And all of them cordially acknowledged him as mentor.

Thus, if I am asked to point to the greatest achievements of William Morris, I will find them in the work of the disciples whom he inspired.

XXV. *The Processes of Bookmaking*

THE first operation in the process of printing is the making of type. And the first step in the making of type is the preparation of the matrix in which the letters are cast. From the earliest stages of the art, and up until a few decades ago, punches were cut by hand on the end of steel billets, from which the temper had been removed to make them easy to work. A so-called counter punch was first cut by hand in the shape of the inside contour of the letter, such as the inside circle of an O. This, after hardening, was driven in the end of the punch, thus depressing the portion corresponding to the inside of the letter, known to typefounders as the "counter." The outside contour of the letter was then made by cutting or filing the outer edges. When the correct shape of the letter was thus punched and engraved on the end of the piece of steel, the latter was hardened by tempering. This completed punch was then driven in copper or some other comparatively soft metal to form the matrix. When this matrix is placed at one end of a

[291]

JOHANN GUTENBERG—THE FIRST BOOKMAKER

FROM AN EARLY WOOD ENGRAVING

rectangular mold, so arranged that the width can be regulated, and molten metal is poured into the mold it is apparent that the resulting cast will bear on one end, in relief, a letter similar in design to that cut on the end of the punch. This cast is a piece of type. Copy is set up for printing by arranging in the proper sequence types of the various letters of the alphabet.

In any book page it is apparent that all the types of all letters are uniform in height, while they vary widely in width, an M, for example, requiring a wider shank or body than an i. The common way of adjusting this width was to "fit" the matrices, that is, to cut them to varying widths, in keeping with the widths of the characters punched in them. When the jaws of the hand mold closed on the matrix, the mold was in consequence set to just the right width for casting the letter in question.

In the latter part of the nineteenth century, an American, Linn Boyd Benton, invented a punch cutting machine which eliminated the laborious and costly process of hand-engraving the steel punch, and made the process of punch production much easier.

Punches so produced were driven in copper the same as before. It was soon found, however, that with this engraving machine, a matrix could be cut in intaglio in the first instance, without going through the intermediate process of punch cutting. It is thus that most type foundry matrices are produced today.

Type casting was for centuries done in a hand mold, the molten metal being dipped from a furnace and as it was poured in the founder gave the mold a quick jerk

[293]

that forced it into the opening and against the face of the matrix. After ejection from the mold the jet, similar to the jets inseparable from all casting operations, was broken off, and the type rubbed and finished by hand. In recent years there have been developed automatic casting machines which perform all the operations of casting and finishing, delivering perfect type at high speed.

Type so cast is laid in a compositor's case, the arrangement of divisions of which is determined—not alphabetically—but according to the frequency with which letters are used. The compartment for the letter e, for example is large and conveniently located, while that for x is smaller and more remote. The first task of the apprentice compositor, therefore, is to learn the "lay" of the case.

With the copy before him and a caseful of type of the desired size the compositor begins to pick piece by piece the letters desired, depositing them in his "stick," a holder which can be set to the width or "measure" of the column or page which he is setting. It is necessary, of course, that the top of the letter be at the top of the line, and to aid the compositor in placing it in the stick in correct position there is a nick or groove in the type to mark the bottom of the letter which he recognizes by sight or touch, as he is carrying the type to the stick. On European type, the nick is at the top.

The letters are set without spacing and, as the line approaches completion and the compositor comes to the end of a word or a suitable point of division within a word, he estimates the space to go between words by dividing the space now left at the end of the line by the number of spacing points in the line. He then begins to drop spaces which he considers to be the right width or less then that width in their proper places. If the line is too tight and the last space will not go in, he has over-estimated, so he removes the spaces already inserted and tries others of lesser width. More often he inserts spaces which he knows are too narrow, and then goes over the line a second time putting in additional thin spaces to make the line come out right. Spacing of hand compo-sition is thus done by the "trial and error" method though a skilful compositor accomplishes it deftly and quickly. It is essential that the lines be spaced to approx-imately uniform tightness for otherwise, when the form of type were locked up for printing the type in some of the lines which were not adequately spaced would fall out. In printers' parlance, the form would not "lift."

Book or magazine composition is first set in "galleys," that is in long columns, so called from the name for the trays on which the type is placed and stored. A first proof, drawn from the newly set type, together with the author's copy is then sent to the proofreader. A "copy holder" reads aloud the original copy indicating all para-graph breaks, punctuation, italicization, and so forth, in a proofroom jargon almost unintelligible to a bystander, while the reader follows the copy in proof. This enables the proofreader not only to correct obvious errors of spelling and punctuation, but also to detect the omis-sion of words or sentences, errors in dates, wrong forms of proper names, and so forth. The errors are marked on the margins of the proof according to a code of symbols, and the proof is then returned to the compositor so that he may make in the type the changes called for by the proofreader. A second proof is then drawn and sent to the proofreader who compares it with the first corrected proof to check whether the changes called for have been accurately made. After this checking, this revised proof goes out to the author.

After the author has read the galley proofs and all desired changes have been made, the type is ready for "make up" into pages. At this point page headings and page numbers are added and when proof next goes out the book is in practically final form for printing.

Setting extensive manuscripts by hand is, of course, a very slow and laborious process and, as the printing industry grew in extent and importance it was only natural that efforts should be made to devise a means of setting type mechanically at greater speed and less cost. This problem intrigued the minds of many and the record of experiments in the field of typesetting machinery is a dizzy one. The failures were myriad. All efforts to take the foundry type used by the compositor and set it up mechanically came to naught. Finally, however, Ottmar Mergenthaler invented a machine that, by the action of a keyboard somewhat resembling that of a typewriter, assembled not type but matrices and, when a whole line was set and spaced, cast this line in one piece of type metal. The machine, which was appropriately called a "linotype" gave a revolutionary impetus to printing. It is often said to have made possible the modern newspaper. As with all new inventions of importance it was expected that thousands of compositors would be thrown out of work. But, again as usual, the industry grew so fast that more men were employed than before.

The next practical machine devised to set type mechanically, was the monotype: the invention of Tolbert Lanston. This machine is made up of two separate units: a keyboard and a caster, and delivers individual types rather than slug lines.

The third device of importance for expediting composition and reducing its cost is one of comparatively recent development: the Ludlow Typograph. In this system matrices are set by hand and type is cast in line form by an exceedingly simple method. The machine was originally devised for setting "display" or advertising composition, one of its principal features being easy change from one type size and style to another. The title page of the present volume is Ludlow-set.

With all three mechanical methods of composition, one great advantage to the printer is unlimited type supply, since he has matrices rather than type. Today machine composition has attained to such high standards of quality that most fine books are now set mechanically. The book set by hand in foundry type is now the rare exception rather than the rule.

When a book has been set—either by hand composition or by machine—and made up into pages it is now ready to print either directly from types or slugs or from plates made from them. The next process is "lock-up," which involves the placing of pages in the position in which they are to print, filling in the spaces between the pages with wood or metal furniture, and locking them in place by the use of "quoins" — wedge-shaped units which are drawn together by the rotary motion of a key engaging in teeth on the facing sides of two quoins. Pulling the angular units together naturally increases the width of the pair and thus exerts pressure to close the form and hold the type in place.

The arrangement of the pages is dependent on two factors: the margins desired on the four sides of the page, and the manner in which the sheet is to be folded. The first printers printed one page of a folio at a time, but they soon learned to print at the same time the two pages of a folio which came on the same side of a sheet. If four leaves of paper were each folded once and gathered together to make a quaternion, or what we should call a "signature" of sixteen pages, it is obvious that pages 1 and 16 would fall on the same side of one sheet and could thus be printed together. If the book were of quarto format and the gathering were to be made up of two sheets folded twice, making again sixteen pages, we find by actually folding two such sheets and numbering the pages, that pages 1, 4, 13, and 16 fall on the same side of one sheet and can thus be printed together. Even this simple combination is difficult to work out without actually folding the paper, and the problems of "imposition" (for such the arrangement of pages in forms is termed) of the modern printer are far more complicated. Modern novels are commonly printed with sixty-four pages in one form on one side of a sheet and sixty-four pages on the other side. A book of 256 pages would therefore be printed in four forms on only two sheets of paper, which in the case of an ordinary novel are 41 by 61 inches in size.

In the imposition of a form the distance between pages determines the relative proportions of the margins, but the general arrangement of the pages is dependent on the working of the folding machine on which the printed sheets are later to be folded, and they must be properly laid for printing in order that the pages, after the sheet is folded, shall follow one another in the proper sequence.

Properly imposed and locked up, a form is now ready to print. The earliest form of hand press used in the early days of printing has already been described. The pressure of a screw was next replaced by pressure through a toggle joint with a spring to return the platen to its original position after the pull was made. The invention of the power press and its development historically makes a fascinating story, but one which we cannot here recount in detail.

Suffice it to say that today most book printing is done on cylinder presses which are known technically as two revolution flat bed presses. The type form is placed on a bed which travels from one end of the press to the other. The ink is carried from a fountain at one end of the press through a series of distributing rollers on to an ink plate which travels with the same motion as the type form. A film of the ink is then taken from the ink plate by the form rollers as it passes under them and immediately thereafter these same rollers contact with the type form, leaving on the type face an even film of ink.

Above this reciprocating bed is a cylinder, the periphery of which revolves at exactly the same speed as the linear travel of the bed. As the bed moves toward the ink fountain end of the press the axle of the cylinder is slightly raised and its surface does not contact with the type, making one revolution without printing. Meantime a sheet of paper has been fed to guides at the top of the cylinder, and half a revolution before the bed reverses its travel grippers on the cylinder seize the edge of the waiting sheet and start to carry it around on its surface. When the front end of the sheet reaches the bottom of the cylinder, which has now returned to a position of contact with the type surface, the bed has started to travel in the other direction, and the paper meets the inked type at the point of impression. As the cylinder completes this revolution the grippers release the sheet which is carried along by tapes and dropped on a delivery board, equipped with joggers which leave the paper in an even pile.

With sheets printed on cylinder presses the next process is folding. This is done on folding machines, the most common type being known as "drop roll" folders. The sheet travels into the folder under the control of tapes and, on reaching a certain point, is struck by a blade at the point where the first fold should be made and carried by this blade in between two knurled rolls which engage the folded edge and carry it through with the fold creased and completed. It is then carried by another set of tapes to the point where it is struck by another blade and the process repeated. When more than four successive folds are required, the sheet is divided in the folder by a slitting roll and each portion folded independently. Another type of folding machine which is tapeless, a development of recent years, is useful for small work or folds of unusual character.

With sheets in folded form the next step is binding. With pamphlets or magazines the signatures are commonly fastened together by wire staples inserted by a stitching machine — with signatures placed one inside the other and "saddle stitched" through the fold or placed one on top of the other in sequence and "side wired" through all of them a short distance from the binding edge. The covers can then be pasted on or included in the stitching.

With the average book, however, the wiring method is not practical. Books of normal size are folded in sixteen or thirty-two page signatures and then gathered in sequence. The principle of hand sewing books will be later described. There are today machines for sewing book signatures. School books are sometimes sewed on tapes but the signatures of the average trade book are usually held together only by the sewing thread. The end leaves, half of which paste down on the inside covers are tipped with a narrow strip of paste to the first and last signatures of the book before they are sewed. After sewing the books are trimmed to the desired size and then rounded and backed. This process gives the curvature to the fore edges of the book and makes a swell at the back which helps the book to fit snugly into its case. To the rounded back of the book is then pasted some crash and paper which extends beyond the back on each side.

Meanwhile the cases are being made. Binder's board, a composition made of fibrous substances or a cheaper substitute known as "chip board" is cut to the right size for the sides. Binder's cloth, if it is to be a cloth bound book, is cut to the appropriate size to cover the boards and paste down on the inside edges. This process is known as case-making and it may be done by hand for small editions or on a case-making machine for quantity work. For board bound books, paper instead of cloth is used to cover the boards.

The cover design is preferably engraved on brass (as is the cover of this volume) and the brass die placed in a stamping press the head of which is heated by electricity or gas flame to keep the brass hot. Gold leaf or some other kind of foil, is either laid on the cover, or pulled over it in roll form, the case in its flat state, already sized, is fed into the press against guides, and the impression applied. Where the hot die strikes the leaf or foil the latter adheres to the cover and the excess material is rubbed off. Many inexpensive books are now stamped with ink, the cases being printed on an ordinary platen press of strong construction, with a heavy ink.

With covers stamped the final process is casing in. This is done by applying paste to the inside of the case and inserting the book. The crash and paper protruding a half inch or so beyond the back are thus pasted to the boards and the end papers which are tipped by a narrow strip of paste to the front and back pages of the book are then pasted over them, thus neatly lining the whole inside area of the case.

Books bound this way in quantity are, technically, not *bound*, but *cased*. In unusual instances, when signatures are sewed on tapes, the ends of the tapes are also pasted to the inside of the case, but the strength of the binding does not exceed the strength of the paste. Though exigent critics may for this reason cavil at modern edition bookbinding the fact is that the average book, so bound, satisfactorily fulfils its purpose. It is only when books so bound are put to extraordinary use — as in the circulation department of a public library — that they fail to measure up to requirements. On the other hand, the mechanical methods make possible the production of books at low cost and so increase their range of circulation and usefulness. According to the law of compensation, for every drawback there is an advantage.

XXVI. *On Type Design*

ACK of good types makes impossible the production of fine books. All the way through this volume, the question of type used by a printer has been inseparable from the discussion of the work of that printer. To produce fine books more is needful than well designed type alone, but good type is a *sine qua non* of good printing.

The first printers gave no thought to type design. Their aim was to produce the equivalent of manuscript books by a quicker and more economical process, and the nearer the printed volumes resembled those turned out from the scriptorium the better. So it was that the types adopted by the fifteenth century printers varied widely, but they varied exactly according to the variation in the prevailing book hand in the countries in which they set to work. The first types did not, therefore, involve a question of type design. They were merely renderings of calligraphic models.

Even Jenson's great roman type followed very closely the humanistic hand then in use by the scribes of northern

Italy. Every art, however, is subject in large degree to the influence of the medium through which it is expressed, and it was inevitable, as typography developed, that the medium of metal cast in the impressions of punches engraved on steel should exert an influence on letter design different from that of a pen-written hand. It is generally considered that Claude Garamond, the French punch-cutter and typefounder of the first half of the sixteenth century, was the first to give conscious expression to this new influence. His types would have been difficult if not impossible to duplicate by penmanship, yet they were perfectly fitted to reproduction in metal and printing on paper. Jenson had given a masterful rendition of the humanistic hand; Garamond had designed type.

The types of Garamond and of his contemporary, Robert Granjon, who cut so many of the italic types of the sixteenth century—exerted a dominating influence over sixteenth and seventeenth century typography. They were the best of the types used by Plantin, and on Garamond's design were based the types in general use by the Elzevirs. (There is a type of modern usage called "Elzevir," but we will look far into the books of the Elzevirs and yet fail to find its model.)

Garamond has been revived in recent years, the first good version being offered by the American Type Founders Company in 1917, which, because of the great enthusiasm with which it was received, was followed promptly by other versions offered by the typesetting machine manufacturers. All these were based on the "Caractères de l'Université," ascribed to Garamond, the punches and matrices of which are one of the principal treasures of the French National Printing Office. It has recently been shown, however, that these types were not those cut by Claude Garamond, but were instead cut by Jean Jannon, a typefounder and printer at Sedan, in the early years of the seventeenth century.

Jannon had been a printer at Paris where he had learned his trade in the Estienne establishment, and where he had been printing with the later forms of types ascribed to Garamond. In 1610, by reason of a sympathy with the cause of Protestantism, he removed to Sedan, where was located a Calvinist Academy, for which he did a certain amount of printing. During the years between 1615 and 1621 he undertook the cutting of a series of types so that he might be equipped to emulate some of the master printers of the sixteenth century, according to his own statement in the preface to his specimen—the first type specimen book known to have been issued in France—but recently discovered and fully reported upon by Mrs. Warde.

Friction which developed a number of years later caused Jannon to leave Sedan and, in 1644, he became associated with a wealthy merchant of Caen in the printing of works in Oriental languages. But they came into conflict with the religious censorship and Jannon's punches and matrices were seized by representatives of the King. These are the "Garamond" types now in the possession of the French National Printing Office.

Always bearing in mind that we are not attempting a

history of printing but only a discussion of the most brilliant achievements in the development of typography which have left a permanent impress on the art, we may say that our next step is to Caslon. Van Dijk, the talented Hollander, had cut many good types. Grandjean at Paris had cut a type which prefigured the "modern" types later destined to sweep "old style" from its pinnacle. But in point of the influence it exerted Caslon's work far overshadowed their accomplishments. As a chapter has already been devoted to the types of William Caslon they need not be further considered here.

Spanish types have always showed a tendency toward calligraphic character, and this is particularly evident in the italic used by Joachim Ibarra of Madrid, the leading Spanish printer of the eighteenth century, in the *Sallust*, generally regarded as his masterpiece. A page from this book is here reproduced.

The "modern" types, with sharp serifs and more pronounced variation in weight between the thick and thin strokes of the letters, as fathered by Baskerville, Didot, and Bodoni, have also been dealt with (Chapter XIX) and require here only a reminder that they stand next in chronological order of development in type design. During the last half of the eighteenth century, however, the characteristics they introduced into type design were carried to extremes and there resulted many types of desperate ugliness.

The typography of this period was, almost without exception, depressing. The only bright point was the "Caslon revival" initiated by the printing in 1844 of

[307]

rebuelta, que perder un punto de su autoridad ; y este mal se havia despues de muchos años buelto a introducir en la Ciudad. Porque haviendose en el consulado de Cneo Pompeyo y Marco Craso restituido a su primèr estado la potestad Tribunicia [49] *: sucedia muchas veces, que ocupando este supremo magistrado gente de poca edad, y de genio ardiente y fogoso, comovian a la plebe acriminando al Senado, y la inflamaban mas con sus liberalidades y promesas ; haciendose ellos por este medio ilustres y poderosos. Oponíaseles con el mayor empeño lo mas-de la Nobleza, socolor de favorecer al Senado ; pero en la realidad por engrandecerse cada uno. Porque, para decirlo breve y claro, quantos en aquel tiempo conturbaron la Republica, afectando deseo del bien comun con coloridos honestos, unos como que defendian los derechos del Pueblo, otros como por sostener la autoridad del Senado : todos ponian su principal mira en hacerse poderosos : ninguno tenia moderacion ni tasa en sus porfias : unos y otros llevaban a sangre y fuego la victoria. Pero despues que Cneo Pom-*

erant, conturbari remp. quam minus valere ipsi malebant. id adeo malum multos post annos in civitatem reverterat. Nam postquam Cn. Pompeio, et M. Crasso coss. tribunitia potestas restituta est; homines adolescentes, summam potestatem nacti, quibus ætas, animusque ferox erat, cœpere, senatum criminando, plebem exagitare ; dein largiundo, atque pollicitando magis incendere ; ita ipsi clari, potentesque fieri. contra eos summa ope nitebatur pleraque nobilitas, senatus sub specie, pro sua magnitudine. namque uti paucis verum absolvam, per illa tempora quicumque rempub. agitavere, honestis nominibus, alii, sicuti jura populi defenderent, pars, quo senatus auctoritas maxuma foret, bonum publicum simulantes, pro sua quisque potentia certabant : neque illis modestia, neque modus con-

G

Lady Willoughby's Diary with types cast in the original Caslon matrices, but the revival was limited in scope.

The next developments of real interest came only with the turn of the twentieth century. We find then dawning a renaissance in typographic appreciation, and the typefounders both served and stimulated the movement by reviving several historic types: first the Bodoni series, then Cloister (a version of Jenson's design), and next Garamond. In addition, an American, Frederic W. Goudy, gave evidence of a native genius for letter design which has seldom been equalled, and he produced in rapid succession a series of types of great beauty. His first type of consequence to be offered commercially was Kennerley, a design clearly original, and embodying some characteristics not before evident in the work of any designer. A proof of Goudy's versatility may be seen in the page from his book *The Alphabet* which is here reproduced, showing his rendition of the letter B in varied forms. This plate also provides an object lesson in the range of type design. All interpretations of the same letter do not look alike, as the U. S. Patent Office holds.

Before discussing further the type production of the past two decades we must consider a new influence in typography with which we have to reckon. The new factor is "display" or advertising composition, in which ideas of varying importance are expressed typographically in types corresponding relatively in weight and size. A glance through newspapers but half a century old will show that display composition is an art of comparatively recent origin. For this the book types—which previously

B corresponds to the second symbol of the Phoenician alphabet, and is the second letter in all European alphabets except those derived from mediaeval Greek —Russian, etc.

INTERPRETATION OF THE LETTER B BY GOUDY

were the only types—would not satisfactorily serve. The first efforts of the typefounders to supply display types were not encouraging. They achieved blackness, but this was concomitant with an ugliness which was staggering.

It was the advertising profession, I believe, which demanded beauty in type as well as emphasis. The demand has been met. Goudy's work alone has exerted a spectacular influence on the appearance of the advertising columns in our magazines and newspapers. And other letter artists have supplemented his work.

We have spoken before of a conscious effort to achieve beauty in letter forms as, in itself, an aim not to be encouraged. But in types for display composition, this rule does not hold good, for in headings containing but twenty letters, for example, set in large type, and surrounded by ample white space, legibility would not be hard to achieve. Conscious and evident beauty in letter forms would in this case be an advantage, for the heading would add to the attractiveness of the advertisement without detracting from the legibility of its brief message. There is, therefore, a decorative quality about most of the new type designs which does not detract from their merit for display composition. But a surprising percentage of them would be most unsuitable for the composition of a book of five hundred pages.

There has been great fertility among type designers in other countries as well as our own. The English founders have been content to limit themselves to the revival of classic faces, but on the Continent invention has run riot.

[311]

Hundreds of new types have been brought out—particularly in Germany—during the past ten years. In the mad effort to achieve originality many weird types have resulted. But among many bad have been a few good. The Cochins and Astrée offered by Peignot in Paris and the roman types designed by Ehmcke, Tiemann, and Koch in Germany are excellent and there are many novelties of much interest, such as the script designed by Lucian Bernhard.

We are living in a productive period so far as type design is concerned. But there are remarkably few candidates of recent birth for election to the ranks of the immortals.

XXVII. *The Title Page*

OR THE FIRST fifteen years of printing there was no such thing as a title page. The scribes had not seen fit to waste a leaf of parchment or paper to communicate facts which could, to their mind, be adequately set forth in three or four lines at the beginning of the text.

This paragraph was frequently in red and usually opened with the word *Incipit*—"here begins," or its equivalent in the vernacular tongues. There were then stated the salient facts regarding the title and authorship of the text which was immediately to follow. The first printers, in this as in other features, followed without question the example set by the scribes. We find, therefore, most of the early printed books starting with an *Incipit*, or *Cy commence*, or *Hier begynneth*.

The early printers printed their text in black and generally left to the hand work of the rubricator the insertion, usually in red, of the headings of chapters or sections, the addition of paragraph marks, and the rather inept practice of marking through capital letters with a pen stroke in red, making them much less readable than if they had been left alone. The rubricator thus quite frequently supplied the *Incipit*, though they were later printed in type.

These introductory paragraphs gave usually the name of the text and the name of the author but never, so far as I recall, the place of printing, the name of the printer, nor the date of issue. They thus performed but one of the functions of the title page with which we are familiar. The most complete statement regarding the authorship, production and place and date of issue was to be found at the end of a volume, in a paragraph which has come to be known as the colophon, a word held by competent authorities to be derived from the Greek word of similar pronunciation defined as "a summit, top, finishing." The first appearance of a printed colophon was in the celebrated Mainz Psalter of 1457 which we have already described.

It will be seen that these terminal paragraphs performed the functions of a title page, but to have to look at the end of a volume for the full title of the book and the name of its author was a clumsy arrangement at best. According to Mr. A. W. Pollard, who has so exhaustively studied the birth pains of the title page, "it is hard to understand how the first printers, who had introduced so mighty a revolution in the art of multiplying books, hesitated for so long over so simple and so sorely needed a reform as the introduction of the title-page."

The first use of a separate page at the beginning of a book to state the title and authorship is found in the

Diß ist die bul zu dutsch die vn=
ser allerheiligster vatter der babst
Pius heruß gesant hait widder
die snoden vngleubigen turcken.

Bul zu dutsch der Babst Pius II printed at Mainz in
1463, and the second in the "Sermon Preachable on the
Feast of the Presentation of the Most Blessed Virgin"
which was printed at Cologne by Arnold ther Hoernen in
1470. This material in the letter was set typographically
like a solid paragraph of text. There was no display.

The first title page with any display arrangement is
a beautiful one indeed. The book was a Calendar, or
Kalendarium, printed by Erhard Ratdolt and his associates at Venice in 1476. Ratdolt was, as we point out
elsewhere, a pioneer in the decoration of books, and in
this volume he does not disappoint his admirers. This
page was printed in two colors, the contents being given
in verse rather than prose, followed by the date of issue,
and the names and native cities of the three men who
collaborated in its production.

The next development is what is known as the "label"
title page, which came into use between 1480 and 1490.
In this form the title of the book in the most abbreviated
possible form was printed at the top of the first leaf of
the book. An early example of such a title page in English occurs in a book printed in London by William
Machlinia soon after 1480:

*A passing gode lityll boke necessarye &
behouefull agenst the Pestilens.*

Interpreting this title phonetically, as is necessary in
reading the English of this period, we find it was a treatise on the plague. Caxton, a near neighbor of Machlinia, did not follow this example, but printed his state-

Lalettera dellifole che ha trouato nuouamente il Re difpigna.

TITLE PAGE OF THE COLUMBUS LETTER

ment of authorship, title, date, and so forth, at the beginning or end of prologue, table of contents, text, or epilogue—anywhere in fact except the obvious place, the first page of the volume, which he left blank.

It was customary with early printed books of importance to have the first page of text embellished with a border in florid and colorful style, supplied by the illuminators. In the development of the art of printing, less and less was left to be supplied by hand. We may, therefore, expect to find books in which such decoration or illustration is printed. An example of this is the *Exposition of the Lamentations of Jeremiah*, printed in Latin by Theodoric Rood at Oxford in 1482. To some such pages illustrations were also added, a charming example being the *Tramisonda istoriata ne la quale si contiene nobilissime battaglie con la vita e morte di Rinaldo*, printed at Venice in 1494. Here decoration and illustration make such inroads on space as to leave room for but eight lines of text.

The next development in the evolution of the title page was a page of illustration of the subject matter of the book, with a short title such as was used on the "label" title pages. An example of such a page (reproduced on page 317) which should have a special interest for American readers, represents the voyage of Columbus in his discovery of the New World. Note the great distance between Spain and the mainland of North America.

An unique form of title page had its origin in France. This consisted of an exaggerated historiated initial, usually the *L* of the French definite article, beginning a title

a mer des
hystoires

A TITLE PAGE USED BY ANTOINE VERARD

set in type of modest size. An impressive example of such a page, in Antoine Verard's *Mer des Hystories* is here shown.

We next encounter pages in which the title of the book is accompanied by a printer's mark, and there was added also, in some instances, an independent woodcut illustration. The former style, as followed by Badius of Paris in 1522 is represented by the title page shown opposite, bearing his celebrated device of a printing press.

Aldus used pages with the title simply set and embellished with his celebrated anchor device. Sometimes he elaborated on the title by giving a brief of the contents of the volume.

In French Books of Hours, title pages follow a style of their own, and are discussed in our chapter on the golden age of typography.

In the second quarter of the sixteenth century we find title pages complete as we know them now. They were especially well set by Robert Estienne, the distinguished Parisian printer.

Once universally adopted as an essential feature of a book, the title page has never been displaced, and never will be. The manner of setting them has varied with different periods and printers, and a good many are reproduced throughout this volume, in discussing the work of eminent printers. The most common fault has been the attempt to list the whole contents of the book on the title page, crowding it to a point not only of ugliness but also of illegibility. The finest printers have always set the simplest pages. The best practice calls for the use of

EPISTOLAE

Gullielmi Budęi, Secretarii Regii,
Posteriores.

Prelum
Ascēsianū

Venundantur Iodoco Badio, cum gratia
& priuilegio in triennium.

THE BADIUS PRINTERS' MARK ON A TITLE PAGE, 1522

TITLE PAGE OF A SIMON VOSTRE BOOK OF HOURS

the fewest possible different sizes of type, consistent with proper display emphasis of the main title. In architecture the maximum weight is at the base, but in a title page the predominant weight is at the top. The principal words in the title should not be divided, and the typography should be planned to meet the requirement.

The prevailing usage is to set title pages in capitals and it is, on the whole, easier to work out an acceptable page with letters which are all the same height than with capitals and lower case. But, as we point out elsewhere, the latter are decidedly more legible, and should be used in cases where they appear to advantage. Simplicity, the right proportional relation between the several blocks of type, and the correct positioning of these blocks on the page, are the main desiderata in title page composition. With books of appropriate character some border or decoration in a mood of restraint is a welcome addition.

The title page is given thoughtful consideration by good book printers, and rightly. For it is, as Mr. Sargent has so aptly termed it, "the door to the book" and it should invite to entrance the visitor approaching the threshold.

XXVIII. *Book Illustration*

T IS a well-established historical fact that men had learned to print pictures before they learned to print books. Our chapters on the block book and on the invention of printing have already explained this seeming paradox so it is not necessary to repeat here the story of the earliest wood-block illustrations. One thing, however, in connection with the work of these primitive craftsmen must not be forgotten as we trace the achievements of their successors, and that is the somewhat astounding fact that in book illustration black and white is a much later development than is color work. But this statement is not to be misunderstood as saying that the earliest printed pictures were produced in color by typographical methods. This was not at all the case. The first printed book illustrations were printed in black and white but no one regarded them as finished pictures. To complete them a miniaturist or illuminator was expected to go over them completely with various colored pigments and perhaps gold foil in such a way as completely to hide all traces of guide to simplify the artist's task. In practice,

of course, not every purchaser could afford to employ the services of an expert book artist; many persons who bought early printed books containing pictures had to be content with having them daubed over with transparent colors by unskilled hands or else to leave them in what was conceived as an imperfect state. And so it came to pass, with the prodigious multiplication of printed books that men's eyes grew accustomed to seeing and even to admiring pictures which were no more than crude outlines of black ink on white paper. Concurrent with the growth of this public appreciation of book-illustration in a brand new medium, there was an attempt on the part of the bookmakers themselves to elaborate and refine this new process. And so we find very early a definite tendency to add detail to the outline figures by multiplication of the printed lines. Just as a draughtsman would interpret gradations of tone and color contrast by pencil strokes so the wood block cutters introduced more and more printing lines into his carved block.

Thus the early history of book-illustration is, in its technical aspect at least, the development of an ever finer line texture and a closer and closer approximation to the perfect facsimile reproduction of a pen-drawing. That such a development involved grave dangers is at once apparent; when a craftsman accepts as his ideal a slavish copying from a model his work is degraded hopelessly. The fine savor of original creation is completely lost. It is no wonder, therefore, that, in the main, the history of printed pictures is a tale of recurrent degeneration from high standards set by successive geniuses who from time to time brushed aside impatiently complicated technique for new and simpler methods.

The earliest medium for the production of printed pictures was the wood block. This, carved down so as to leave in relief only what it was desired to produce in black upon the paper, gave a printing surface which could be locked in the press, inked, and printed as simply as an equivalent area of type. But wood is at once softer and has a coarser grain than metal. If it is cut in too fine a line repeated impressions are bound to crush or break it. We, therefore, find very early an attempt to substitute for wood carved metal but this, being harder to carve, had distinct limitations.

The next attempt to overcome the deficiencies of wood was the introduction of plate engraving. In this process the printing lines are incised, not elevated above the non-printing surface. This allowed an almost infinitely refined texture and at the same time reduced vastly the amount of drudgery required in preparation. Indeed, with this method it was no unusual thing for the designing artist himself to engrave the plate, whether it was cut with a graver or etched with acid. But these advantages were more than offset by new difficulties in printing. A plate engraving cannot be produced on the same press or at the same time with type impressions. After inking, the non-printing surface must be wiped clean in such a way as to leave every incised line filled with ink, and the paper to draw this from these hollows must be impacted with many times greater pressure than is necessary for the ordinary printing press. Furthermore, even

POLIPHILO QVIVI NARRA, CHE GLI PARVE AN-
CORA DI DORMIRE, ET ALTRONDE IN SOMNO
RITROVARSE IN VNA CONVALLE, LA QVALE NEL
FINE ERA SERATA DE VNA MIRABILE CLAVSVRA
CVM VNA PORTENTOSA PYRAMIDE, DE ADMI-
RATIONE DIGNA, ET VNO EXCELSO OBELISCO DE
SOPRA. LA QVALE CVM DILIGENTIA ET PIACERE
SVBTILMENTE LA CONSIDEROE.

L A SPAVENTEVOLE SILVA, ET CONSTI-
pato Nemore euaso, & gli primi altri lochi per el dolce
somno che se hauea per le fesse & prosternate mébre dif-
fuso relicti, me ritrouai di nouo in uno piu delectabile
sito assai piu che el præcedente. Elquale non era de mon-
ti horridi, & crepidinose rupe intorniato, ne falcato di
strumosi iugi. Ma compositamente de grate montagniole di non tro-
po altecia. Siluose di giouani quercioli, di roburi, fraxini & Carpi-
ni, & di frondosi Esculi, & Ilice, & di teneri Coryli, & di Alni, & di Ti-
lie, & di Opio, & de infructuosi Oleastri, disposti secondo laspecto de
gli arboriferi Colli. Et giu al piano erano grate siluule di altri siluatici

with the added labor of double printing the effect of plate engraving is quite different from that produced by relief printing, and it is never congruent with genuine typographic work.

Only these two processes, carved relief blocks and incised plate engravings, were used in the production of book illustration during the first three and a half centuries of European printing, and there was no essential improvement in either process between the years 1500 and 1780. At the latter date an Englishman, Thomas Bewick, discovered that many of the difficulties of wood block work could be obviated if one used an end grain surface. Up to that time wood-engravers had worked only on side grain, with the lines of cleavage parallel to the printing face. By cutting his blocks across the log instead of lengthwise Bewick found it possible to produce as fine and as true a line as the lightest copper plate engraving. A long line of his disciples, in Britain, America, and Germany carried on Bewick's technique in a crescendo of achievement down to the eighteen nineties.

In the meantime a German, Senefelder, had introduced a third and entirely new method of picture printing. He used neither a raised nor a sunken printing surface but a perfectly flat plane on which the ink was distributed to the desired blacks and withheld from the desired whites by the antipathies of oil and water. Because the first plates used for this process were slabs of a fine grained limestone it is still known as lithography. The results produced by this new method were entirely satisfactory for certain purposes and it is still used widely for certain classes of work. Like plate engraving this process is simple and direct enough for original artists to produce the printing element themselves, but it has the same disadvantage of requiring a special press and a separate impression.

Along with the vast discoveries in the natural sciences during the nineteenth century, various means were devised for producing printing surfaces by photo-mechanical methods. With the advent of photography the exact reproduction of visual objects became a simple and speedy process. Today by purely physical and chemical manipulation the color pictures are produced, though usually it must be confessed, with artistic value in inverse proportion to the degree in which mechanical devices have been substituted for the human eye and hand.

Since nearly every chapter of this volume involves a discussion of illustrated books the reader will be able, with this general outline of the course of development, to reconstruct for himself the details of the history of book illustration. We shall attempt to give him here only a few of the outstanding names.

Of the illustrated books of the fifteenth century German are the most numerous and Italian the finest. France also made a notable contribution more resembling Italian than German work but marked by distinctive national characteristics of its own. Of all the books produced on German soil during this period the most famous are the *Schatzbehalter*, the *Nürnberg Chronicle*, and the *Breydenbach*. These are all done in a finished technique which, while it accomplishes much in elaboration, has lost something of the charm one finds in such illustrations as those produced at Augsburg in the seventies.

In Italy the best illustrated book of this century is undoubtedly the *Hypnerotomachia*, though here again a more conscious artistry has nothing of the direct effectiveness shown in such earlier and more primitive work as the Florentine editions of Savonarola's tracts.

The blocks of the *Hypnerotomachia*, however, provide an excellent example of observance of one of the cardinal principles of good book illustration: that the plates should key in color and weight of line with the color and weight of the type, so that both form a harmonious ensemble.

All these books were ornamented with the wood cut. Indeed only two attempts were made during this century to apply plate engraving to book decoration: the *Dante* printed at Florence in 1481, and a Roman edition of Ptolemy's *Geography*.

During the sixteenth century both methods were employed and carried to a high standard of excellence. Germany still specialized on the wood block. The *Thewerdanck* of 1517 is probably the finest book ever achieved by that nation in the point of successful welding of decoration and typography in a unified design. In Italy social and civic degeneration was reflected in a sad retrogression from its former high typographical standards. France, on the other hand, had forged ahead and in the work of Geofroy Tory equalled or even surpassed the achievement of the *Thewerdanck* designs.

From this point on there was a strong tendency to in-

81

MEydelhart was vol böser list
    Dann Er aus vil vrsachen wist
  Wurd Er wider dem Tewren mann
  Geleich ein anndre schalckheit tan
  So mocht Ers newr böser machen
  Darumb Er still stund in sachen
  Ein klein zeit bis Er kunndt ermessen
  Das Tewrdannck des het vergessen

HOW KING
MARKE FOVND
SIR TRISTRAM

ILLUSTRATION BY AUBREY BEARDSLEY IN "MORTE D'ARTHUR,"
LONDON, 1893-1894

crease the use of plate engraving in book production. Even such artists as Dürer and Holbein were drafted to this service. France, however, has the palm for achievements in this method. There Cochin, Gravelot, and Eisen in the late eighteenth century carried line engraving to a standard that will probably never be surpassed.

In our own period and in English speaking lands book illustration has again been restored to its place as one of the fine arts. William Morris led the way and by his example inspired others to even greater achievements than he himself could attain. To name but a few of the host, there are Aubrey Beardsley, the Englishman, as was Walter Crane, with Pyle and Pennell, Ruzicka and Lewis, our own countrymen. And in France also some distinguished work has been done in recent years, the illustrations in fine books receiving much more attention than the typography. The multicolor wood engravings by Schmied, for example, are among the finest of their kind.

XXIX. *The Decoration of Books*

URING our historical review of the work of outstanding printers we have heard a good deal about book decoration. We will see that this decoration usually falls within one or another of the following classes: (1) initial letters; (2) page borders; (3) headbands and tailpieces.

The earliest decorative initials known appeared in the Mainz indulgences of 1454 and 1455, but they were plain letters cut on metal, in which decorative element was modest indeed. The next instance of printed book decoration is, of course, very important: the magnificent initials in two colors in the Fust and Schoeffer *Psalter* of 1457, which supplied in finished form what most of the fifteenth century printers left space for, to be filled in by the illuminators. Though these were repeated in later editions of the same book, printed initials were not used in other books printed by the same firm. It is thought these Psalter initials were cut on metal in two parts which were inked separately, put together again, and printed in one impression.

[334]

BOOK DECORATION

Decorative woodcut initials made their appearance in the books of three different printers in the same year: 1472, being used by Gunther Zainer and Johann Bämler at Augsburg and by Johann Koelhoff at Cologne. In Gunther Zainer's Bible of 1477, appear pictorial initials, which are here used for the first time.

It will be recalled that Erhard Ratdolt at Venice used the first decorative title page in 1476 and in that year and the one immediately succeeding there appeared in his books woodcut initials and borders which were so fine that they still serve as models to be copied by printers seeking to embellish their work. His decorative blocks were undoubtedly designed by his partner Bernhard Maler or Pictor (painter), whose name denotes his particular talent. Ratdolt was a pioneer in book decoration and his work has never been much improved upon.

The motifs in Ratdolt's decoration were wholly floral. Other printers made use of human figures and animals, urns and trophies, jardinieres and birds, with borders or wreaths of floral character. At Lyons grotesques and fabulous animals appear in the backgrounds. A characteristic initial used at Paris is represented by the calligraphic L used so often in one form or another on title pages (see page 319).

Much of the best printing ability in the fifteenth century was expended in the production of liturgical books. The high point in the missals was the Canon of the Mass which begins, as we may recall, *Te igitur clementissime pater*, calling for an initial T which was always particularly splendid.

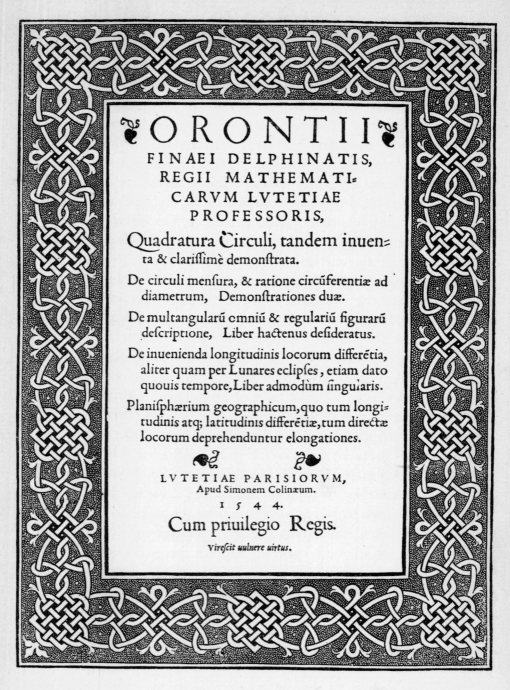

❧ ORONTII ❧

FINAEI DELPHINATIS,
REGII MATHEMATI=
CARVM LVTETIAE
PROFESSORIS,

Quadratura Circuli, tandem inuen=
ta & clarissimè demonstrata.

De circuli mensura, & ratione circūferentiæ ad
diametrum, Demonstrationes duæ.

De multangularū omniū & regulariū figurarū
descriptione, Liber hactenus desideratus.

De inuenienda longitudinis locorum differētia,
aliter quam per Lunares eclipses, etiam dato
quouis tempore, Liber admodùm singularis.

Planisphærium geographicum, quo tum longi=
tudinis atq; latitudinis differētiæ, tum directæ
locorum deprehenduntur elongationes.

LVTETIAE PARISIORVM,
Apud Simonem Colinæum.

1544.

Cum priuilegio Regis.

Virescit uulnere uirtus.

BORDER DESIGN USED BY COLINES, 1544

BOOK DECORATION

In the early sixteenth century great artists like Albrecht Dürer and Hans Holbein turned their talents occasionally to book decoration. In France, also, two names loom large. One was that of Geofroy Tory whose work we have already considered. His initial letters and page borders have never been surpassed. The other was that of Bernard Salomon, *le petit Bernard*, who executed for de Tournes of Lyons, fine borders in arabesque style which have served many printers of later generations as models.

Headbands and tailpieces appeared in the sixteenth century and perhaps earlier, some of the finest ever produced being used by the Estiennes and their contemporaries during the "Golden Age" of typography. An example of a headband of this period as used by Bruce Rogers in *The Centaur* is reproduced on page 369.

Decorative effects could be obtained by another method than engraving — by the assembly of decorative units cast like type. In 1924 I called attention for the first time to the earliest known use of such ornaments by G. and A. Alvise at Treviso in 1471. From this date on they grew in popularity and reached a high point of development in England, strange to say, during the sixteenth century. A typical example of their use for a title page border is shown on the following page.

Woodcut borders for title pages were popular through the sixteenth, seventeenth, and eighteenth centuries, but generalizing to some extent, the earlier were the better. Later on the border overshadowed the title page of the book, almost to the point of extinction.

[337]

DISERTISSIMI
VIRI ROGERI
ASCHAMI ANGLI,
REGIÆ OLIM MAIESTA-
TI A LATINIS EPISTOLIS,
familiarium Epistolarum libri
tres, magna orationis elegantia cōscripti, nunc
denuò emendati
& aucti.

QVIBVS ADIVNCTVS EST
COMMENDATITIARVM, PETI-
toriarum, & aliarum huius generis si-
milium Epistolarum, ad alios Princi-
pes & Magnates conscripta-
rum, Liber vnus.

HVC ACCESSERVNT PAV-
ca quædam eiusdem R. A. Poemata,

ITEM ORATIO E. G. DE VITA
& obitu R. A. & eius dictionis elegantia.

LONDINI.
℣ Pro Francisco Coldocko,
ANNO. 1581.

TITLE WITH BORDER OF TYPE ORNAMENTS

BOOK DECORATION

After leaving the sixteenth century there is a long jump to the next distinguished accomplishment in book decoration—to William Morris, whose work has already been described and illustrated. Even his borders and initials were strongly reminiscent of Ratdolt.

All through the history of book decoration the striking point is that the motifs remain almost entirely floral, with the exception of a few arabesques and entrelacs. The modern decorative artists are now introducing some new elements of decoration which afford at least a welcome change. Whether any of them will win permanent adoption into the armory of bookmaking we cannot yet predict. What we can say is that the best of our contemporary work is still highly traditional in its inspiration.

XXX. *The Art of Bookbinding*

THE production of texts designed for continued use and preservation made necessary some covering which would protect them yet, at the same time, permit convenient consultation or reading. The form of this covering was of course determined, to a large extent, by the form of the book. Assyrian clay tablets of the eighth century B. C., were enclosed in cases stamped with a short title. Egyptian papyrus rolls were enclosed in wooden cases.

At Pompeii were found "diptychs" which consisted of two wooden leaves bound together at one side by leather thongs which served as hinges—in other words, in the form of a double photograph frame made for traveling. The facing sides were hollowed out and filled with wax, on which the text was scratched with a stylus. One such diptych, recording a financial transaction, is dated A. D. 55, and is the oldest existing Latin manuscript. During the next few centuries, some extremely handsome diptychs for presentation to personages of importance were made of ivory and elaborately carved.

The usual form of writing a papyrus, in columns with the writing itself parallel to the length of the roll, made it possible to fold the roll accordion fashion, with the folds coming in the spaces between the columns. Since the reverse side of the roll was blank, this method brought blank sides of the resulting pages facing each other, and printed sides facing each other, presenting an ensemble much resembling a modern book. When we paste the blank sides together or pierce the book at one side and fasten it together with ties, the resemblance becomes even more marked. Oriental books are still bound in this way.

With the coming of paper and parchment, the book made up of folded sheets became more logical, and we find this type of book from the fifth century on. The sheets were folded once, and four or more of these folded sheets were arranged inside of one another so as to make what is known as a gathering or quire. A stitch through the fold would thus hold all of them. When the practice arose of sewing a number of these gatherings, with the threads passed around two or more thongs of leather at the back of the book, the essentials of modern binding came into being.

These thongs at the back needed protection, and the first move was to paste over them a covering of leather. But the vellum leaves would then tend to curl and, in use, the pages would become worn at the corners. The obvious remedy was to apply thin wooden boards front and back and by lacing into them the protruding ends of the thongs on which the book was sewed, a hinged joint was conveniently obtained.

[341]

The rough leather then pasted on the back came over a short ways on the boards in order to give a neat finish. The next step was to extend this leather to cover the whole area of the boards. On books of value, on the text of which had been expended much pains to make them beautiful, it was only natural to make the further effort to decorate the leather covered sides of the binding.

In the tenth century Suidas gives us confirmation in picturesque form of the use of leather in the binding of books. He tells us that the Golden Fleece, which was the object of search by Jason and the Argonauts, was really a book bound in sheepskin which taught the art of making gold. There is a still earlier reference (450 A. D.) to large square books of the Byzantine emperor's instructions, bound in red, blue, or yellow leather, bearing a gilt or painted portrait of the emperor.

The earliest form of embellishment of bindings invoked the art of the goldsmith and jeweler. Bindings covered with gold, silver, and precious stones were probably Byzantine in origin but were introduced farther westward earlier than the sixth century. Seneca and other Roman philosophers criticized the extravagant ornamentation of books. In this connection may be recalled the plaint of St. Jerome: "Your books are covered with precious stones, and Christ died naked before the door of His temple."

The oldest binding now extant is on a copy of the Scriptures in Greek bound in two plates of gold bearing a cross set with precious stones and cameos, which was given by the Queen of the Lombards to the Basilica of

St. John the Baptist at Monza at the end of the sixth century. A binding of the seventh century, of boards covered with velvet and embellished with silver, is preserved in the Laurentian Library at Florence.

It will be recalled that there was a brilliant school of manuscript writing and illumination in Ireland in the fifth, sixth, and seventh centuries (see page 36). Most of the bindings of this period, were, however, quite plain, for the ecclesiastics using the books had to travel in sparsely settled territory and it was needful for the books to be light in weight and to lack obvious attraction for bandits. For books presented to churches, however, richly decorated "book shrines" were provided.

Though most of the Irish bindings were plain, some elaborate work was done. Dagaeus, a monk of the sixth century, is reported to have been adept with both leather and metal. The Molaise Gospels of the eleventh century were bound in bronze plates with silver and gold ornaments riveted on.

In England the monastic organizations became interested in bookbinding, Durham and Winchester being the centers where the finest work was done. As a matter of fact, in the thirteenth century, the English binders gained supremacy over their Continental confrères.

The earliest decoration of leather bindings (without the aid of the goldsmith) was by means of points and lines impressed or stamped into the leather. The next development, which probably took place from the tenth to the twelfth century, was the cutting of special stamps or punches in iron or some other metal, with which to decorate the leather "in blind," that is, without the use of gold leaf which had not yet come into use. Most of these "tools" were cut in intaglio so that impressions from them gave a cameo effect. With a limited number of these tools it is apparent that a wide variety of combination and arrangement could be achieved. Incidentally such tools, though now in relief rather than intaglio, constitute the equipment of the fine binder of today. These punches had still another great advantage in that they could be stamped hot, making a deeper impression, changing slightly the color of the leather, and giving, all in all, a more effective result.

Manuscripts were costly and it had been thought appropriate to enshrine them in costly bindings. But with the invention of printing at the midpoint of the fifteenth century, a new situation confronted the binders. Books were produced in quantity. Some were of course handsome and important and demanded a fine dress, but many were cheap and of small importance comparatively and required only the most utilitarian form of binding. The ordinary run of books were thus bound in sheep, calf, and goatskin and stamped in blind.

The next great forward step in the art of bookbinding was the introduction of gold tooling. In Europe this appeared first in Italy, toward the end of the fifteenth century, coming almost certainly from an Eastern source. In gold tooling an adhesive size is first applied to the leather, then sheets of gold leaf beaten exceedingly thin are laid down. The heated tools are next pressed down where it is desired to have the decoration appear, and where the heat and pressure are applied, the gold leaf adheres to the leather, the excess gold not so impressed being afterwards rubbed off. The affinity of gold, properly applied, for the leather is remarkable, and once on will practically never come off.

Aldus Manutius, in the bindery operated in conjunction with his printing office, was the first to make use of gold tooling in an extensive way. From his use of it the decorative unit known as the Aldine leaf is named. Arabesques and entrelacs were also used on his bindings.

Books with metal clasps and bosses were manifestly not designed to be kept standing in bookshelves. They were laid singly on a shelf or kept on a reading desk or lectern, to which they were sometimes chained. Backs of early printed books were never decorated—not even the title appeared on them. Quite often this was lettered on the fore-edges of the volume. When books became more utilitarian and had to take their place with other books on shelves any protruding elements had, of necessity, to be eliminated.

The influence of Jean Grolier in the early sixteenth century made a profound impression on bookbinding design. The typical binding executed for Grolier was made up of interlaced strapwork in symmetrical geometric design, with incidental decoration of leaves and florets. The bindings done for the Italian collector Thomas Maioli at about the same period were similar in general character and probably finer than those of Grolier. The cover design of the present volume is a typical Maioli pattern.

Persian and Arabic influence is clearly discernible in

the development of a style known as "Venetian" bindings in the early years of the sixteenth century. Dutton thus describes the manner of their making. "The board was coated with a paper composition and the center and corners were then cut out in the desired shapes. Then the entire board, both the recessed panels and the upper ground, was covered with a thinly pared leather which took the form of the cut-out recesses. This leather was then coated with a colored lacquer and lastly decorated and painted with arabesques in gold."

All color on bindings up to this time had been applied by paint or lacquer, but the Venetian binders soon adopted the Oriental practice of superimposing leathers of different colors, a practice known as inlaying, and one still in use today for imparting color and brilliance to fine bindings.

From this point on, we can only touch briefly on the work of several of the most important binders, who have left a definite impress on binding style. Nicholas Eve was at work in France late in the sixteenth century. The bindings done under his supervision are characterized by the use of all-over or diaper patterns of small units, such as fleurs-de-lis, tears, or two lambdas (representing the initials of Louise de Lorraine, wife of Henri III). His name is also associated with the so-called "fanfare" style, in which the space was broken up into geometric compartments which were filled in with shaded or azured tools of a floral character.

Clovis Eve followed in the post of "binder to the

King" after the decease of his brother Nicholas, but there is little specific evidence regarding bindings which he executed.

Our next figure of note is a mysterious personage: Le Gascon. There has been some question as to whether such a person ever existed, but Thoinan has proved, by documentary evidence, that such a binder and gilder was at work in Paris in the second quarter of the seventeenth century and that his work was well regarded.

At any rate a very definite style of binding is named for him—a style in which the lines of the decoration are not continuous, but are broken up into a succession of fine dots. In fact all the elements are rendered as fine dots rather than solids, by the use of what are known to binders as "pin-head" tools. This made for a style of great delicacy.

Antoine Michel Padeloup, referred to as Padeloup le jeune, was the most renowned member of a large family of binders. He worked in Paris during the early part of the eighteenth century, his style being characterized by lace pattern borders of great luxuriance.

Nicolas Denis Derome was the most brilliant of another large family of binders which contributed to the art no less than eighteen members by the name of Derome. Many of Derome's bindings resemble Padeloup's and it is possible that he may have taken over the business and the tools of the latter. Derome is best known, however, for his dentelle borders—borders with salients toward the center. In these he introduced a small bird with outstretched wings. He also drew on the grammar of ornament of other crafts for other dentelle designs.

Passing now to England, we find the name of Thomas Berthelet first on the list of eminent binders. It was he who introduced into England the art of gold tooling. In addition to his binding activities he was named King's Printer in 1530. Many of his designs were executed in gold on white leather or vellum, the style being copied from Continental binders. Some of his bills which have come down to us describe a volume "bounde after the Italian fascion" or "after the fascion of Venice." One of his books bound for Edward VI shows the first use in England of a decorative doublure—that is, the lining or facing of the inner side of the cover. In this instance, the inside cover is lined with calf and decorated with gold and colors.

The next English binder of eminence was Samuel Mearne who in 1660 became bookbinder to the King. His name is associated with the "cottage pattern" in binding, so called because of the pent-like arrangement of lines at the top, bottom, and sides. Sprays and branches, combined with lacework, fill in the spaces, or small tools are used in fan ornament. Though the craftsmanship is not of the highest order, the bindings have much of charm.

Until the time of Roger Payne, there was no notable change of style in English binding. His tools, which were original in character, he is said to have designed and engraved himself. According to Dutton, "they consisted of crescents, stars, leaves, acorns, running vines and circlets of gold, and were placed at intervals in the spaces to be decorated, the field being studded with gold dots. He was the first English binder who attempted to make his ornaments appropriate to the character of the book on which they were to be employed." Payne, who worked in London towards the end of the eighteenth century, put in many of his bindings a description of the loving care he expended upon them. He was, unfortunately, a drunkard, but in spite of his failings, he made a major contribution to the art of bookbinding.

Little attention has been given to the history of book-binding in the United States and even the name of the first independent American bookbinder was until recently unknown. But two or three months ago I showed that Edmund Ranger of Boston should be credited with that distinction. On the title page of a book printed at Cambridge, Mass., in 1672: "Christs Famous Titles," we find this imprint: "Printed by M. J. for Edmund Ranger, bookbinder near the Dock, and Joseph Farnham, near the Red Lion in Boston, 1672." And the next year on the title page of the first American temperance tract, we find him again listed as "bookbinder," but with less specific address. It is evident that Ranger had business relations with both of the printers working in Cambridge at this time, and it is more than likely that he bound the books turned out by their presses. Unfortunately, we know of no binding which can be definitely ascribed to him.

Having briefly traced the historical development of the art of bookbinding, it remains to consider some of the present-day aspects. The stronghold of "fine binding" today is in England. There are located several establishments with a complement of conscientiously trained craftsman, and a labor cost infinitely less than for similar work in the United States. There are, however, in New York and Chicago several shops operating with London-trained finishers whose work is of high standard but whose costs are necessarily high.

The fine binders of today work in the same manner as their predecessors for centuries back. The signatures are sewed on cords, and these cords are interlaced into the boards (now made of composition) which, in the next step, are covered with leather. A flexible back is greatly to be desired so that a book will open easily and lie flat and close easily and stay closed. It is a rule of informed binders to trim the books they handle just as little as possible, in books printed on deckle edge paper confining this trim to the top only, which is then frequently gilded. Many binders in ages past have mangled books in a distressing way by cutting down their margins so radically that there are almost no margins left. When a book already severely cropped is to be rebound, the fine binder "rough gilds" the edges before he starts his work so that he may avoid the necessity of further cropping.

The sewing, gilding of edges, covering, and so forth, are known as "forwarding;" the decoration of the cover as "finishing." The design is first made up on paper with inked impressions of the tools, and when the arrangement has been worked out to satisfaction, it is transferred to the leather by light impressions through the paper pattern onto the leather which has previously been dampened to soften it. The portions of the cover thus lightly impressed are then sized and the gold leaf is laid. This is so thin that the impressions show through clearly. The finisher, thus having a guide for his work, makes a second and more vigorous impression with his hot tools which causes the gold to adhere to the leather. The volume is then pressed between polished plates to impart a smooth and brilliant surface to the leather, and the book is now ready for delivery to an expectant collector.

Almost all binding in England and the United States is wholly traditional in character and there is in evidence practically no inventiveness in design. Books are executed in the style of one or another of the masters whose work has been discussed and their merit appears to hinge on how faithfully those styles are reproduced.

Toward the end of the nineteenth century, a great service to the cause of bookbinding was rendered by T. J. Cobden-Sanderson—a disciple of William Morris.

This remarkable man, who gave up a career in the legal profession to become a bookbinder through choice, made consequential contributions to the art, particularly in introducing new forms of design and freeing the binders from a too-servile allegiance to the classical styles. His motifs of decoration, while still within the bounds of conventionalism, were much more naturalistic than the tools which had been used by his predecessors. His pupil, Douglas Cockerell, writes: "Before his time there had been few attempts to combine tools to form organic patterns. Mr. Cobden-Sanderson's tools were very elementary in character, each flower, leaf or bird being the impression of a separate tool. These impressions were combined in such a way as to give a sense of growth, and yet in no way overlapped the traditional limitations and conventions of the craft. Mr. Cobden-Sanderson got his results by sheer genius in the right use of simple elements."

There is an entertaining story told of Cobden-Sanderson's rejoinder to a lady client who came to protest a charge of six pounds for binding a book on which, as she pointed out, there was little gold tooling. "Madam," replied the master binder, "I charge as much for my restraint as for my elaboration."

The main present source of original ideas in bookbinding design—as in book printing design—is on the Continent. German artists are binding books with entire freedom from the restrictions of tradition, and they are being followed by a few on this side of the ocean who are interested in the modern movement. Many of the results are weird but many of the designs show much promise. From the free experimentation, however, there is bound to result much good. As in all fields, the best course will be found in a synthesis of the best elements in the old leavened by the best elements in the new.

XXXI. *Private Presses*

OOKMAKING is a fascinating craft. A book can be a thing of beauty and a vehicle of world-changing ideas. It is not surprising, therefore, that men and women, seeking a hobby for their amusement or burning with some intellectual or artistic ideal should seek to express themselves by setting up presses of their very own. A private press, then, is a printing establishment, usually a very small one, which aims to produce books for other motives than commercial profit.

Ever since the fifteenth century when Johann Müller (Regiomontanus) printed at Nürnberg astronomical works which he and his friends had written, the private press has played a part in the production of books. In the early days of the craft, however, both the commercial printer and the state authorities frowned upon this form of book production. This was especially true in England during the sixteenth and seventeenth centuries, when private presses had the dangerous habit of issuing books which the Star Chamber deemed "naughtie & seedi-tious." The Martin Marprelate tracts, a series of Puritan attacks upon the bishops, for instance, were the product of a printing office which, in an unsuccessful attempt to avoid detection, was moved from place to place in a wagon. Needless to say, the typography of private presses working under these conditions was extremely poor. When a man of wealth, however, took up printing as a hobby, as did Horace Walpole with his Strawberry Hill Press, better results were obtained, and when competent artists and craftsmen, such as John Baskerville and William Morris, set up private presses the result was truly revolutionary.

Since the death of Morris his ideals have, to a large degree, been fostered and propagated by private presses. This is partly because such an establishment, printing only a limited number of copies addressed to a discriminating clientèle and regarding profits as a secondary consideration, can carry out experiments which a commercial plant would not dare attempt. The private press, also, is able to perform the different processes of book-making by hand and in its endeavor to obtain Morris' results is able to use Morris' methods.

The first important disciple of the typographical messiah was Charles Ricketts who in 1896 issued from the Vale Press an edition of Milton's *Early Poems*. The actual printing of the Vale Press was done at the Ballantyne establishment under the immediate supervision of Mr. Ricketts who designed the type and cut most of the borders, ornaments and initials. The decoration is greatly

[354]

influenced by Morris but the types are modeled upon those of Nicholas Jenson and Johann of Spire. The most famous production of the press is the *Works of Shakespeare* (1900-1903) in thirty-nine volumes. After continuing for seven years, the operation of the press was terminated in 1904, with a *Bibliography of the Vale Press* by Ricketts and then, fearing lest, drifting into the hands of unskilled printers the type should "become stale by unthinking use," the punches and matrices were thrown into the Thames and the letters melted down.

The Eragny Press at Hammersmith was started in 1894 by Lucien Pissarro, a French painter and engraver. He used, at first, the Vale type of his friend Ricketts but in 1902 he began the use of the Brook type, designed by himself and based upon the Vale letter. The designing, wood-engraving and printing of the books of the Eragny Press are all the work of Pissarro and his wife, Esther. His productions are famous for their beautiful colored wood block prints; in fact, as one critic has pointed out, "Mr. Pissarro's aim is rather to print illustrations with a suitable text than to print an illustrated book."

The Ashendene Press of C. H. St. John Hornby, situated at Chelsea, is the most important private press now in operation and, although it eschews the elaborate decoration of the Kelmscott books, in general plan its productions follow those of the earlier press quite closely. The first book of the press, *The Journal of Joseph Hornby* (1895), was printed in the Caslon letter and this character and various sizes of the Fell type obtained from the Oxford University Press were used until 1902. St. John

Dic & argutae properet Neaerae
Murreum nodo cohibere crinem;
Si per invisum mora ianitorem
    Fiet, abito.
Lenit albescens animos capillus
Litium et rixae cupidos protervae;
Non ego hoc ferrem calidus iuventa
    Consule Planco.

FAUNE, Nympharum fugientum amator,
   Per meos finis et aprica rura
Lenis incedas abeasq; parvis
    Aequus alumnis,
Si tener pleno cadit haedus anno,
Larga nec desunt Veneris sodali
Vina craterae, vetus ara multo
    Fumat odore.
Ludit herboso pecus omne campo,
Cum tibi Nonae redeunt Decembres;
29

Hornby, however, admired the type which Sweynheym and Pannartz had employed in their press at the monastery of Subiaco, a letter which exhibits many of the characteristics of both the gothic and the roman forms. With the aid of Emery Walker and Sidney Cockerell, he designed an alphabet modeled from the Sweynheym and Pannartz *Lactantius* of 1465 and named it Subiaco type. An example of this beautiful letter may be seen in the pages of the *Carmina Sapphica* of Horace here reproduced. Walker, the associate of Morris, became the "godfather" of the press and it is largely because of his influence that it continues the Kelmscott tradition. Only the thinnest spaces are used and the page presents an appearance of rich even black, sometimes enlivened with passages in red or blue and with colored initial letters either printed from wood blocks or added by the hand of the rubricator. *The Dante* of 1909, the *Malory* of 1913 and the *Spenser* of 1923, three large and imposing folios, are superbly executed examples of the work of this press.

The Essex House Press was an expression of a desire to put "idealism in industry." Founded in 1898 by the Guild of Handicraft under the leadership of C. R. Ashbee, the establishment acquired two of the printing presses and the empty type cases of the Kelmscott Press. Plans were made to complete the *Froissart* which Morris had begun and to print some of the works which he had planned to undertake, but these designs were never carried out. The first productions of the Essex House Press in Caslon type are delightfully simple but later works are printed in characters designed by Ashbee. These may be

¶ THE DOVES PRESS was founded in 1900 to attack the problem of Typography as presented by ordinary Books in the various forms of Prose, Verse, and Dialogue and, keeping always in view the principles laid down in the Book Beautiful, to attempt its solution by the simple arrangement of the whole Book, as a whole, with due regard to its parts and to the emphasis of its capital divisions rather than by the addition & splendour of applied ornament.

II

¶ The Books selected for this purpose have been chosen partly for the sake of the particular typographical problems presented by them, but partly also in view of the second object of the Press, viz., to print in a suitable form some of the great literary achievements of man's creative or constructive genius. To-day there is an immense reproduction in forms at once admirable & cheap of all books which in any language have stood the test of time. But such reproduction is not a substitute for the more monumental production of the same books, and such a production, expressive of man's admiration, is a legitimate ambition of the Printing Press & of some Press the imperative duty.

III

¶ THE ENGLISH BIBLE is a supreme achievement of English Literature, if not of English

8

PAGE OF THE CATALOGUE OF THE DOVES PRESS

dismissed as interesting but unsuccessful experiments and the later work of the establishment is greatly handicapped by their use. The woodcuts, however, are always excellent. The best known production of the Essex House Press is the *Prayer Book of King Edward VII* (1903).

The Doves Press, to which we now turn, was established at Hammersmith by Emery Walker and T. J. Cobden-Sanderson. These two typographical artists cut a remarkable roman letter based on that of Jenson, a very beautiful type in spite of the rigid descender of the y which tends to direct the eye to the lefthand corner of the page and thus tends to make reading somewhat difficult. The books of the Doves Press are characterized by a majestic simplicity. Free from all ornament, save for an occasional colored initial, they form a contrast to the works of Morris and show the influence of the Kelmscott Press chiefly in their close spacing. The Doves Bible (1903-1905), the masterpiece of the press, is a monument of dignity and restraint. The five large quarto volumes of this work presented no small task to the single compositor who so skilfully put it into type.

In 1909, Walker retired from the partnership and Cobden-Sanderson continued the press alone until 1916 when he printed the *Catalogue Raisonné of Books Printed and Published at the Doves Press* in which he bade his press an eternal farewell. A page of this beautiful book is here shown. After the last leaf had been printed he took in his arms the type, matrices and punches of the Doves Press and threw them into the Thames, with this invocation: "May the River in its tides and flow, pass over them to and from the great sea for ever . . . untouched of other use."

Another recently founded English private press deserves mention. The Golden Cockerel Press at Waltham Saint Lawrence in Berkshire has, under the direction of Harold Taylor, produced some quaint and unusual books and the Shakespeare Head Press at Stratford-on-Avon has issued a Shakespeare and other fine books.

In America, Morris speedily gained many enthusiastic admirers who imitated his typographical style with great zeal but little taste. Few, indeed, are the type-specimen books issued in the United States during the late 90's which do not contain an ugly blotchy, black type with some fantastic ornaments intended to accompany it. These found a ready market among printers who supplied themselves with some thick paper and a quantity of red ink and set out to do artistic printing, but succeeded only in perpetrating inconceivable typographical monstrosities.

The Elston Press at New Rochelle, New York, however, was more fortunate in its results. Its books were frank, but by no means servile imitations of those of the Kelmscott Press. In type, ornament, illustration and design *The Vision of William Concerning Piers the Plowman*, printed in 1901, for example, closely follows the Kelmscott *Chaucer* but by 1904 the edition of Longus' *Daphnis and Chloe* issued by this press, though it retains the main characteristics of a book printed by Morris in Golden type, still, in the use of a title-page and in other features shows some degree of independence.

PRIVATE PRESSES

The Roycroft Shop at East Aurora, New York, was part of the organization which flourished under the direction of the odd but talented Elbert Hubbard. The shop in its typography copied many of the obvious features of the Kelmscott books but unfortunately allowed numerous faults, chief of them, a certain cheap eccentricity, to creep into their productions.

The books designed by Thomas B. Mosher, although somewhat out of the scope of this chapter, deserve mention because of their influence on American typography. Mosher did not himself own a plant but he designed and supervised the printing of the many excellent books which he published.

The Village Press was founded in July, 1903, and was first located in the barn of its proprietor at Park Ridge, Illinois. The working force of the establishment consisted of the owner, Frederic W. Goudy, his wife, Bertha, and a promising young apprentice by the name of Will Ransom.

Goudy had begun life as a bookseller but gradually succumbed to his love for the graphic arts and after doing some commercial lettering and advertising work, set up, in 1895, the Booklet Press, in Chicago where he printed the *Chap Book*. To this office came Will Ransom filled with a desire to learn the art of designing types and soon the two enthusiasts decided to found a private press. A new face, the now famous Village type, was cut by Goudy and the work of the press was begun with Mrs. Goudy doing most of the composition. In March 1904, the press was moved to Hingham, Massachusetts, and two years later to the Parker Building in New York City where it was destroyed when that building burned. The Village Press, however, was re-established and is still in operation at Marlboro-on-Hudson, N. Y.

The Village Press is important because it was the training ground of a great type designer. The intrinsic merit of its productions, though sometimes marred by traces of advertising technique, is high. Besides the excellence of their type, the books show much skill and originality in design.

Perhaps the most interesting private press in America is that operated by Dard Hunter in a room of his home at Chillicothe, Ohio. Dard Hunter was taught the art of printing by his father and later worked for seven years at the Roycroft shops, then, dissatisfied with the condition of American typography, he went to Europe where he studied papermaking and type design in England, Germany, and Italy. Upon his return to America, he began with the equipment of a three-hundred-year-old Wiltshire paper mill, some ancient typefounder's tools, and an old hand press, to make all the implements needed in his private press. He succeeded in manufacturing excellent paper from fine Irish linen and in cutting a roman type somewhat resembling that of Jenson. Hunter has printed three books of his own: *Old Papermaking* (1923), *The Literature of Papermaking* (1925), and *Primitive Papermaking* (1927). For these he wrote his own copy, made the paper, designed, cast, and set the type, and printed, bound, and published his books. His works are said to be the first books printed in modern times which were produced entirely by the labor of one man.

Germany also has a number of interesting private presses. Best known of these is the Bremer Press whose two special types, an Italianate roman and a magnificent Greek were designed by its director, Dr. Wiegand. Although, by their uniform character, Bremer books are apt to seem monotonous, they display sound craftsmanship and good taste. The superb edition of the *Iliad* and *Odyssey* of Homer will stand as a lasting testimonial to the merit of this press.

The Officina Serpentis, established in 1911 by Tiffenbach, is still under the Kelmscott influence. A letter based upon that of Peter Schoeffer is employed, with ornaments and initials in keeping with the type but rather too archaic in character for present-day use. The books of the Officina Serpentis also lack variety but the technical work is always good, especially in the clear beauty of the red and black printing inks.

The Ernst-Ludwig Press, founded in 1907 by the Kleukens brothers, still continues to issue simple and dignified books printed in an austere and classical style. The Janus Press, started in the same year by Dr. Carl E. Poeschel also continues to issue a few books of high quality with types and initials designed by Walter Tiemann.

In Holland, the Zilverdistel Press at The Hague has produced, under the direction of J. F. van Royen, some excellent books. The press has two fine special types. The first is a letter designed by Lucien Pissarro, based upon old Dutch handwriting, which has an effect not unlike that of the Ashendene face. The second is a roman closely resembling the Doves Press font. In composition, too, as well as in its type faces, the Zilverdistel Press shows the influence of English typography.

Such, then, is the history of the modern private press. In England, it has produced many outstanding books. In the United States, however, it has not been so successful. American genius, it would seem, takes kindly to work under commercial conditions and its best typography has been produced in offices doing a wide variety of work.

Private presses have produced during the last thirty-five years but an infinitesimally small proportion of the printed matter of Europe and America and, considered by themselves, they are of minor significance. The private press, however, has been the pioneer and the pathfinder of modern typography. The books of private presses made by the loving care of printers devoted to their art, form models which the commercial craftsman has learned to copy and, because of this, typography has reaped a great benefit. The private press, then, has performed a real service in the task of bringing closer to realization the dream of William Morris, a world redeemed from ugliness.

XXXII. *Modern Fine Printing*

MAKING an effort to appraise our own situation with respect to standards of bookmaking, it is comforting to be able to render an encouraging report. Much book printing of a high order of excellence is being done and—a point even more gratifying—it is being done, not by one or two, but by a considerable number of printers.

There are some practical reasons which contribute toward bringing about this "renaissance" of fine bookmaking which is now upon us. In the first place economic conditions have made possible a radical increase in the number of collectors of fine editions. This has provided printers interested in producing fine books with a wider circle of patrons, and the number of volumes calculated to be fine books appearing within any calendar year has increased to a surprising extent.

In the second place we are blessed with a number of printers of true genius, the more important of whom were profoundly influenced and inspired by the example

[365]

of William Morris. When the grain of such influence falls on fertile soil we are bound to reap rich harvests.

The most important figure in modern fine printing in the United States is Bruce Rogers, whose books are collected enthusiastically by an ever-widening circle of amateurs, with a consequent steady appreciation in the market value of his books. This market situation is not artificial, however, because his work is deserving of the esteem in which it is held, its most commendable feature being variety.

With many of the modern private presses, to have seen one of their books is almost equivalent to having seen all of them. Instead of using one type only and sticking to one style, Rogers has used a myriad of types and has adapted his style to the subject in hand. He must be regarded as a traditionalist, for practically all his work follows the the typography of one classic school or another, but in following the masters a native inventiveness bubbles, as it were, to the surface and we have traditional typography plus a verve which captivates us.

Rogers' abilities as an artist carry him through the whole range of the book arts. He draws his own decorations, designs his own types, makes the typographical arrangement, oversees the composition with a critical eye, and creates the style of binding. He is thus practically independent of assistance from others. In recent years he devoted considerable attention, with gratifying results, to a rather fanciful and often playful use of type ornaments. We can conceive no more masterful use of such ornament than in the title page of *Pierrot of the Minute*

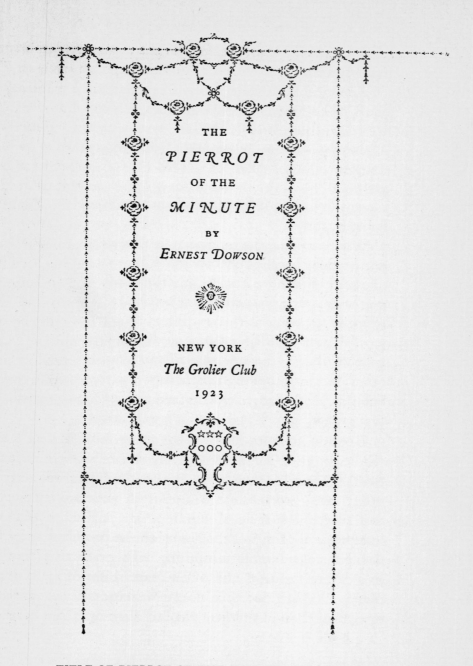

THE
PIERROT
OF THE
MINUTE
BY
Ernest Dowson

NEW YORK
The Grolier Club
1923

TITLE OF PIERROT OF THE MINUTE, BRUCE ROGERS

(here reproduced)which he did for the printers' series of the Grolier Club. In the book, the title page is printed in two colors: rose and black.

His most celebrated book is, perhaps, a mere pamphlet entitled *The Centaur* which, partly because of its perfection as a piece of typography and partly because of the extremely limited edition in which it was printed, has risen to dizzy heights in the auction room. A page from this booklet, in the composition of which the Centaur type, designed by Rogers in faithful imitation of the roman type of Jenson, was used for the first time, is here shown in slight reduction.

This is no place for a biography of Bruce Rogers, but we may recall that his first noteworthy work was done at the Riverside Press in Cambridge, Massachusetts, between the years 1903 and 1912, during which period he issued fifty books of a standard not heretofore known in this country. Since the termination of that connection he served for some time as printing adviser to the Cambridge (England) University Press. After his return to this country he became typographic adviser to the Harvard University Press and designer of books for the printer, William E. Rudge, in whose office his books are produced, these two relationships being in effect at the present writing.

The other master of typography in America is Daniel Berkeley Updike, the moving spirit of the Merrymount Press of Boston. Updike, unlike Rogers, is an employing printer and in addition to winning fame as a designer of books, he has made a success in building up a printing

THE CENTAUR. WRITTEN BY MAURICE DE GUÉRIN AND NOW TRANSLATED FROM THE FRENCH BY GEORGE B. IVES.

I Was born in a cavern of these mountains. Like the river in yonder valley, whose first drops flow from some cliff that weeps in a deep grotto, the first moments of my life sped amidst the shadows of a secluded retreat, nor vexed its silence. As our mothers draw near their term, they retire to the caverns, and in the innermost recesses of the wildest of them all, where the darkness is most dense, they bring forth, uncomplaining, offspring as silent as themselves. Their strength-giving milk enables us to endure without weakness or dubious struggles the first difficulties of life; yet we leave our caverns later than you your cradles. The reason is that there is a tradition amongst us that the early days of life must be secluded and guarded, as days engrossed by the gods.

My growth ran almost its entire course in the darkness where I was born. The innermost depths of my home were so far within the bowels of the mountain, that I should not have known in which direction the opening lay, had it not been that the winds at times blew in and caused a sudden coolness and confusion. Sometimes, too, my mother returned, bringing with her the perfume of the valleys, or dripping wet from the streams to which she resorted. Now, these her home-comings, although they told me naught of the valleys or the streams, yet, being attended by emanations therefrom, disturbed my thoughts, and I wandered about, all agitated, amidst my darkness. 'What,' I would say to myself, 'are these places to which my mother goes and what power reigns there which summons her so frequently? To what influences is one there exposed,

office of the highest standard. He is not himself a designer of type, though his judgment undoubtedly influenced in great degree the drawings of the several special types designed for his use. In planning books he has relied almost entirely on the use of type alone, but the results he accomplishes in this medium are little short of remarkable. I can recall, in the history of typography, none who used type more skilfully or with a surer hand.

Strange to say, the collectors of modern fine printing are not awake to the merits of Updike's printing, and in failing to acquire examples of his work while they are still to be obtained are, I feel sure, missing an opportunity. While his work is appreciated now it is of the type which will be appreciated to a greater extent by generations to come.

Updike is a student of type history as well as a typographer of renown, and he has made a contribution to the literature of typography which will not soon be superseded. His *Printing Types*, in two volumes, constitutes an invaluable text book for all who use type and in writing it, he rendered a lasting service to the profession of which he is a distinguished exponent.

Passing to the Pacific Coast we find at work a number of printers of high ideals and a good deal of ability. John Henry Nash of San Francisco has printed many fine books, most of them in a style more ornate than those of the two printers already discussed, but this characteristic gives his work an individuality it might not otherwise have. It is no merit to copy the work of others, while the courage of a trail blazer always deserves commendation.

[370]

FINE PRINTING

The Grahborn brothers, Henry Taylor, the Johnsons, and others are also printing in a way to add to the typographic renown of the state of California.

In New York a comparative newcomer to the printing fold has been turning out many distinguished books. Elmer Adler, who navigates the ship of the Pynson Printers, was first attracted to typography as an avocation which in a gradual metamorphosis became his vocation. His standards of execution are high and the design of his books gives evidence of much originality in the use of type. In alliance with the most distinguished American publisher he has contributed to the beauty of many books of general circulation. Adler is still a young man and we may expect much fine work from his hand.

From the Yale University Press is coming much typography of a distinguished character. The reason is not far to seek. We find it in the person of Carl Purington Rollins who directs the destinies (typographically) of that Press. His work is characterized by a catholicity of taste tempered by a natural tendency to spontaneity. He has done many inexpensive books superlatively well— which, from my point of view is high praise.

The late Walter Gilliss, with whom I was privileged to collaborate in the production of a number of notable volumes, was a typographer of distinguished ability. He was a traditionalist in every sense of the word but his judgment in the use of type, the selection of sizes, and the spacing of matter on a page was sure to an uncanny degree. His name is assured of a permanent place in the roll of fine printers in America, along with his colleague of earlier years, Theodore L. DeVinne. Judged by present standards, DeVinne was not a great printer, but judged by the standards of his own period he towered head and shoulders above his fellows. He also rendered a service of no less importance by his studies and writings on the history of the printing art.

The encouraging feature of our present typographic status is the number of men all over the country who are doing printing of a high degree of excellence. The leaders are not traveling a lonely road but are only at the head of a column of enlisted men whose faces are turned in the same direction. In the zeal of the young men with a deep interest in fine typography we cannot fail to find fair augury for the future of bookmaking.

XXXIII. *Towards the Golden Book*

HE fifth centenary of the invention of printing will soon be upon us. In the preceding pages we have followed the work of the best printers for nearly five centuries, and have discussed their aims and their accomplishments, their successes and their failures. Inspired by their example, warned by their errors, guided by their experience: towards what goal are we directed? As we have sat at the feet of the masters of typography, what lessons have we learned? What constitutes, to borrow the words of Cobden-Sanderson, the "Ideal Book or Book Beautiful"?

Before considering in detail, however, the features which make for fine bookmaking, I am going to define the scope of the discussion and radically delimit its field. In thinking of books in their larger aspect we must think of those bought and read by the "reading public" —a class growing larger and larger each year. This automatically excludes "precious" books, in the making of which the design and printing are almost ends in themselves, and the text and its dissemination regarded as elements of secondary importance.

But, it will immediately be objected, do not a large proportion of the books to which we have devoted our attention in the present volume fall within the special class thus disqualified? The answer to this is affirmative. Bodoni, for example, and William Morris did not produce books for reading but for exhibition. Whatever features in their work contributed towards making more books better constituted their fundamental contribution to the cause of bookmaking.

We shall always have enthusiasts who will devote their effort to the production of books in limited editions, produced almost without regard for cost. It is well that this should be the case, for such work is the equivalent of the laboratory experimentation of the chemist, testing the validity of principles to be applied on a scale ten thousand times as great in producing a product which shall stand the test of market conditions.

It seems, however, that the book designer of high ideals should be imbued with a zeal for public service—with an ambition to bring beauty into books which touch the lives and influence the esthetic standards of readers counted in millions instead of in tens or hundreds.

To be of true importance in the work of the world, books must be read, and as a condition precedent thereto they must be sold. This injects into the planning problem certain economic considerations for, if good bookmaking is to become and continue possible, books must be produced at a cost within reason and sold at a price within reason and yet yield to the publisher a profit which will justify his investment in brains and money (emphasis on the first-named ingredient!). Fortunately, fine bookmaking from the point of view of artistry does not necessarily mean expensive bookmaking, but it does require genius in planning and careful supervision in execution.

Granting our rather paradoxical definition of objective: the fine making of common books, let us chart the beacons by which we shall steer our course.

A book should, first of all, be consonant in spirit and form with its character and purpose. This means, for example, that if it is intended to be read for the pleasure of the reader it should be of moderate size, should open easily and be held open easily. The weight of such a book also should be no greater than necessary. The English publishers have been particularly successful in keeping the weight of books within a moderate limit, largely because of their convenient supply of paper made from Esparto grass, which seems to be native and exclusive to Scotland.

It would very naturally be inappropriate in a book designed with this object in view to provide extravagant margins. The margins should be correct in relation to proportions, but they should not be excessive.

If the book, on the other hand, were a scientific treatise illustrated with detailed plates, it is obvious that the scale in which the plates could best be reproduced would determine the format of the volume. A book of this character might be a quarto or folio as these requirements might dictate.

[375]

Light weight and moderate size, though desirable characteristics in books for continuous reading, should not be gained at too great a sacrifice in type size—for ease in handling will never justify difficulty in reading.

One of the most frequent errors in the planning of books (and in the planning of all other printing for that matter) is setting lines of type too wide. There is nothing that slows up reading and induces eye-strain more than type lines too long for the type size in which they are set. The lines in a book in ten point should not, for example, be much over three inches wide; while one in twelve point or fourteen point should not exceed in measure four and a half inches. One authority lays down the rule that no line should be longer than one and a half times the length of the lower case alphabet of the type in which it is set.

Another essential of an ideal book is ample white space between lines, so that the eye may have a guide in carrying back from the end of one line to the beginning of the next. With types with descenders and ascenders of normal length, set in lines of the right width, no spacing between lines, or leading as the printer calls it, is necessary. But with types with abbreviated descenders leading is absolutely essential.

A word as to materials. The greatest problem concerns paper. We hear a great deal about the quick disintegration of modern papers, but this relates particularly to newspapers which are, for obvious reasons, printed on the cheapest paper which can be manufactured. Very cheap book paper will discolor badly in five or ten years but a fair grade of book paper, sold at a price within the reach of the average publisher, will last long enough for all practical purposes. In the printing of a document which, by reason of its character, is likely to be consulted for the next two hundred years or more, an all rag paper should be used. Such paper can be obtained at a price between two and three times the cost of a fair grade of book paper, so its use in books which demand it does not involve a prohibitive expense.

Several important newspapers have begun to publish special editions on rag paper for preservation in libraries. This is a wise provision as the newspaper is an historical record of the most fundamental character. The greatest complaints about book papers come also from libraries whose books are used not by one reader but by hundreds. Under this undue strain it is natural that books manufactured primarily for the individual reader should go to pieces. The newspapers have suggested a solution: that a special library edition of important and even of unimportant books should be printed on rag paper and specially bound. The libraries could well afford to pay the extra cost of materials, which would amount to less than the present cost of replacement copies. This special library edition could also be bought by collectors of first editions.

Hand-made paper is still the best paper but as it costs ten times more than a good machine-made paper, it can hardly be considered for any books addressed to a wide audience. For practical considerations good typographic design, a large enough type size, ample leading, fair margins, and the like, are of more importance than an investment in permanence of paper stock where that particular quality may never be required.

The theorists do a great deal of talking about the degradation incident to machine production. It is beyond denial that the change from a hand to a mechanical method of production generally results at first in lower standards of execution. But as the machine process becomes perfected, the printers interested in a high standard of work can regain that standard in machine operation. In presswork, for example, I can see no characteristic in hand press printing which cannot be obtained with careful and competent operation of a modern power press. The first type composition by mechanical process was of poor quality indeed, but there can now be produced by machine excellent typesetting, in faces of good design, well spaced and well cast. And the difference in cost between setting body matter by hand and machine is, of course, spectacular.

It seems to me, therefore, that the book artist of the present and future should take advantage of the economies of mechanical processes while insisting upon a high standard of product. When men of real ability turn their attention to obtaining the best work by the most effective means, real progress will be sure to result. The cause of fine bookmaking will not be served by a stupid loyalty to antiquated methods.

Most of the points we have so far discussed concern soundness of design. They correspond to the basic principles of architectural construction. But what have we in bookmaking to correspond to the architectural elements of ornamentation—elements which contribute nothing to the strength of a building or to its usefulness but contribute greatly to its beauty?

The principle of "fitness to purpose," about which we hear so much, will prevent us from making bad books, but to make great books we must pass the boundary of negative rules and give rein to creative impulses.

Some authorities urge that as the purpose of books is to be read, legibility is the primary consideration, and that any features which do not promote legibility are excrescences and tend to diminish rather than increase the merit of the book. That a book "unfitted to purpose" is wrong, and that an illegible book is pernicious, all will be ready to admit. It is further true that a logically planned book, like a logically planned building, has in it many elements of beauty. But these principles alone will not suffice to produce the best designed books of which we are capable. Were they carried to their logical conclusion we would never have a headband, an initial letter, a border or decoration on a titlepage, or any of the other "excrescences" by which we can do so much to make a book charming.

So, I believe, in many books beauty is an end in itself to be sought in bookmaking beyond and additional to "fitness to purpose." This word *many* implies that there are some books in which beauty is fundamentally a desideratum and others in which it is not a factor of material importance. When we attempt a classification, the distinction appears to lie between a work of utility only and a work of literary art. Even the most enthusiastic

[379]

typographer could hardly summon much enthusiasm regarding the embellishment of a dictionary or a trade directory or a cable code book though he might have much enthusiasm in their sound typographical design. For works of this character, legibility and convenience of consultation can be the only features sought.

But when we turn to works of creative literary art: novels, poetry, essays, and the like, a different situation prevails. It is not essential to the physical actualities of life that such books should be read. They are read for pleasure: for gratification of our artistic perceptions. They are, in other words, food for the spirit. Can we not then enjoy them esthetically at the same time not only for the text we read but also for the beauty of their appearance, which we perceive likewise through our eyes? I think so. I believe it is a crying shame that so much beautiful literature of the present day comes to us in such unesthetic form as it does.

The object of any work of art is to evoke an emotion. Does a poem of real moment run a better chance of gaining its object if it comes to us in the crowded columns of a newspaper or on a page not only clear typographically but beautiful as well? We react to art not through one sense only at a time. It is on rare occasions that we can see a work of art in any medium independent of its environment. We sense unconsciously other impressions than that of the object nominally holding our attention. This is certainly true of books, or so many people would not appreciate finely made books. And it is worthy of note that the modern books most in demand by present-day connoisseurs are those, not of the severely plain school, but those in which the creative fancy of the designer has made his contribution to the book as a work of art, helping—in only a small degree perhaps—to present it in the manner best calculated to gain the appreciation of the individual of good taste. As a picture frame executed by a master of the framing art can help present a great oil painting in a more favorable way to those who view it than to show the canvas stretched bare over its frame, so can the artist in bookmaking present to the reader an *opus* in the literary field in a way favorable to its esthetic appreciation.

Were legibility the only factor worthy of consideration, we are wasting our time in type design. Having at our disposal a round old style, such as can be found in any linotype shop, we can stop there. Garamond is a beautiful type. But it is not as legible as a rounded old style. Kennerley is a type of much charm but as to readability the same comment applies. Yet types of real beauty have a function of importance in bookmaking.

Then there is the element of variety. I do not believe in standardization in book plan or design. There is in progress a crusade to effect standardization in sizes of printed matter. Such a course deadens interest and increases the monotony of our reading matter. In other applied arts we have decided that standardization is depressing. In architecture, we do not design all houses of the same shape and size. In town planning and landscape work we endeavor to attain variety rather than uniformity. I believe the same principles apply to book design.

The unofficial standardization in novel format, I must confess bores me. I should find very refreshing a novel a little taller or a little wider or a little thinner than usual. I believe a publisher would find it worth while commercially to break away from this standard and do a little pioneering.

Individuality is, therefore, a desideratum. So long as a book is not freakish the more it has in the way of personality the better.

We can conceive a committee of experts in typography and book design meeting in council and determining upon the most logical form of novel. They might fix, by common consent, on a good type-page size, the paper size, the face and size of type in which the text should be set. They could select the type for chapter headings, running heads, and the like. Acting solely on the principle of "fitness to purpose" they would eschew decoration. Let us then presume the publishers adopted this as a standard novel format. I can conceive reading the first novel under this plan and appreciating its legibility and the logic of its plan. When I had read the fourth novel so standardized in format I should be losing some appreciation of its merits, and after the twentieth I am sure I would be wishing they would print the twenty-first in red ink! No, there are other desiderata in reading purposed for esthetic enjoyment than legibility.

The appreciation of charmingly designed books being so general among readers, it seems a wonder that publishers have made so little attempt to beautify their books of general trade circulation. It would be so simple to lend a little more grace to the average novel, and the effort would be all in the composition. Paper can remain cheap, cloth inexpensive. Still, with but a little expenditure in taste, a book can be made charming instead of bleak. A good set of initial letters can add marvelously to the grace of a book. An individual treatment of chapter headings—a line of type ornaments perhaps, or two or three properly chosen rules—can help vastly toward making a book a thing of beauty rather than a drab succession of gray-appearing sheets. Perhaps we can even devise some new and good forms of book decoration.

I believe, therefore, in good book decoration, sparingly but feelingly used, and in putting more into books than the bare demands of fitness to purpose. Sound in kind and right in measure, decoration will add to the beauty of books in everyday use. It will make them more worthy the attention of those accustomed to high standards of artistry in other objects of daily use. It will make them more pleasing to read. It will sell more books.

A title page particularly offers opportunity for a touch of grace in the way of decoration. The copy on the modern title page is usually brief and simple and after this is set in type ample space remains for other uses. Too much decoration is, of course, worse than none at all, but a little, tastefully applied, is generally a help except in cases where the subject and character of the book demand severity and simplicity of treatment.

Bindings of modern books offer a wide range of opportunity to the book designer. Here again variety and individuality are, I think, virtues. In the past books have looked too much alike and, in general, have been too drab. Binding cloths are available in a wide range of colors, but they are plain colors without pattern other than in the texture of the surface finish. Decorative binding cloths are beginning to appear in Europe and it is only a matter of time when they will come into use here.

Lacking such cloths a number of the up-to-date publishers have had recourse to decorated paper covering the boards of the binding. Many of these papers are charming and their use has raised the average of attractiveness in publishers' books. The only drawback is that paper over board sides makes a much less durable binding, though with a cloth backbone the result is fairly satisfactory. In the book proper the binding is now the gayest feature so far as design is concerned.

In present-day commercial book design, however, there is an item in the conception of which fancy can run riot: the jacket. The attractiveness of the jacket is said to have an important influence on the sale of the book, for the volume is clothed in its jacket when it stands on the table or shelf of the bookseller. Naturally a jacket which arrests attention runs a far better chance of being, in the first instance inspected, and in the second instance sold, than a book which plays the part of the shrinking violet among its neighbors.

Whatever the plan and design of a book, however, a vital requirement in any book worthy of approbation is a high standard of workmanship in its manufacture. If the type is not well spaced and accurately positioned on the page, if the printing on the two sides of a leaf or sheet do not register accurately, if the presswork is care-less and the binding slipshod—all the efforts of a book designer go up in smoke.

One aspect of workmanship is proofreading, and we all know how an otherwise fine book will be marred for us by a succession of stupid errors. On the other hand, a book giving evidence of painstaking correction is a joy.

The average printer has little conception of the care necessary to the making of a fine book. He is prone to regard illustrated catalogues and color printing as "fine" work while "book work" is in many offices a synonym for thoughtless haste and indifference. We cannot expect good books to come into being without an ample meed of thoughtful care and supervision.

The modern movement which has been manifesting itself in other forms of art is at last making some impres-sion on typography. It is well that this is the case for arts need from time to time an infusion of new blood if stag-nation is not to set in. It is too early to estimate just what permanent effect the modern experiments will have on book design, but it is likely to be of consequence. The standards evolved in centuries of fine bookmaking will never be supplanted, but they will be modified and vital-ized by the best work in the new spirit. The book designer who expects to do distinguished work cannot depend alone on reproduction of past styles. He must keep his eyes open for the best elements in the modern work, and make use of such as prove of true worth.

Books were not made more beautiful by the invention of printing, but beautiful books were duplicated in quantity and, through the wider consequent circulation, became—instead of decorations on the shelves of the wealthy and powerful—vital forces in moulding the thought of the people. From this precedent our thesis is logically derived. The fine making of common books—is not this an ambition to challenge the imagination of the bookmaker of idealism—a crusade in which we can enlist with a will?

Let me vision for you a book of the future, yet in no way beyond the bounds of practicality. It is convenient to handle, easy to read, the execution is workmanlike, the materials are good but not extravagant, the design a thing of beauty, revealing the hand of an artist. Into its makeup will go the gold refined from ore mined by many generations of printers of genius, wrought into a work of art by the taste and skill of its designer. It is in this direction and along these paths that we shall seek and find the "Golden Book."

NOTES AND INDEX

Notes

NO attempt will be made in this volume to give a bibliography of the subjects dealt with, for the scope is so wide that such a bibliography would require an undue allowance of space. I will give, therefore, references to works of which extensive use has been made in the preparation of some of our chapters, and comments on some special points in question.

Initial letters and headbands used throughout the volume, aside from those made by the typefounders and composing machine companies, have been taken from *Ars Typographica*, from a booklet printed by Norman T. A. Munder for the American Writing Paper Company, and from a book on Letterheads recently published by Crane & Company. Many have been made specially for me by various artists, among them: Clarence P. Hornung, Paul Ressinger, Frank Powers, and Aaron Bohrod. A number of unusually handsome examples have been reproduced from Bruce Rogers' edition of *Geofroy Tory*.

PAGE 9

Primitive methods of writing have been concisely described by James H. Breasted in "The Physical Processes of Writing in the Early Orient and their Relation to the Origin of the Alphabet," in *American Journal of Semitic Languages and Literatures*, Chicago, 1916, Vol. 32, p. 230-249. To this article I am largely indebted for the information in this chapter.

PAGE 12

The original reproduction of the Assyrian relief showing the scribes at work is in Patterson-Kleinmann, 88/89—Layard, Monuments of Ninevah, I, 58.

PAGE 14

This statement regarding the origin and manufacture of papyrus is based on the statement by G. Moeller, *Hieratische Palaeographie*, I, p. 4-7.

PAGE 17

For a discussion of the form of the stylus, see A. T. Clay, "Documents from the Temple Archives of Nippur," Philadelphia, 1906, p.

[389]

17-20; and L. Messerschmidt in *Orientalische Literatur-Zeitung*. Also A. T. Clay, in *Geographical Magazine* for April, 1916.

PAGE 18

The best authority on the alphabet and its origins is a recent volume by Jensen, with excellent plates showing the derivation of the various scripts:

JENSEN, HANS. Geschichte der Schrift. Hannover, Orient-Buchhandlung Heinz Lafaire, 1925.

Other authorities are:

TAYLOR, ISAAC. The alphabet. 1883. (Revised edition, 1899.)

CLODD, E. The story of the alphabet. n. d. [*cerca* 1900].

ROBERTS, E. S. Introduction to Greek epigraphy, 1887-1905.

PAGE 19

For full information on the Cretan scripts see:

EVANS, ARTHUR J. Scripta Minoa, I. Oxford, 1909.

EVANS, ARTHUR J. Cretan pictographs and pre-Phoenician script. London and New York, 1895.

For critical discussion of Evans' hypotheses, see:

KLUGE, H. Die Schrift der Mykenier, Eine Untersuchung über System und Lautwert der von Arthur J. Evans entdeckten vorphönizischen Schriftzeichen. Cöthen, 1897.

The Sinai script was first reported upon by Gardiner in:

GARDINER, ALAN H. The Egyptian origin of the Semitic alphabet. *Journal of Egyptian Archaeology*, vol. 3, p. 1, 1916.

On this see also Sethe, who accepts Gardiner's theory:

SETHE, Die neu-entdeckte Sinai-Schrift und die Entstehung der semitischen Schrift. *Nachrichten der Gött. Ges. der Wissenschaften*, 1917, p. 437-475.

On the text of the Sinai inscriptions see:

GRIMME, Althebräische Inschriften vom Sinai. Darmstadt, 1923.

On the character of the early Semitic alphabets and writing, consult:

E. SCHAEFER, "Die Vokallösigkeit der Phoenizischen Alphabets. *Zeitschrift für Aegyptische Sprache*, vol. 52 (1915), p. 95-98. Also A. REINACH, *Revue Epigraphique*, n. s. Vol. 2, (1914), p. 130-155.

PAGE 22

This illustration and the two following are reproduced from Frederic W. Goudy's article on the roman alphabet in Vol. II of *Ars Typographica*.

PAGE 26

The information in this chapter on the beginnings of papermaking is based largely on:

CARTER, FRANCIS H. The invention of printing in China and its spread westward. New York, 1925.

PAGE 27

The discovery of the fabric containing fibers of the paper mulberry

NOTES

tree is reported by Sir Aurel Stein, *Serindia* p. 674, note 22.

PAGE 28

The document reproduced facing p. 28 is TXII, a ii 2 of the finds recorded by Sir Aurel Stein. The size of the original is 9½ x 16⅜ inches. It was found in a brown silk envelope. Details regarding these Sogdian documents are recorded in his *Serindia*, p. 670 and p. 776.

PAGE 29

The information on early European papermaking is derived in large degree from:

HUNTER, DARD. Fifteenth century papermaking. *Ars Typographica*, New York, 1926, vol. 3, p. 37-51.

Other authorities on early Chinese printing are:

STEIN, SIR M. AUREL. Serindia. London, 1921.

KAMESO, ASAKURA. [History of early printing in Japan.] *In Japanese.* Tokyo, 1909.

SATOW, SIR ERNEST. On the early history of printing in Japan. *Transactions of the Asiatic Society of Japan*, 1882, vol. 10, p. 48-83, 252-259.

HULLE, HERMANN. Ueber den alten chinesischen Typendruck und seine Entwicklung in den Ländern des Fernen Ostens. Berlin, 1923.

PELLIOT, PAUL. Une bibliothèque médiévale retrouvée au Kan Sou. *Bulletin de l'Ecole Française d'Extrême Orient*, 1908, vol. 8, p. 525-527.

CURZON, ROBERT. Printing in China and Europe. *Miscellanies of the Philobiblon Society*. London, 1860, vol. 6, p. 1-33.

PAGE 36

Much of the material in this chapter is drawn from the delightful book by Madan, to which the reader is referred for a more extended treatment of the subject.

MADAN, FALCONER. Books in manuscript, London, 1920.

PAGE 43

This chapter is based to a large extent on the fundamental work by Professor Carter.

CARTER, FRANCIS H. The invention of printing in China and its spread westward. New York, 1925.

PAGE 49

This block-printed book of 1187 and other examples of East Asiatic printing in the collection of the Newberry Library are described in:

LAUFER, BERTHOLD. Descriptive account of the collection of Chinese, Tibetan, Mongol, and Japanese books in the Newberry Library. (Publications of the Newberry Library, No. 4.) Chicago, [1914].

The account of Pi Shêng's invention was by Shên Kua, a contemporary writer regarded as authentic. The passage is here quoted from Carter, *op. cit.*, p. 160-161.

PAGE 57

For further information on early woodcuts and block-books see Thomas F. Carter, *The Invention of Printing in China* (New York, 1925), Joseph Cundall, *A Brief History of Wood-Engraving* (London, 1895), Campbell Dodgson, *Catalogue of Early German and Flemish Woodcuts in the British Museum* (London, 1903-11. 2v.), Alfred W. Pollard, *Fine Books* (London, 1912), and William H. Willshire, *Descriptive Catalogue of Playing and Other Cards in the British Museum* (London, 1876).

PAGE 58

Manuscript entries upon two criblé engravings on metal offer good evidence that these prints were made in 1406. See Henri Delaborde, "Notice sur deux Estampes de 1406 et sur les Commencements de la Gravure" in *Gazette des Beaux Arts*, 2. ser., I (1869), 238-253

PAGE 66

The initial and headband on this page were designed by Will Ransom and are here used through his courtesy.

PAGE 67

The following works are referred to:

FORRER, R. Die Zeugdrucke der byzantinischen, romanischen, gothischen und späteren Kunstepochen. Strasbourg, 1894.

FORRER, R. Die Kunst der Zeugdrucks von Mittelalter bis zur Empirezeit. Strasbourg, 1898.

FORRER, R. Les imprimeurs de tissus dans leurs relations historiques et artistiques avec les corporations. Strasbourg, 1898.

DEPIERRE, Jos. L'impression sur tissus, spécialement l'impression à la main, à travers les âges et dans les divers pays. Mulhouse, 1910.

PAGE 68

This important block which belongs to J. Protat, a printer of Mâcon, France, has been described and reproduced by Bouchot. See: BOUCHOT, H. Un ancêtre de la gravure sur bois. Paris, 1902.

PAGE 69

Regarding the thirteenth century manuscript with the stamped initials, see:

FLEURY, ED. Les manuscrits à miniatures de la Bibliothèque de Laon, 1863, Part II, p. 4ff.

For the origins of oil paints, consult:

CH. DALBON. Les origines de la peinture à l'huile, 1904, p. 35-98.

C. LOUMYER. Les traditions techniques de la peinture médiévale, 1920, p. 153-160.

PAGE 70

The binding stamped with letter stamps in relief belongs to the Verein für Nassauischer Altertumskunde. It has been described by Gottfried Zedler in his *Gutenberg Forschungen*.

On binder's stamps in use prior to the invention of printing, consult:

FALK, FRANZ. Der Stempeldruck vor Gutenberg. *Zentralblatt für Bibliothekswesen*, Leipzig, 1900, Beihefte, vol. 8, p. 73-79.

NOTES

Husung, Max J. Neues Material zur Frage des Stempeldrucks vor Gutenberg. *Gutenberg Festschrift*, Mainz, 1925, p. 66-72.

Theele, Joseph. Einzeltypenstempel auf Kölner Einbänden. *Gutenberg Jahrbuch*, Mainz, 1926, p. 9-13.

PAGE 71

This entry of 1398 appears in the *Archives de la Côte-d'Or*, série B, No. 11673, cited by Dehaisnes: Histoire de l'Art dans les Flandres, vol. 2, p. 770.

Extracts from the Paulirinus manuscript have been published by Kemke in the *Centralblatt für Bibliothekswesen*, 1890, p. 144-149.

PAGE 73

The literature on the invention of printing is extremely voluminous, and we can make reference to a few only of the more important works. The most important sources are the *Veröffentlichungen* of the Gutenberg Gesellschaft, the *Gutenberg Jahrbuch*, the *Gutenberg Festschrift* of 1900 and of 1925, the books by J. H. Hessels, the recent volume on the Coster question by Zedler, and the files of the *Zentralblatt für Bibliothekswesen*.

On the invention controversy, consult the following:

Bauer, Friedrich. Das Giessinstrument des Schriftgiessers. Ein Beitrag zur Geschichte der Schriftgiesserei. Hamburg und München, 1922.

Bauer, Friedrich. Wer hat die Buchdruckerkunst erfunden?

Castellani, C. L'origine tedesca e l'origine olandese dell' invenzione della stampa. *Zentralblatt für Bibliothekswesen*, vol. 6, p. 50; vol. 7, p. 332.

Haebler, Konrad. Warum tragen Gutenbergs Drucke keine Unterschrift, *Zentralblatt für Bibliothekswesen*, 1902, vol. 19, p. 103.

Hessels, J. H. Gutenberg, was he the inventor of printing? London, 1882.

Junius, Adrian. Batavia. Leiden, 1588.

Kruitwagen, Bonaventura. Die Ansprüche Hollands auf die Erfindung der Buchdruckerkunst. *Gutenberg Festschrift*, Mainz, 1925, p. 353-370.

Linde, Antonius van der. De Haarlemsche Kosterlegende. The Hague, 1870.

Linde, Antonius van der. Gutenberg. Geschichte und Erdichtung. Stuttgart, 1878.

Mori, Gustav. Was hat Gutenberg erfunden? Leipzig, 1922.

Muller, G. H. Die Quellen der Costerlegende. *Zentralblatt für Bibliothekswesen*. 1911, vol. 28, p. 145 ff.

Pollard, Alfred W. Gutenberg, Fust, Schoeffer and the invention of printing. *The Library*. 1907, vol. 8, p. 69.

Someren, I. F. van. De Gutenberg-Legende. *Het Boek*, 1914, vol. 3, p. 1-10.

Zedler, Gottfried. Die neuere Gutenbergforschung und die Lösung der Costerfrage. Frankfurt a. M., 1923.

Zedler, Gottfried. Von Coster zu Gutenberg. Der holländische

Frühdruck und die Erfindung des Buchdrucks. Leipzig, 1921.

On Gutenberg and his life and work consult:

BORKEL, ALFRED. Gutenberg. Sein Leben, sein Werk, sein Ruhm. Giessen, 1897.

DEGEORGE, L. L'Imprimerie en Europe au XVe et au XVIe siècle. Les premières productions typographiques et les premiers imprimeurs. Paris, 1892.

DELISLE, LEOPOLD. A la mémoire de Gutenberg. Paris, 1900.

DZIATZKO, KARL. Was wissen wir von dem leben und der Person Johann Gutenbergs? In: Sammlung bibliothekswissenschaftlicher Arbeiten, vol. 8. Leipzig, 1895.

FIRMIN-DIDOT, A. Histoire de la typographie. Paris, 1882.

GOTTSCHALK, PAUL. Die Buchkunst Gutenbergs und Schöffers. Mit einem einleitenden Versuch über die Entwicklung der Buchkunst von ihren frühesten Anfängen bis auf die heutige Zeit. Berlin, 1918.

HESSELS, J. H. The so-called Gutenberg documents. *The Library*, n. s., 1909-1910.

HUMPHREYS, H. NOEL. A history of the art of printing. London, 1867.

LINDE, ANTONIUS VAN DER. Geschichte der Erfindung der Buchdruckerkunst. 3 vols. Berlin, 1886.

MADDOX, H. A. Printing, its history, practice and progress. London, 1923.

MEISNER, HEINRICH, and JOHANN LUTHER. Die Erfindung der Buchdruckerkunst. Zum 500. Geburtstag Gutenbergs. Bielefeld, 1900. (Monographien zur Weltgeschichte. Vol. XI.)

MORTET, CHARLES. Les origines et les débuts de l'imprimerie d'après les recherches les plus récentes. Paris, 1922.

REQUIN. La question de l'imprimerie à Avignon à 1444 et 1446. Marseille, 1902.

REQUIN. L'imprimerie à Avignon. Paris, 1890.

SCHORBACH, KARL. Die urkundlichen Nachrichten über Johann Gutenberg. *Zentralblatt für Bibliothekswesen*, 1900, Beiheft, vol. 8, p. 153-319.

SCHUBERT, ANTON. Zur Geschichte der Familie Waldvogel. *Zentralblatt für Bibliothekswesen*, 1899, vol. 16, p. 500.

HESSELS, J. H. The Gutenberg fiction. London, 1912.

On the early printing of Mainz, consult:

DE RICCI, SEYMOUR. Catalogue raisonné des premières impressions de Mayence (1445-1467). Mainz, 1911. (Veröffentl. der Gutenberg-Gesellschaft.)

DZIATZKO, KARL. Gutenberg's früheste Druckerpraxis. Leipzig, 1890.

FREIS, ERNST. Zum Rubrikenverzeichnis der 36-zeiligen Bibel. *Zentralblatt für Bibliothekswesen*, 1918, vol. 35, p. 167.

HUPP, OTTO. Ein Missale speciale, Vorläufer des Psalteriums von 1457. München, 1898.

HUPP, OTTO. Zum Streit um das Missale speciale. Mit Nachwort von P. Schwenke. *Zentralblatt*

NOTES

für Bibliothekswesen, 1918, vol. 35, p. 255.

PERTZ. Uber die gedruckten Ablass-briefe von 1454-55. *Abhandl. d. Berl. Akad. d. Wiss.*, 1856, Phil. Kl., p. 707.

PREISENDANZ, KARL and PAUL SCHWENKE. Zwei neue Exemplare der Ablassbriefe von 1455. *Zentralblatt für Bibliothekswesen*, 1919, vol. 36, p. 175.

SCHWENKE, PAUL. Ein neues Datum für den 31-zeiligen Ablassbrief von 1454. *Zentralblatt für Bibliothekswesen*, 1909, vol. 26, p. 30; 1910, vol. 27, p. 219.

SCHWENKE, PAUL. Johannes Gutenbergs 42-zeiligen Bibel. Ergänzungsband zur Faksimile-Ausgabe. Leipzig, 1923.

The best works on the early Cambridge (Mass.) press are:

RODEN, ROBERT F. The Cambridge press (1638-1692). New York, 1905.

LITTLEFIELD, GEORGE E. The early Massachusetts press, 1638-1711, 2 vols. Boston, 1907.

A more recent contribution to the subject, on which the present chapter is largely based, is:

McMURTRIE, DOUGLAS C. Die ersten Drucke in English-sprachigen Nord-Amerika. *Gutenberg Jahrbuch*, Mainz, 1926, p. 136-143.

PAGE 74

The summary of the Junius story is based on that given by Kruitwagen in the article listed below:

KRUITWAGEN, BONAVENTURA, O. F. M. Die Ansprüche Hollands auf die Erfindung der Buchdruckerkunst. *Gutenberg Festschrift*, Mainz, 1925, p. 353-370.

PAGE 140

The standard work on Caxton is the two-volume treatise by William Blades. One of the best short essays is that by George Parker Winship, which has been of much help in the preparation of this chapter, from it being quoted the quotations from Caxton's prologues. The chapter in Pollard's *Fine Books* on "Printing in England" (1476-1580) is full, explicit, and authoritative.

Much entirely new documentary material bearing on Caxton's activities on the continent has been recently discovered by W. J. Blyth Crotch and published in March, 1927, in an article listed below.

CROTCH, W. J. BLYTH. Caxton on the continent. *The Library*, London, 1927, n. s., vol. 7, pp. 387-401.

PAGE 155

For further information regarding bibliographies of incunabula see Robert A. Peddie, *Fifteenth Century Books, a Guide to their Identification* (London, 1913), David Murray, *Bibliography, Its Scope and Methods* (Glasgow, 1917), and Alfred W. Pollard, "Incunabula," in *Encyclopedia Britannica*, 11 ed. XIV, 369-70. For a discussion in English of the *Gesamtkatalog der Wiegendrucke*, see *The Library Journal*, LXI (1926), 426, 7.

PAGE 160

For further information on the subjects treated by fifteenth century books see Robert Steele, "What Fifteenth Century Books Are About" in *The Library* (1903-1905, 1907) n. s., Vol. 4, p. 235-254; vol. 5, p. 337-58; vol. 6, p. 137-155; vol 8, p. 225-238; and Alfred W. Pollard "Introduction" to the *Catalogue of Books Printed in the Fifteenth Century, now in the British Museum* (London, 1905), vol. 3, p. ix-xxvii.

PAGE 170

For further information see Arthur A. Tilley, "Estienne," in *Encyclopedia Britannica* II. ed., IX, 798-800; G. H. Putman, *Books and Their Makers in the Middle Ages*, New York, 1897-1898. 2 vols.; D. B. Updike, *Printing Types*, Cambridge, 1922; 2 vols.; A. J. Bernard, *Geofroy Tory*, Cambridge, 1926; A. W. Pollard, "The Books of Hours of Geoffroy Tory" in *Bibliographica*, London, 1895, I., 114-122.

PAGE 201

The best reference work on this subject is:

COHEN, HENRI. Guide de l'amateur de livres à gravures du XVIIIe siècle. Sixième édition, revue, corrigée et considerablement augmentée par Seymour de Ricci. Paris, 1912.

Other books which may be found useful are:

HIND, A. M. A short history of engraving and etching. London, 1911.

BERALDI, J. H. Estampes et livres, 1872-1892. Paris, 1892.

LEONIE, J. Bibliography of the 18th century art and illustrated books. London, 1898.

PAGE 225

Our main source of information regarding Spanish-American printing history is J. T. Medina's series of bibliographical studies, of which the following has been of especial assistance in the preparation of this chapter:

MEDINA, JOSE TORIBIO. La imprenta en Mexico (1539-1821). 8 vols. Santiago, 1907-1912.

PAGE 250

The best source on Franklin's work as a printer is:

OSWALD, JOHN CLYDE. Benjamin Franklin, printer. Garden City, 1917.
See also:

LIVINGSTON, LUTHER: Franklin and his press at Passy. New York, 1914.

ADAMS, RANDOLPH G. The passports printed by Benjamin Franklin at his Passy press. Ann Arbor, 1925.

Regarding the possibility that the first Mexican printer was Esteban Martín, Iguiniz, the leading Mexican bibliographer of the present day has this to say: "It is known from documentary evidence that the first viceroy of New Spain, Don Antonio de Mendoza, and the first archbishop of Mexico, Don Fray Juan de Zumárraga, during the years 1535-1537, carried on the necessary negotiations for the establishment of this noble art in the country whose

NOTES

civil and ecclesiastic government had been entrusted to them."

And further: "In the middle of June of the year mentioned [1539] it appears that citizenship was conferred upon Esteban Martín, a printer by trade; but for lack of documents it is not clear whether he practised his trade before the arrival of Pablos. Trustworthy authors assure us that the first book produced by the Mexican presses was the 'Escala espiritual' by San Juan Clímaco, translated into Spanish by Fray Juan de la Anunciación, a monk of the Order of St. Dominic, and that it was printed in 1535. Was there a printing office before the one established by Juan Pablos? Again the lack of documentation does not permit us to clarify this point, which, for the rest, lends itself to many conjectures."

These quotations are from the following article:

IGUINIZ, I. B. La imprenta en Mexico durante la Dominación Española. *Gutenberg Festschrift*, Mainz, 1925, p. 122-124.

PAGE 266

This chapter is based in large degree on the excellent books by Dr. Charles L. Nichols of Worcester listed below, supplemented by considerable study on my own part of the Isaiah Thomas papers in the collection of the American Antiquarian Society.

NICHOLS, CHARLES LEMUEL. Isaiah Thomas, printer, writer and collector. Boston, Club of Odd Volumes, 1912.

NICHOLS, CHARLES LEMUEL. Bibliography of Worcester. Worcester, 1900.

PAGE 276

The best source of information regarding the work of William Morris as a printer is the volume by H. Halliday Sparling listed below. Sparling was secretary of the Kelmscott Press and Morris' son-in-law and had available most of the records of his work. The book errs on the side of enthusiasm, being frankly a eulogy, but it contains a wealth of material.

SPARLING, H. HALLIDAY. The Kelmscott Press and William Morris, master-craftsman. London, Macmillan and Co., 1924.

STEELE, ROBERT. The revival of printing. London (Riccardi Press), 1912.

PAGE 304

The standard authority on type design, and one destined to be standard for many years to come, is:

UPDIKE, DANIEL BERKELEY. Printing types, their history, forms, and use, 2 vols. Boston, 1922.

PAGE 306

The sources of present Garamond type designs are discussed fully in the following article, in which was presented new documentary material of value, together with reproductions from Jannon's specimen printed at Sedan, 1621.

PAGE 310

BEAUJON, PAUL [*pseud. of Mrs. Frederic Warde*]. The "Garamond" types, sixteenth and seventeenth century sources considered. *The Fleuron*, No. 5, Cambridge, 1926, p. 131-179.

The plate is reproduced from Frederic W. Goudy's *The Alphabet*.

PAGE 313

This chapter is based largely on Alfred W. Pollard's very excellent treatise entitled: *Last Words on the History of the Title Page*. From this volume also three of the illustrations are reproduced.

POLLARD, ALFRED W. Last words on the history of the title page. London, 1891.
See also:

BAMMES, REINHOLD. Der Titelsatz, seine Entwicklung und seine Grundsätze. Leipzig, 1911.

DE VINNE, THEODORE L. A treatise on title-pages. New York, 1902.

PAGE 315

The unique copy of the "bul" is now in the John Rylands Library, Manchester, England.

PAGE 353

Information on private presses is at present scattered in many places. Considerable information may be found in Robert Steele's *The Revival of Printing* (London, 1912). On September 3, 1927, Will Ransom began a series of articles on private presses in the *Publishers' Weekly*.

PAGE 340

On the history and art of bookbinding consult:

COCKERELL, D. Bookbinding and the care of books. London, 1901.

DUTTON, MEIRIC K. History of the art of bookbinding. Norwood, Mass., 1926.

GRUEL, L. Manuel de l'amateur de reliures. Paris, 1877.

HORNE, H. P. The binding of books. London, 1894.

PRIDEAUX, S. T. Historical sketch of bookbinding. London, 1893.

PRIDEAUX, S. T. Bookbinders and their craft. London, 1903.

PRIDEAUX, S. T. Modern bookbindings. London, 1906.

ZAEHNSDORF, J. W. The art of bookbinding. London, 1880.

McMURTRIE, DOUGLAS C. The First American bookbinder. *Bookbinding Magazine*, New York, 1927, vol. 6, no. 6, page 22, 24.

Index

Adler, Elmer, typographer, 371.

Adolf, Archbishop of Mainz, appoints Gutenberg his courtier, 86.

Aldus Manutius, printer and publisher at Venice, 123; his Greek types, 125; his italic, 126, 127; his printers' mark, 128.

Alost, first printing at, 113.

Alphabet, origin, 18.

Alvise, G. and A., 337.

American Antiquarian Society, founded by I. Thomas, 244, 274.

American Type Founders Company, 305.

American Weekly Mercury, founded by Andrew Bradford, 261.

Andreae, Johannes, statement regarding invention of printing by, 103.

Andrews, Eben T., letter to Isaiah Thomas, 244.

Ars Moriendi, block book, 62, 64.

Arts and Crafts Exhibiiton, first, 276.

Ascensius, Jodocus Badius, printer at Paris, 180, 320.

Ashendene Press, the, at Chelsea, 355.

Austria, first printing in, (at Vienna) by Stephan Koblinger, 115.

Avignon, early attempts at writing artificially at, 101.

Badius, *see* Ascensius.

Balearic Islands, first printing in (at Valdemosa), by Nicholas Calafat, 115.

Bamberg, first printing at, 107.

Bämler, Johann, of Augsburg, 335.

Barbier, Jean, printer at London, 150.

Baskerville, John, printer at Birmingham, 205, 206, 307; private press of, 354; originates wove paper, 33.

Batchelor, Joseph, of Little Chart, papermaker, 287.

Baxter, Richard, his "Call to the Unconverted," 245.

Bellaert, Jacob, first known printer at Haarlem, 78, 113.

Benton, Linn Boyd, inventor of punch cutting machine, 293.

Bergel, Arnold, reference to Fust-Gutenberg lawsuit, 105.

Berthelet, Thomas, introduction of gold tooling in England by, 348.

Beughem, Cornelius, bibliographer of incunabula, 155.

Bewick, Thomas, improver of wood cutting, 328.

[399]

Bible, fifteenth century editions of, 162.

Bible, 42-line, 90; rubrication completed, 94; facsimile of, 95; a method of production of, 96.

Bible, 36-line, 98.

Bible, transmission of, 39.

Biblia Pauperum, block book, 61, 65.

Binder's stamps, in use before invention of movable type, 70.

Binding, oldest, now extant, 342.

Blades, William, his study of William Caxton, 158.

Block books, 57, 66.

Block prints (Heiligen), 58.

Bodoni, Giambattista, Italian printer and typefounder, 217, 221, 307, 309.

Book, constituents of a fine, 375-386.

Book, decoration of, 334.

Books of Hours, 183, 186.

Bookbinding, earliest forms of, 340.

Bookbinding in England, 343.

Bookbinding in Ireland, 343.

Bookbinding of today, 350.

Book illustration, early history of, 324, 325.

Bookmaking, processes of, 291.

Bookmaking, the renaissance of fine, 365.

Booklet Press, the, 361.

Boston Gazette, 250.

Boucher, 202.

Boustrophedon writing, 24.

Bradford, William, first printer of Pennsylvania, 247; first printer of New York, 248; first printer of New Jersey, 248, 254.

Bradshaw, Henry, bibliographer of incunabula, 157.

Braud, Denis, first printer in New Orleans, 248.

Breasted, James H., on Assyrian methods of writing, 17.

Bremer Press, the, 363.

Breydenbach, his *Peregrinations*, 329.

Brito, Jean, pretender as inventor of printing, 101.

Bruges, first printing at, 114.

Brun, Pedro, printer at Tortosa and Barcelona, 115.

Brunet, J. C., bibliographer, 157.

Budapest, first printing in, 115.

Bul zu dutsch der Babst Pius II, first known book with title page, 314.

Burne-Jones, Sir Edward, 281, 284.

Buyer, Barthelemi, patron of first printing at Lyons, 112.

Calafat, Nicholas, first printer in Balearic Islands, 115.

Campbell, bibliographer of Dutch incunabula, 158.

"Caractères de l'Université, 306.

Carbo, Ludovicus, statement regarding invention of printing by, 103.

Carter, Thomas F., on block printed playing cards, 52; on transmission of block printing from China to Europe, 51.

Caslon, William, English typefounder, 197; his type design, 199.

Castaldi, Pamfilo, pretender as inventor of printing, 101.

"Catecismo Mexicano", 229.

Catholicon, colophon of, 99.

Catterson-Smith, R., 288.

INDEX

"Caves of the Thousand Buddhas," early printing discovered in, 45

Caxton, William, his printing at Bruges, 114; first English printer, his early history, 140; his Troy translation, 142; learns printing, 143; partnership with Colard Mansion, 144; his service to English literature, 150.

Cennini, Cennino, on textile printing, 67.

Chaucer, Geoffrey, the works of, 284.

"Chaucer" type, third type designed by William Morris, 284.

China, invention of paper in, 27; origin of printing in, 43.

Claudin, Anatole, historian of French printing, 113.

Clay tablets, as writing material, 17.

Cobden-Sanderson, T. J., disciple of William Morris, 351; establishes press, 358.

Codex Sinaiticus, 41.

Cohen, Henri, bibliographer, 201.

Colines, Simon de, printer at Paris, 177.

Cologne Chronicle, 74, 104.

Composition, book and magazine, 295, 296.

Composition, hand, 294, 295.

Connecticut, New London, press comes to, 1709, 248.

Constantinople, first printing in, 115.

Coornhert, Dirck, reference to printing at Haarlem, 78.

Copinger, Walter A., bibliographer of incunabula, 156.

Cornelis, bookbinder at Haarlem, 78.

Coster, Lourens Janszoon, claimed to be inventor of printing, 74; innkeeper and chandler, 78; manuscript pedigree of family, 78.

Cracow, first printing of, 115.

Crantz, Martin, early printer at Paris, 112.

Crete, evidence of early alphabetic writing in, 19.

Cromberger, Juan, printer at Seville, Spain, principal of first printing office in Mexico, 225.

Davis, James, first printer of North Carolina, 248.

Day, Matthew, second printer in the U. S., 239.

Day, Stephen, first printer in America, 236.

Delaware, Wilmington, in 1761, printing comes to, 248.

Denham, a merchant in Philadelphia, 257.

Denmark, first printing in (at Odensee) by Johann Snell, 115.

Dépierre, Joseph, researches in the history of cloth printing, 67.

De Vinne, Theodore L., American printer of eminence, 372.

Deventer, first printing at, 113.

De Worde, Wynkyn, successor to William Caxton, 148.

Dialogues, produced by Henri II Estienne in 1578, 176.

Diamond Sutra, earliest printed book, 46.

Dibdin, Thomas Frognall, librarian of Earl Spencer and bibliophile, 156, 210.

Didots, French printers, 217, 307, 318.

[401]

Didot, François, founder of the French line of printers, 218.

Didot, François Ambroise, French printer and typefounder, 218, 219.

De Ricci, Seymour, editor of Cohen bibliography, 202.

Derome, Nicolas Denis, famous binder, 347.

Dinckmut, Conrad, 132.

"Diptychs," 340.

Donatus, editions of, produced at Mainz, 88.

Dorat, *Les Baisers*, 202.

Doves Press, the, at Hammersmith, 358.

Dunne, Hans, goldsmith, supplies Gutenberg with printing material, 71.

Dunster, Henry, his relations with the early Massachusetts Press, 242.

Du Pré, Jean, producer of first illustrated book in France, 138.

Dürer, Albrecht, 333, 337.

Dziatzko, documents relating to Gutenberg published by, 87; study of 42-line Bible by, 94.

Edelstein, the second illustrated book, 129.

Egmond Chronicle, on invention of printing, 79.

Eisen, 202.

El Fayyûm, Egypt, discoveries of documents at, 51.

Elieser, Rabbi, first printer in Lisbon, 115.

Eliot, John, Rev., promoter of early printing in the Indian tongue, 241.

Elston Press, at New Rochelle, N. Y., 360.

Elzevirs, 305.

Engraving, plate, 326.

Eragny Press, the, at Hammersmith, 355.

Ernst-Ludwig Press, the, 363.

"Escala Spiritual," printed by Martin, 228.

Espinosa, Antonio, expert type cutter, 232, 233.

Essex House Press, the, 357.

Estienne, Charles, brother of Robert, 175.

Estienne Family, 171.

Estienne, François, publisher at Paris, 175.

Estienne, François II, printer at Paris and Geneva, 176, 177.

Estienne, Henri II, printer at Geneva, 176.

Estienne, Robert, printer at Paris, 172.

Estienne, Robert II, "Printer to the King," 176.

Evans, Arthur, on Cretan origin of alphabet, 19.

Eve, Clovis, binder at Paris, 347.

Eve, Nicholas, bindings of, 346.

Falk, Franz, on early binder's stamps, 70.

Fêng Tao, his instrumentality in printing the Confucian Classics, 48.

Fernandez, Fray Alonso, 228.

Fichet, Guillaume, patron of first printing at Paris, 102; statement regarding invention of printing by, 102.

Fischer, documents relating to Gutenberg published by, 87.

Flores, Doña Francisco, first woman printer at Oaxaca, 234.

INDEX

Forrer, R., researches in the history of cloth printing, 67.

Fournier, Simon Pierre, typefounder at Paris, 203.

Fowle, Daniel, first printer of New Hampshire, 248.

Franciscus, Magister, statement regarding invention of printing by, 103.

Franklin, Benjamin, his apprenticeship, 230; his arrival in London, 256; his return to America, 257; his partnership with Meredith, 259; on his own, 259; publications of, 260; commissioner to France, 264; establishment of private press, 264; "I, Printer," 265.

Franklin, James, pioneer printer of Rhode Island, 248, 253.

"Freeman's Oath," first printing in the American colonies, 237.

Friburger, Michael, early printer at Paris, 112.

Fust, Johann, advances money to Gutenberg, 85; lawsuit with Gutenberg, 85; later printing by, 100.

Fust and Schoeffer, publisher's list of, 100; Psalter of, 334.

Gaguin, Robert, letter of Fichet regarding invention of printing addressed to, 102.

Garamond, Claude, 182, 183, 221, 287, 305; his types used by Estienne, 174.

Gardiner, Alan H., on Sinai script, 19.

Gelthus, Adam, statement regarding invention of printing by, 104.

Georgia Gazette, first newspaper in Georgia, 248.

Georgia, Savannah, in 1763, printing comes to, 248.

Gering, Ulrich, first printer at Paris, 112.

Gilliss, Walter, 371.

Glover, Jose, Reverend, father of printing in U. S., 235.

Golden Age of typography, 170.

Golden Book, the, towards, 373.

Golden Cockerel Press, at Waltham Saint Lawrence in Berkshire, 360.

Goudy, Frederic W., types of, 309, 310, 311; designer and cutter of types, 309; and Bertha, establishes private press, 361.

Graesse, biblographer, 157.

Grahborn brothers, the, 371.

Granjon, Robert, 305.

Gravelot, 202.

Green, Samuel, 241.

Green, Timothy, one of the first printers in Vermont, 248; succeeds Thomas Short, 1713, 248.

Grolier, Jean, influencer of, on bookbinding, 345.

Guicciardini, Lud., reference to printing at Haarlem, 78.

Gutenberg, Johann, 74, 84.

Gutenberg documents, 87.

Haarlem, first printing at, 113.

Haebler, Konrad, his *Typenrepertorium*, 157; his studies of Spanish incunabula, 114; on work of German printers in foreign lands, 108; hypothesis regarding first printing in Italy, 110.

Hain, Ludwig, bibliographer of incunabula, 156.

Han, Ulrich, 136.

Heiligenleben, first illustrated book printed at Augsburg, 130.

Helmasperger Instrument, 85, 105.

Herbst, Johann, statement regarding invention of printing by, 103.

Herculaneum, recovery of manuscripts at, 42.

Hess, Andreas, first printer in Budapest, 115.

Hessels, J. H., Documents relating to Gutenberg published by, 87; combats Ottley's views on order of Speculum editions, 83.

Heynlin, Jean, patron of first printing at Paris, 102, 111.

Hieroglyphics, 9.

Higman, Jean, printer of Paris, 171.

History of Printing in America by Thomas, 273.

Hochfeder, Caspar, first printer in Cracow, 115.

Holbein, Hans, 333, 337.

Holland, primitive printing, examples of, 79, 80, 82.

Holland, first printing in, 113.

Holland, primitive types of, 80.

Hooper, William Harcourt, wood engraver, 281.

Hopkins, Daniel, letter to, from I. Thomas, 268.

Hornby, C. H. St. John, private press of, 355.

Hubbard, Elbert, director of the Roycroft Shop, 361.

Humery, Kunrad, loans printing equipment to Gutenberg, 86.

Hungary, first printing in (at Budapest), by Andreas Hess, 115.

Hunter, Dard, 362.

Huvin, Jean, printer at London, 150.

Hypnerotomachia Poliphili, 136, 327, 330.

Ibarra, Joachim, leading Spanish printer of the eighteenth century, 307.

Ideographic writing, 9.

Initials, decorative, earliest, 334.

Illumination, 39.

Illustrated books of the fifteenth century, 329.

Incipit, the, 313.

Incunabula, subject of, 155, 160.

Indulgences, first dated examples of printing, 91.

Ink, or varnish base, 69.

Invention of movable types, European, 66, 73.

Invention of movable types, Chinese, its sterile outcome, 56.

Ireland, early manuscript writing, 36.

Iserin Thure, Anna zu der, breach of promise suit brought by, 86.

Italy, first printing in, 110.

Jacobszoen, Jacob, printer at Delft, 113.

Jaenecke, celebrated ink-maker, 287.

Jannon, Jean, typefounder and printer at Sedan, 306.

Janus Press, the 363.

Japan, earliest block printing in, 44.

Jenson, Nicholas, printer at Venice, 117; his early history, 118; his roman types, 119; his gothic types, 122; formation of company, 122; his will, 123, 304; maker of coins, 71.

Joannis, documents relating to Gutenberg published by, 87.

Johann of Paderborn, first printer at Alost, 113.

John of Cologne, partner of Jenson at Venice, 123.

INDEX

Johann of Speyer, first printer at Venice, 110.

John of Westphalia, *see* Johann of Paderborn, 113.

Johnson, Marmaduke, early printer at Cambridge, Mass., 242.

Johnston, James, first printer of Georgia, 248.

Junius, Hadrianus, author of first published account of invention of printing at Haarlem, 75.

Keimer, Samuel, establishes press at Burlington, New Jersey in 1728, 248, 255.

Keith, Sir William, 255.

Kells, Book of, 37.

Kelmscott Press, the, 360.

Kennerley, designed by Goudy, 301.

Mentelin, Johann, printer at Strasbourg, 107.

Ketalaer, Nicholaus, printer at Utrecht, 113.

Keysere, Pieter de, early printer at Paris, 112.

Kleukens brothers, the, 363.

Koblinger, Stephan, first printer in Vienna, 115.

Koelhoff, Johann, of Cologne, 33.

Köhler, documents relating to Gutenberg published by, 87.

Korea, movable type printing in, 55.

Kruitwagen, B., on Junius' account of invention of printing at Haarlem, 78.

Lactantius, Subiaco, 1465, facsimile of, 109.

Lanston, Tolbert, "monotype" invented by, 297.

Le Bé, Guillaume, 221.

Le Febvre, Jacques, editor for Henri Estienne, 172.

Leempt, Gerardus, printer at Utrecht, 113.

Leiden, first printing at, 113.

Léon de Laborde, documents relating to Gutenberg published by, 87.

Le Robert, Jean, purchase in 1446 of Doctrinale by, 83.

Leroy, Guillaume, first printer at Lyons, 112.

Letter stamps, in use on moulds for casting, 70.

Lettou, John, early English printer, 150.

Lignamine, J. P. de, statement regarding invention of printing by, 103.

"Linotype," invention of the, 296.

Lisbon, first printing in, 115.

Lithography, introduction of, 328.

Liu Pin, on early Chinese block printing, 47.

London, first printing at, 146.

Louisiana, New Orleans, in 1768 or earlier, printing comes to, 248.

Ludlow Typograph, the, 199, 297.

Luther, Martin, translation of Bible by, 171.

Machlinia, William, printer at London, 150, 316.

Martin, Esteban, printer of "Escala Spiritual," 228.

Madan, Falconer, on methods of the scribes, 37; on Tischendorf's researches, 40.

Maioli, Thomas, Italian collector, 345.

Manual de Adultos, 230.

Manuale Sacramentorum, 233.

Manutius, Aldus, gold tooling first used by, 345.

Mainz, sack of, bearing on spread of printing, 108; examples of early printing produced at, 87.

Maittaire, Michael, bibliographer of incunabula, 156.

Malouel, Jehan, cutting stamps for pictures, 71.

Mansion, Colard, printer at Bruges, 114, 144.

Martin Marprelate tracts, the, 354.

Martinez, Antonio, printer at Seville, 115.

Maryland, St. Mary's City, 1685, printing comes to, 247.

Massachusetts Spy, 267.

Matthaeus, first printer at Saragossa, 114.

Mearne, Samuel, English binder of eminence, 348.

Medina, J. T., 228, 229.

Meditations of Cardinal Turrecremata, first illustrated book in Italy, 136.

Mendoza, viceroy, patron of early printing in Mexicon, 225.

Mentelin, Johann, pretender as inventor of printing, 101.

Meredith, Hugh, partner of Ben. Franklin, 259.

Mergenthaler, Ottmar, "linotype" invented by, 296.

Merrymount Press, the, of Boston, 368.

Miniatures, in manuscripts, 39.

Moabite Stone, early example of alphabetic writing, 21.

Machlinia, William, 316.

Mohammedan world, barrier to spread of printing, 49.

Mongol Empire, influence on spread of printing, 49.

Monk Makario, first printer in Rieka, 115.

Montenegro, first printing in (at Rieka), by the Monk Makario, 115.

Moreau le jeune, 202.

Morris, William, a typographical Messiah, 276; papers designed by, 287, 339; private press of, 354.

Mosher, Thomas B., designer of books, 361.

Müller, Johann, 353.

Nachmias, David and Samuel ihn, first printers in Constantinople, 115.

Nash, John Henry, typographer, 370.

Newberry Library, example of early Chinese block printing in collection of, 49.

New England Courant, 251.

New Hampshire, Portsmouth, in 1756, printing comes to, 248.

New Jersey, Perth Amboy, 1723, first printing in, 248.

New York, 1693, first printing in, 247.

North Carolina, Newbern, in 1749, printing comes to, 248.

Notary, Julian, printer at London, 150.

Nürnberg Chronicle, 134, 329.

Oberlin, documents relating to Gutenberg published by, 87.

Odensee, first printing in, 115.

Officina Serpentis, the, 363.

Osler, William, his bibliography of medical incunabula, 158.

Ottley, W. Y., views on order of Speculum editions, 82.

Oxford, first printing at, 148.

INDEX

Oudry, J. B., 202.

Pablos, Juan, first printer in Mexico, 225.

Padeloup, Antoine Michel, renowned member of a large family of binders, 347.

Palmart, Lambert, first printer in Spain (at Valencia), 114.

Palmer, Matthias, statement regarding invention of printing by, 103.

Palmer, Samuel, printer of London, 257.

Pannartz, Arnold, pioneer printer in Italy, 108.

Panzer, George W. F., bibliographer of incunabula, 156.

Parchment, its origin, 16.

Parker, James, establishes a press in Woodbridge, New Jersey, 248.

Paulirinus, Paulus, early metal engraver, 71.

Paper, coated, 33; early methods of manufacture, 29; its origin, 26; laid and wove, 33; manufacture by machine, 32.

Papermaking, its bearing on the invention of printing, 66; introduction into the Rhine district, 67.

Papyrus, 1, 341; method of fabrication, 14; manner of use, 15; supplanted by paper, 29.

Paris ordinance forbidding card playing in, 58.

Payne, Roger, changes style of English binding, 348.

Peddie, Robert A., his concordance to bibliographies of incunabula, 158.

Pellechet, Marie, bibliographer of incunabula, 156.

Pelliott, Paul, discovers wooden types of early Chinese origin, 54.

Pennsylvania, 1685, first printing in, 247.

Pennsylvania Gazette, 260, 261.

Period typography, 7.

Perry's Spelling Book, 272.

Pfister, Albrecht, second illustrated type-printed book by, 129.

Phillips, Jr., Eleazer, first printer of South Carolina, 248.

Phoenicians, authors of the alphabet, 18.

Phonographic writing, 9.

Pictographic writing, 9.

Pictor, Bernhard, 335.

Pigouchet, Phillippe, 186.

Pine, *Horace*, 204.

Pi Shêng, Chinese inventor of movable types, 53.

Pissarro, Lucien, private press of, 355, 364.

Plantin, Christopher, printer at Antwerp, 188; "appointed Printer to the King of Spain," 189; Polyglot Bible, 190, 305.

Playing cards in Europe, 57.

Playing cards, their Chinese origin, 52.

Poeschel, Dr. Carl E., founder of Ernst-Ludwig Press, 363.

Poland, first printing in, 115.

Pollard, Alfred W., on identity of printer of 42-line Bible, 96, 314; on Junius' account of invention of printing at Haarlem, 78.

Polyglot Bible, 190, 191.

Pompeii, recovery of manuscripts at, 42.

"Poor Richard," 263, 264.

Portugal, first printing in (at Lisbon), by Rabbi Elieser, 115.

Press, Kelmscott, 280.

Press, screw, 69.

Prince, Edward, type cutter and engraver, 280.

Private presses in America, 360; in Germany, 363; in Holland, 363.

Proctor, Robert, bibliographer of incunabula, 157.

Psalter of 1457, 96; methods of printing initials in, 97; colophon of, 97, 314.

Puerto, Alonso del, pioneer printer at Seville, 115.

Pynson Printers, the, New York, 371.

Pynson, Richard, printer at London, 138, 150.

Ranger, Edmund, first independent American bookbinder, 349.

Ransom, Will, 361.

Ratdolt, pioneer of book decoration, 316, 335.

Read, Deborah, 254.

Reichling, Dietrich, bibliographer of incunabula, 156.

Requin, Abbé, publishes documents on writing artificially at Avignon, 101.

Rhode Island, 1727, printing comes to, 248.

Ricardo, Antonio, first printer at Lima, Peru, 234.

Ricketts, Charles, 355.

Rieka, Montenegro, first printing in, 115.

Rodriguez, 230.

Rogers, Bruce, most important figure in modern fine printing, 366, 368.

Rollins, Carl Purington, typographer of the Yale University Press, 371.

Roman alphabet, early examples of, 23.

Rood, Theodoricus, first printer at Oxford, 148.

Ruppel, Berthold, first printer at Basel, 111.

Rusch, Adolf, printer at Strasbourg, 107.

Sallust, 307.

Salomon, Bernard, 337.

Samarkand, introduction of paper making at, 28.

Schatzbehalter, 134, 329.

Schelhorn, documents relating to Gutenberg published by, 87.

Schmidt, documents relating to Gutenberg published by, 87.

"Schoolmaster-Printer," first printer at St. Albans, 148.

Schöpflin, documents relating to Gutenberg published by, 87.

Schorbach, Karl, documents relating to Gutenberg published by, 87.

Schreiber, W. L., on method of production of earliest Dutch printing, 84.

Schwenke, Paul, study of 42-line Bible by, 94.

Scribes, Egyptian, 11, 12; mediaeval, methods of, 38; writing equipment, 13.

Scriptorium, description of, 37.

Senckenberg, documents relating to Gutenberg published by, 87.

Senefelder, inventor of lithography, 328.

Seville, first printing at, 114.

Shu, Empire of, early printing in, 48.

INDEX

Short, Thomas, establishes press at New London, Conn., 1703, 248.

Sieben Leiden vom Christi, thought to be earliest example of Italian printing, 110.

Sinai Script, 19.

Snell, Johann, first printer in Stockholm, 115; first printer in Odensee, 115.

Song Hyon, on casting of early Korean types, 55.

South Carolina, Charleston, in 1731, printing comes to, 248.

Spain, first printing in, 114.

Spanish types, 307.

Speculum Humanae Salvationis, block book, 64.

Spindeler, Nicolaus, printer at Tortosa and Barcelona, 115.

St. Albans, first printing at, 148.

Stamped initials, 68.

Stein, Sir Aurel, discovers early specimens of paper, 27; discovers specimens of early printing, 45.

Stockholm, first printing in, 115.

Stoll, Johann, early printer at Paris, 112.

Story of the Glittering Plain, first book printed at the Kelmscott Press by William Morris, 281.

Strasbourg, first printing at, 107.

Strasbourg lawsuit, in which Gutenberg is involved, 85, 105.

Stylus, use in cuneiform writing, 16.

St. Catherine, Convent of, 40.

St. Christopher, first dated European woodblock, 58, 59.

St. Sebastian, woodcut of 1437, 60.

Subiaco, first printing at, 108.

Sweden, first printing in (at Stockholm), by Johann Snell, 115.

Sweynheym, Conrad, pioneer printer in Italy, 108.

Switzerland, first printing in, 111.

Taylor, Henry, 371.

Textile printing, 68.

Thewerdanck, the, 330.

Tiffenbach, establishes the Officina Serpentis, 363.

Tischendorf, Constantine, discovers Codex Sinaiticus, 40.

Title page, the, 313; early, printed in England, 316; first books with, 314, 316.

Tooling, gold, introduction of, 344, 348.

Torresanus, Andreas, in possession of Jenson's types, 123.

Tortosa, first printing at, 114.

Tory, Geofroy, 172, 180, 181, 182.

Trajan column, lettering on, 23.

"Troy" type, second designed by William Morris, 281.

Ts'ai Lun, traditional inventor of paper, 27.

Tun-huang, discoveries of early printing at, 45.

Turkey, first printing in (at Constantinople), by David and Samuel ihn Nachmias, 115.

Type casting, 293.

Type design, 304.

Type, earliest known use of decorative units cast like, 337.

Types, metal, in Korea, 55.

Types made of china, invented by Pi Shêng, 53.

Uglheimer, Peter, receives bequest of Jenson's types, 123.

Usher, Hezekiah, first American publisher, 242.

[409]

Updike, Daniel Berkeley, typographer, 368, 370.

Utrecht, Bradshaw's provisional assignment to this city of primitive Dutch printing, 82.

Vale Press, 354.

Valencia, first printing at, 114.

Van Dijk, type cutter, 307.

Van Royen, J. F., director of the Zilverdistel Press, 363.

van Zuren, Johann, reference to printing at Haarlem, 78.

Vascosan, Michael, "Printer to the King," 180.

Veldener, Jan, printer at Louvain, 114; in possession of Speculum blocks, 81.

Vellum, its origin, 16.

Venice, first printing at, 110; ordinance prohibiting playing cards and prints in, 57.

Vérard, Antoine, French publisher, 138.

Vergil, Polydore, statement regarding invention of printing by, 104.

Vermont, Westminster, in 1780, printing comes to, 248.

Viart, Guyonne, widow of Jean Higman, 171.

Vienna, first printing in, 115.

Village Press, the, at Park Ridge, Ill., 361.

Virginia, Jamestown, forbids operation of press, 247.

Voulliéme, bibliographer of Cologne, 158.

Waldfoghel, Procopius, silversmith, 71; engaged in a process of writing artificially, 101.

Walker, Emery, 277, 358.

Walpole, Horace, the private press of, 354.

Wang Chieh, printer of earliest known printed book, 46.

Wang Cheng, describes early wooden types, 54.

Warde, Mrs., type specimen book of Jannon, discovered by, 306.

Wendelin of Speyer, second printer at Venice, 111.

Wernher, Adam, statement regarding invention of printing by, 103.

Wiegand, Dr., director of the Bremer Press, 363.

Wimpheling, Jacob, statement regarding invention of printing by, 104.

Wood blocks, 326.

Woodcuts, 57.

Woodcut, earliest dated, 44.

World Judgment, fragment of, 88.

Writing, earliest known example of, 11.

Yale University Press, 371.

Yemantszoen, Maurice, printer at Gouda, 113.

Zainer, Gunther, printer of Augsburg, 335.

Zell, Ulric, authority for statement in Cologne Chronicle, 75.

Zedler, Gottfried, on early binder's stamps, 70; on method of production of earliest Dutch printing, 84.

Zilverdistel Press, the, 363.

Zumarraga, Archbishop, patron of early printing in Mexico, 225.

Zwolle, first printing at, 113.